In Search of Radical Theology

John D. Caputo, *series editor*

PERSPECTIVES IN
CONTINENTAL
PHILOSOPHY

JOHN D. CAPUTO

In Search of Radical Theology
Expositions, Explorations, Exhortations

FORDHAM UNIVERSITY PRESS
New York ■ 2020

Fordham University Press has no responsibility for the persistence or accuracy of URLs for external or third-party Internet websites referred to in this publication and does not guarantee that any content on such websites is, or will remain, accurate or appropriate.

Fordham University Press also publishes its books in a variety of electronic formats. Some content that appears in print may not be available in electronic books.

Visit us online at www.fordhampress.com.

Library of Congress Cataloging-in-Publication Data available online at https://catalog .loc.gov.

Printed in the United States of America

22 21 20   5 4 3 2 1

First edition

To Maya and Matthew
    Our children's children, our hope against hope

Contents

Like a Devilish Knight of Faith:
A Concluding Quasi-Theological Postscript

Preface

Aside from the Introduction, which was written for the present volume with the express purpose of introducing the very idea of a radical theology, the essays collected together here have been previously published, and, while discontinuous in terms of content, they are continuous in their intent. Setting out from different contexts, addressed to different audiences, expressed in different voices, each is variously set on staking out the parameters of what I call "weak theology" or, more recently, "radical theology," something of a successor to the "radical hermeneutics" with which I started out many years ago.

Other than some editing to reduce repetitions and update footnotes, I made no effort to rewrite these essays. I intimate no invisible hand working them all together unto one, make no pretense that they are a seamless line of argument. I think their occasional quality a virtue, not a vice. I do not seek to impose the overarching unity of a monograph but to propose the more oblique unity of a common point of view which is being variously reinvented. I have set them out in an order that seems best to me, but, truth to tell, they can be read in any order that suits the reader's needs.

I start with an address to a distinguished gathering of Catholic theologians and philosophers assembled to discuss the "challenge of God." Catholicism is the world in which I was born and which I have borne with me over the years, even if Catholics who read things like *First Things* can hardly bear to hear me described as Catholic. To them I say, may the first be last. Under the flag of a radicalization of what I call the "Catholic Principle," I offer an account of the resistance Catholicism throws up against its own idea of tradition. This I place in collaborative juxtaposition with what is called the "Protestant Principle" by Paul Tillich, who is my favorite official theologian. I set this essay in the context of the firing of a gifted campus minister a few years ago by a Catholic academy in the Archdiocese of Philadelphia. The cause? Loving someone of whom the archbishop did not approve. Need I say more? I do, in this piece.

"Proclaiming the Year of the Jubilee" (chapter 2) addressed quite a different audience, a mix of both academics and non-academics, variously activists and artists, theists, post-theists, and atheists, straight and not so straight, men and women, of various persuasions, or better, of various *un*persuasions, including "nones" who no longer believe the old religion, who continue to believe something, but are in search of just what. Here I adopt a sometimes playful, taunting voice, full of atonal Derridean chords like ghosts and specters—all these deathly tropes are deadly serious and important to me—where radical theology is described as "hauntology." The invitation was to say in more or less intelligible American English (even though we were in Belfast) what radical theologians are talking about when they read unreadable papers at each other at the American Academy of Religion.

Next, I put a scholarly essay on Jacques Derrida (chapter 3), which follows closely the changing fortunes of religion and the name of God in the course of his work. Derrida is my favorite unofficial theologian. Derrida would never permit himself to be called a theologian. He told me that he would be "intimidated" by such a thing. (I smiled.) So let us say, instead, he is my favorite slightly atheistic, quasi-Jewish, somewhat Augustinian *agent provocateur* in matters theological. He is, in short, a "devilish knight of faith," a perfect model for radical theology. In fact, for philosophy. Indeed, for life in general! For me, weak or radical theology may be variously described in Derrideanese as the deconstruction of classical or confessional theology, as the specter that haunts classical theology, or as the reinvention of the event that stirs within the various confessional traditions, or even as devilish hermeneutics. Whichever way I end up putting it, I always have Derrida up my academic sleeve, a self-styled rogue, who had the devil in his eye. This piece is followed with a more wide-ranging essay on the unorthodox, maybe even mischievous but always serious interest continental philosophers take in Augustine, and specifically pursuing the way the *Confessions* has been differently taken up and reimagined by not only Derrida but also Heidegger, Lyotard, and Marion (chapter 4).

Needless to say, such a project, which keeps several balls in the air at once, has not been without its critics, who, coming felicitously from opposing camps, help me calibrate more carefully just where radical theology fits (or resists being fitted). Some, coming over one side of the hill (the orthodox side), charge my "religion without religion" with a fear of the concrete determinate religious traditions. To speak of fear is to make a psychologistic charge, which invites a psychologistic response, which is that they are afraid of the indeterminate, of the unforeseeability of the future, of the irretrievability of the past, in short, afraid of radical theology. This camp charges me with being an atheist, insinuating that radical theology does not take "real" religion seriously (chapter 5), while the other camp, coming over the other (secular) side of the hill, accuses me of *not* being an atheist (chapter 6). One thinks I do not take Augustine seriously and the other takes me to be Augustine redux, serving up the sheep of classical orthodox Augustinian Christianity clothed in the garments of a declawed Derridean wolf. I was writing these responses pretty much at the same time, rejoicing in the delicious symmetry of my critics, which allowed me to step aside and let them crash into each other. Although I still have not decided which one of these criticisms is more wrong, I am grateful to both camps for making me a better radical theologian. By showing their common but mistaken assumptions, about both deconstruction and God (whom I do not confuse), I can pinpoint exactly where on this hill I make my stand, where to locate the hill I would die on, although, of course, like Bartleby, I would prefer not to.

One point running through all the essays is that, unlike modernist critiques of religion, radical theology is theology, not a drive-by shooting of theology. It does not debunk but reinvents the theological tradition. This pervasive point can be seen throughout, but especially in the essay that deconstructs modernity's construction of a Pure (ahistorical) Reason (the upper case is meant to mock the uppity pretentiousness) by way of the postmodern conception of the truth of the event. The presentation of this truth, which looks a little impure to Pure Reason and mad to Enlightenment Rationality, was made to a conference in Stockholm on madness, reason, and religion (chapter 7). The point to take away is that radical theology is a double weakening or deconstruction—of supernatural theology on the one hand and of transcendental reason on the other, and therefore of the settled distinctions between faith and reason, the religious and the secular, the defining binaries of modernity. After that, I deploy Kierkegaard's witticism about the knight of faith who looks like a tax collector as a trope for radical theology itself, arguing that radical theology needs to adopt the disguise of the "philosophy of religion"—this was written for a conference in Montreal on the future of the continental philosophy of religion—in order to make itself look respectable. The challenge for radical theology is to earn a spot in the curriculum, given that the "radical" makes it suspect among the confessional seminaries and the "theology" renders it suspect among the university seminars (chapter 8).

Next comes a short piece that reflects the current state of the art of radical theology, where the torch has been passed to a new generation—Generation X—of radical *political* theologians, sent in to replace aging white male deconstructionists who will mercifully go unmentioned. Delivered at a Westar Institute session of the American Academy of Religion, I analyze what I call Trumptime as a way to bring to bear the weight of radical theology upon the idolatry of White Christian Nationalism (chapter 9). After any discussion of Trump we look for hope, hope against hope, so this essay is followed by an address to a society of pastoral theologians in Pasadena for whom radical means effecting radical change. Radical theology is a radicalization of hope, which is a deeply resonant political figure, where the deepest hope takes place when things look hopeless (chapter 10).

I conclude with a eulogy to Derrida, written shortly after his death (2004)—to Jacques, who loosened my tongue. Derrida and Kierkegaard's pseudonyms together, the one in tandem with the other, gave me what it was not theirs to give, my voice. Conspiring in the title of this little eulogy, they inspire everything I do.

Introduction
What Is Radical Theology?

We live in a world in which traditional religion is making itself unbelievable. The mainstream churches are emptying; their seminaries are closing. The "nones" are waxing; the nuns are waning.[1] Meanwhile, secular rationality is proving itself increasingly calculating and heartless. The one cannot suffer the other, and both are insufferable. We need help. Can anyone change the conversation? Evidently, someone did. In recent decades, we have witnessed the emergence of an odd, irregular, and unclassifiable discourse that is not far from what in the past we called theology. Make no mistake. This is not your grandfather's divinity school; this is not seminary theology. But neither is it the old secularism. Old barriers between the religious and secular, first erected by the learned despisers' critiques of religion in the nineteenth century, are coming down, and a new genre of quasi-theological, cross-disciplinary literature—sometimes described as "theory"—appears to have lifted the ban on theology and allowed it to be part of the conversation.

For the theologians, it started back in the 1960s when, drawing variously on Tillich, Bultmann, and Bonhoeffer, on the one hand, and Hegel and Nietzsche, on the other, the famous (and for the orthodox infamous) band of "death of God" theologians burst on the scene. They pulled off a public relations coup we have not seen since—they got academic theology on the TV talk shows and the cover of *Time* magazine.[2] This was a brilliant but fast-moving storm that blew out as fast as it blew in, but it presaged a wave of creative thinkers who would ignore the boundaries traditionally drawn between theology and philosophy, indeed between philosophy, theology, literature, politics, psychoanalysis—and anything else. While pinning down what "postmodern" means is a fool's errand, whatever it means, this border-crossing unclassifiability is part of it.

Dare we say that theology is no longer banned from the court? That the *odium theologiae*, which for the better part of two centuries has been sustained by secular intellectuals, including today's so-called new atheists, has at last become itself odious? How did we get here? How did I get here?

For philosophers like me, it started with Heidegger's work published after World War II, which had adopted a mystical tone gravitating around his notion of "overcoming onto-theology,"[3] which could well be the hashtag for the transformation of continental philosophy launched in the 1960s. Emmanuel Levinas, one of Heidegger's fiercest critics, creatively transcribed basic elements of biblical spirituality into a stunningly original account of ethics, which Jacques Derrida, who wrote a brilliant study of Levinas in 1964, called "jewgreek," a perfect word he borrowed from James Joyce. Derrida himself, gradually making more explicit use of Levinas as his work progressed, began to unfold—hauntingly, I would say—what he called a "religion without religion."[4] Gianni Vattimo announced he believed he believes. Foucault set off a flurry of studies of the genealogy of religion. Even the Catholics got into it. Jean-Luc Marion spearheaded a radically phenomenological redoing of Catholic mystical theology. By the last decade of the twentieth century, a wave of philosophers was undulating in theological waters, where they were joined by radical feminists, Lacanians, decolonialist and race theorists. Around the turn of the twenty-first century a trilogy of original work on Saint Paul was published by Giorgio Agamben, Alain Badiou, and Slavoj Žižek, which looked like an updated rendition of the 1960s death of God squad. American process theologians, never intimidated by orthodoxy, added a dose of Deleuze to panentheism and produced a new materialism, where what is dead is not God but matter, the old inert dumb matter, replaced by quantum waves as mysterious as the *mysterium tremendum*. Today, theorists wonder whether medieval angelology is not resurfacing in the new information technology.

Dare theology raise its head out of its foxhole? Are we to think that religion is not confined to right-wing rural fundamentalists with White Christian Nationalism on their mind? Have the most cerebral, sophisticated, urban, international, left-wing, and avant-garde intellectuals—hitherto the heart of a very resolute anti-religion—themselves gotten religion? However we describe it, something is going on. The old disdain of the intellectual elite for theology is attenuating, while the (not so very) "new atheists" are trotting out an obsolete and boring (and Islamophobic) nineteenth-century materialism. Writing the history of all this work would require a completely different book, several of them, but the point is plain. The old borders are collapsing, and theology, a certain theology, is alive and well among thinkers whom the orthodox would consider secularists or atheists.[5]

It was in this context that in 1997 I published *The Prayers and Tears of Jacques Derrida* (about Derrida), and that led in 2006 to *The Weakness of God* and in 2013 to *The Insistence of God* (both about God, not Derrida). The first, a plea for a prayerful, if not theological, Derrida, was a prolegomenon to the next two, in which I ended up calling weak or radical theology what I started out calling radical hermeneutics. Borrowing a phrase from Kierkegaard, I finally established in these three books the point of view of my work as an author, of which the essays collected here are a sampling. So it is incumbent on me to set out how I understand radical theology. This will have all the limitations of being my version, reflecting an undisguised pedigree in biblical and Christian sources.[6] But that, I think, is as it should and inevitably must be. As I hope to show, radical theology declines to answer the question, *what is it?* There should be as many radical theologies as there are theological and cultural traditions to radicalize. But I am getting ahead of myself. Let's start from the top.

Theology as Inflection, Not Genuflection

One way to approach radical theology—I think both the most useful and most accessible way—is to distinguish it from confessional theology. By confessional theology I mean what we ordinarily just call theology, period, plain and simple, without the adjective, the sort of thing the various religious communities do in their seminaries. Of this, radical theology is the radicalization. Where seminary theology is a genuflection, radical theology is the inflection. It is constituted by the distance it creates between itself and confessional theology, the disturbance it creates within confessional theology. Radical theology is that by which confessional theology is *inwardly disturbed*. The disturbance is not coming from outside; it is down in its *roots*, even if, especially if, confessional theology refuses to acknowledge it. The task of radical theologians, then, is to identify and incite that disturbance, not to quell it; to disclose that distance, not to close it. Their word to the confessional theologians is Augustinian: *Nolite foras ire*; do not go troubleshooting elsewhere; the disturbance is here at home. My ideal radical theologian is a whistle-blower, an insider alerting everyone that there is trouble inside the corporation. Radical theology is a disturbance of the peace, appearing just where there should be a sword, not peace.

The *radical* in radical theology means that confessional theology is exposed to instability and the instability goes all the way down. So "radical" here does not mean theology's unshakable foundation, the classical sense, but the opposite, a deep-down inner instability. That is the disturbance. But the *theology* in radical theology means that this groundlessness, while unnerving, is itself theological, and not another drive-by shooting typical of modernity. The disturbance constitutes the stuff (*die Sache*) of a radical theology, requiring an unnerving faith that runs deeper than the reassuring beliefs cultivated in the seminary hothouse. Confessional belief is eroded by doubt; radical faith is steeled by doubt. *Pace* Luther, we are saved by doubt, by what our radical Tillich would call the dynamics of doubt.[7]

For an explanation, I will admit that is all *un peu* polemical. So to clarify more carefully what I mean, I will elaborate two fundamental differences between radical and confessional theology. The first I call the "disciplinary difference" between the two communities who practice radical and confessional theology (I). The second I call the "theological difference," which establishes the difference conceptually, in strictly theological terms (III). The first has to do with the institutional *location* of the difference; the second with its internal *logic*. The first identifies where radical theology can be found; the second, how it can be defined. In between these two sections I insert a discussion of the "event," which holds the key to both differences (II). At the end, I ask what difference this difference makes, what good radical theology does (IV). Is it primarily a negative undertaking? Is it strictly academic? Does it have any use? Of course, I will be forced to complicate this distinction as I go along. Inasmuch as I am setting up theology as radical theology's straight man, literally (orthodox and patriarchal), I must beware both of caricature and of creating a new binary opposition, which is exactly the sort of thing radical thinking sets out to disturb.

I.
THE DISCIPLINARY DIFFERENCE

In the historical confessional theologies, the theologies that actually exist, that are housed in churches and synagogues, mosques and temples, in seminaries and religious institutions of learning, in religious journals and publishing houses, the theologians report to their respective denominational communities. The task of the confessional theologians is to clarify the founding texts and oldest traditions, to defend the community against its critics, to interpret the evolving tradition in the light of new circumstances. Historically, in the early Christian church, the theologian in chief was the bishop, who was a teacher, not a bureaucrat in a downtown office. The theologian, who was not an academic, theologized in concert with the congregation. The criterion of *truth* is whether the theologian has tapped into something in the spirit of the community, and whether the community can truly recognize itself in the theology. If the link between the two cannot be made, then the theologian is de-linked, cut loose from the community. Or the opposite. Often enough, as history testifies, the community, which never was just a pure unity, adheres to the theology and severs itself from the larger community; then a new breakaway community is formed, based on a new take on the truth of the spirit.

Where are radical theologians found? Too often, alas, on the unemployment line, which I say only half in jest. It is not by accident that I open this collection with a story of the firing of a friend of radical theology.[8] When they do find work, it is often in a secular university, doing "theory" in the humanities center or the religion or comparative literature departments, where tenure protects them from the unemployment line, provided they can find a job to begin with.[9] Of course, they can also be found, hiding in plain sight, in the seminaries and theology departments of religious institutions—where they represent the inner disturbance. Not surprisingly, the major figures in the early death of God movement all encountered job trouble. However they are employed, radical theologians report to anyone and everyone who is willing to listen, with or without religion or theology in the standard sense. The criterion of truth here is, in principle, whether *anyone anywhere* in the culture, in any culture, can recognize himself or herself in what the radical theologians say.[10] Radical theologians do not observe the usual distinctions between religion and the secular, or faith and reason, theology and other disciplines. By reserving the right to ask any question, to borrow an expression from Derrida, they expose the power play in what calls itself "religion" and "secular"; they delight in finding a religion in this secularity (Tillich) and a religionlessness in this religion (Bonhoeffer).

For radical theologians the founding texts and ongoing traditions of the confessional communities are resources for their reflections but without *normative authority*. These sources are formative, not normative. No revelation is special; no book is inerrant; no bishop is infallible; no people particularly chosen. Everyone and everything must present its credentials and address in a meaningful way the world in which we actually live today. Meanwhile, back in the seminaries, confessional theologians are too often occupied answering questions that no one is asking. But lacking normative authority does not mean that the concrete historical communities are dispensable. On the contrary, because in this approach radical theology is marked by the inflection, it depends on these texts and theological traditions. Without the latter, the very idea of radical theology might never have arisen, no more than we would have been likely to look for roots where there was no tree. The historical confessional traditions are where theology is found *in actu exercitu*, in action, in the flesh, and as such they supply the subject matter of radical theology. Without these communities, there would be nothing to *radicalize*, nothing to reflect on and inflect, in short, nothing for radical theologians to *do*. They would be radically unemployed.

Almost. That raises the next point, which involves qualifying this distinction without altogether disqualifying it. The first rule in radical thinking is, when you see a distinction, deconstruct it, lest it become a monster.

Three Qualifications

This distinction between confessional theologians and radical theologians needs to be qualified on three points in particular. First, the distinction misleads us into thinking that, since the confessional bodies are concrete, determinate, and historical, radical theology must be abstract, indeterminate, and ahistorical, as if the confessional traditions are the existence of which radical theology distills the essence.[11] This I reject, radically, root and branch. The confessional traditions are not specimens etherized on the table of radical theologians who seek to identify the species. Radical theology has no such prodigious head. It does not pretend to some overarching ahistorical standpoint. It does not proceed from above; it works from down below, seeking to inhabit from within, to feel about not for a quiddity but for a quickening form of life, by way of the most micrological investigations. As the *repetition* of real, existing historical traditions, radical theology on this approach will always bear the mark of the tradition that is being radicalized, always carry along within itself the trace of the determinate historicality of the historical movement it inhabits. Radical theology will always also be a radical Christianity, a radical Judaism or Islam, a radical Paul, a radical Luther, a radical Buddha, and so on. We can always trace its ancestry, detect its theological pedigree, derive the tradition from which it arrives. *What is it?* It is this dissemination, this proliferation, wary of every "what," eluding every "is."

The goal of abstracting an eternal truth untainted by temporality, a universal unscathed by particularity, is the misguided project of the Enlightenment philosophers, of whom radical theologians strive earnestly to be the "post-." Their unfortunate influence is too much felt in what traditionally passes itself off as the "philosophy of religion," which is an artifact of the modern university and speaks an artificial language, not a naturally religious one. The upshot of the philosophy of religion is what Hegel calls a bad infinity, endless anthologies gathering proofs for the existence of God, the freedom of the will, the immortality of the soul, and the problem of evil, on the questionable premise that this will keep undergraduates occupied and off their smart phones. The philosophy of religion acts as if religion—as if this word were historically innocent, as if there is one such thing called in Christian Latin "religion"[12]—were a cluttered heap of concepts, propositions, and arguments in need of sorting out by a SWAT team of logicians sent in by the philosophy department.

Radical theologians root through the various confessional traditions in search of a disturbance going on within them; confessional theologians, like Bartleby, would prefer not to. It is not a matter of making abstraction *from* but of getting traction *in* them. This demands the most meticulous knowledge of a given tradition, finding tiny crevices and openings in the tradition through which tangled roots can be detected. There is always more to confessional theology than the latter is prepared to admit. Confessional theology contains something that it cannot contain, a recess that it cannot reach, an excess that it cannot corral in canons and definitions, a resistance that it cannot put down. The space between this concealed depth and the seemingly stable surface of the institution is the source of an anxiety that confessional theology passionately seeks to silence with authoritative doctrine, firm belief, solemn or enthusiastic rite.

That said—beware of caricature—nothing pleases me more than the many local communities living on the borders of their confessional body, defying its authoritarianism, exposing its hypocrisy, hanging on by a thread before the letters of expulsion and excommunication arrive in the mail. They are my heroes, my intended audience (and the ones who usually invite me to speak).

Second, this is clearly not a clear distinction, and here we begin to transition into the logic of the difference. The relationship between radical theology and confessional theology is not clear-cut but interactive; it is not binary but circular. Their *rela*tion is a *circu*lation, and if we cut off this circulation, they would both turn blue. Radical theology depends on the confessional theologies it inhabits, haunts, and disturbs, even as the confessional theologies depend on the radical theological stream by which they are both nourished and disturbed. It is just because they give visible and audible reality to their radical sources that their confessional creeds have any credibility at all; if they cut off this circulation, they become monsters. My premise—my wager, my suspicion, my hope—is that pastors and congregations alike implicitly understand, if they let themselves think about it, that they trade in symbols, and that the symbols of confessional religion are at bottom sustained by what the symbols are symbols of. Radical theology is a confessional theology that has come to understand itself. By the same token, the thoughts that radical theologians think would likely never have gotten in their head at all but for the grace (*sola gratia!*) of the confessional traditions. There would be no radical Jesus if Christianity did not preserve his memory. Without these traditions, they would trade in volatilized and empty abstractions; they would be talking only to one another and not really talking about anything.

Third, as the work of Paul Tillich has shown, the circulation I describe is actually wider than I have so far allowed. For radical theology can be found where the word "theology" is not to be found at all, in the depths of the so-called "secular" culture. Radical theology is found wherever matters of "ultimate concern" are raised—in art and science, in ethics, politics, and everyday life. Radical currents circulate throughout the culture at large, which is why radical theology can also be described as "secular theology." This means that, in principle, we could talk about radical theology without so much as even mentioning confessional theology or even religion. In principle, we could begin anywhere in the culture and, if we dig deep enough, hit radical theological soil.

Then why did I begin with this distinction? The reason is, as I said above, I think this is both the most accessible and useful approach. I am focusing on the accessible part now, and I take up the useful part in the final section (IV), where I address the danger religion poses to itself and to everyone else. Without the confessional traditions, radical theology would have a hard time getting off the ground. The reason for bothering with "religion" at all, is that, in actual fact, it is in the confessional traditions that the trace of radical theology is most readily detected, the scent easiest to follow, and without them we would lose something deeply important. My reasoning here is completely Tillichian. Tillich famously said that God is the ground of being and not an alien being, but nonetheless we are alienated from God, and in this state of alienation, what we call "religion" fills a vital need. There are no temples in the heavenly Jerusalem, but you will have noticed that this is not the heavenly Jerusalem. This is an alienated and wounded world, and so we need to set aside a place where we can explicitly attend to the ground of being, telling its stories, singing its songs. Is it just an accident that this notion of an elemental religion found everywhere in the depths of the culture is the product of a theologian? Without religion in the narrow sense, radical theology would be like a Romantic poet without a meadow or a stream. It could be done, but it would that much harder.

I should mention that philosophers will recognize this circulation as the circularity of the hermeneutical circle,[13] which Heidegger redescribed as the "ontological difference" between Being and beings: Being is always the Being *of* beings, and beings are what they are only *in* their Being. Just so: Radical theology is the radical theology *of* a historical theological tradition; a historical theology is always rooted *in* radical sources. Theologians will recognize this circulation as the circularity of what Tillich called the unconditional and the conditional. The unconditional (the subject of radical theology) does not exist; it is the depth dimension *of* what does exist, of *whatever* exists, religious or secular. What does exist does so as a conditional form of its unconditional content.[14] Each one depends on the other; one will never be found without the other. Armed with these provisos let us proceed to stake out the distance that differentiates them.

II.
A THEOLOGY OF EVENT

In the version I advance here, the distance between radical theology and confessional theology arises from a disturbance the source of which is the *event*. Events are the coming of what we cannot see coming, which is its Derridean accent. Events are not what happens, the conventional understanding of the word, but what is going on *in* what happens, which is its Deleuzian accent.[15] The event has several recognizable features.

Instability. Events are not what is present but what is being promised and remembered in the present. They are not what is happening, but what is being recalled and what is being called for in what is happening. By exposing the present to the future and leaving it unprotected from the past, the present is deprived of stability, but that instability is the condition of its mobility, without which the present would petrify. Confessional theology is what happens, occupying a relatively stable place in space and in time. Events are what is going on *in* theology, representing the restlessness that theology, not without trying, is unable to arrest. Instead of *correcting* theology when it thinks it goes wrong, adjudicating it from above, as do the philosophers of religion, radical theology listens in on what is going on in theology, working from below, *detecting* something restlessly astir there. That is the event.

No Essence. There is no such thing as *the* event. Events are not essences but the hint of something promised, a trace of something from time immemorial disturbing our sleep. Events are not essences but disturbances. They are more like a specter than a spirit, more like a whisper than an essence. There are as many different events as there are different historical communities, different historical memories and expectations, different historical dreams and hopes, prayers and aspirations. Do not contract the event to some concrete historical figure or community. That would close the distance, shut down its promise, take the future away from the present. Just so, do not extract some essence from the history. There are two rules here: First, never underestimate the powerless power of the event, of a dream or a memory, to shatter our horizon of expectation; and second, never contract the pulsation of the event to any particular form it takes; never freeze the event into one effect it produces, now or in the past, and not in the future either, for there is no ideal essence up ahead that we are heading for asymptotically. In the domain of events, if someone asks what is this or that—like what is radical theology?—the most rigorous answer is: We don't know; it's not over yet. The most we can do is to give examples. To announce an essence is to pronounce the time of death. Essences are discovered only at autopsies.[16]

Infinitival Distance. What is precisely eventive in events is their open-endedness, their resistance to closure. The various confessional theological effects—the beliefs and practices, the structures and constructions—found in the history of theology are all in varying measure finite.[17] The event, by contrast, is *infinitival*—not infinite, as in classical theology. Because the event is eventive, not entitative, it is neither a finite nor an infinite entity. In the order of events, we have to do not with the infinite but with the infinitival. The axiom of radical theology, if it had one, is that confessional theology is separated from radical theology by an infinitival distance, which means the gap can never be closed, structurally, in principle. Closure is neither its inspiration nor its aspiration; closure is not its Idea in the Kantian sense. Closure would spell death and disaster. No finite form or figure is finished, however finely wrought. No belief or doctrine found in a historical community is ever simply given, is ever simply present. This is an axiom not in the strong sense of a logical rule, but in the weak sense of *axioma*, what we treasure, prize, and appreciate axiologically.[18] According to this axiom, to be appreciated for what it is, whatever presents itself—a theology or anything else—must be put in the infinitive; it must come attached with a coefficient of infinitivity. Were a historical tradition to proclaim justice, this will always turn out to be, more radically considered, a justice-*to-come*, a coming year of the jubilee, because justice, if there is such a thing, does not exist, not as such, although various acts, people, or laws may be variously and intermittently just or unjust. When we announce the year of the jubilee, the fiftieth year, no one is counting.[19] The event admits not of a *concept* of justice, which assumes we have some finite ideality in our grasp (*capere*), but at most of a *song* to a justice-to-come. And what is that song if not a *hymn*, and what is that hymn, if not a *prayer*? And what is that prayer if not the stuff of a more radical *religion*, a religion before or beyond, without or within religion in the usual sense, a religion of the event?

Temporality. Events do not take place *in* time; events are the *timing of* what takes place in time, of what happens. In speaking of the event (*événement*), the accent falls on the to-come, *à-venir, zu-kommen*, on the future, *l'avenir, die Zukunft*. Derrida distinguishes a radical and unforeseeable future from the future-present (*le futur*), the future we can foresee will become present.[20] We can and must prepare for the future of our children, of the nation, of the planet, which are gravely serious matters. But this is made difficult because the future-present is haunted by the "absolute" future, the *un*foreseeable one, the coming of what we cannot see coming, for which we cannot be prepared, which shatters our horizon of expectation. For better or for worse. So the radical future has a disturbing and ambiguous quality, a spectrality. On the one hand, it is not what happens but what *promises* to happen, for which we are hoping, sighing, dreaming.[21] On the other hand, it is not what happens but what *threatens* to happen, our worst nightmare come true. Openness to the event is openness to the promise/threat, which is risky business. We feel that today. The whole world is spooked. Will AI kill us or cure us? Will humanity end up being enslaved by creatures of its own making? What are we doing to our planet? What kind of life will our children and grandchildren have? What will be left after Trump is finally gone? To have hope in the future-present is to hope for what is possible, but in the sphere of events we hope against hope, in *the* impossible.[22] Radical theology describes a radical hope and faith, an absolute prayer or aspiration. Its first, last, and constant word is "come, *viens, oui, oui*," which would be found on the first page of radical theology's book of *un*common prayer, if it had one.

Post-theism. The event is not God. The event is not a being, not even the Supreme Being (theism); it is not the ground of being or the Being of beings (panentheism); it is not even the God beyond Being (negative theology). For all its "not this, not that," for all the similarities in semantic resources and syntactical strategies, even if they are kindred spirits, or kindred specters, even if radical theology is never far from mystical theology,[23] still, the event is not the *Deus absconditus* no more than it is the *Deus revelatus*. To all such entities and ontologies, to all such Gods and Godheads beyond God, the right theological response is atheism. But in its departure from theism, panentheism and hyper-theism, such atheism provides the point of departure for a new post-theism, a pivot to a post-theology.[24] This atheism is not the end of theology, but the beginning of a radical, spectral—or, as I like to say—weak theology, where the event is not God, but the name of God is the name of an event. Adieu to the futile debate between the theists and the atheists, adieu to the antinomy and antagonism between the supernaturalists and the reductionistic naturalists. The various theisms and atheisms mythologize the event, conflating it with a mythological entity, with a divine power, and then idly debate whether or not there is one.

The Call. The event goes under indefinitely many names but its least limiting, most evocative name is what I like to call a *call*, the event of the call, the call the event pays on us, what is getting itself called in and under the name.[25] The call does not exist; the call calls for existence. The call does not exist; the call calls. The call is not an existent. The call is not an essence (a stable presence of which we could form a concept). The call is issued as a solicitation or summons for something more nascent than an essence, something which has not yet achieved existence, before any essence has been formed, before any existence has been brought forth. Its proper modality is prophetic, calling for the coming of what it cannot see coming. The call solicits; it does not command, nor does it hold up an ideal *eidos* to be gradually realized in existence. The call calls for something that is neither a what nor a that, neither a *quid sit* (what it is) nor an *an sit* (whether it is), but a *how* and a *when*? How long, O Lord?

Insistence. Events have neither essence nor existence but *insistence*, which is the modality proper to the calling of a call. The call is not a law of essence underwriting the course of nature and history, or a supreme being (existent) who calls everything into being. It calls prior to both supernatural faith and also natural reason. Radical theology is weak theology because in it the essence and existence of God weaken into God's insistence, the being of God weakens into the may-being (*peut-être*) of God, the omnipotence of almighty God into the might-be of the event that is being called for, that is being recalled, in the name (of) "God," which may or may not come to be.

The Spirit. The call is the radicalization of the Spirit, the spectralization of the Spirit, the weakening of the Spirit into a spectral call. The call supplies the phenomenological content or, let us say, provides the haunto-phenomenological credentials lying behind or within the strong theological figure of the Spirit. The Holy Spirit, the great Spirit, is one of religion's oldest, deepest images (*Vorstellung*, symbol). The spirit inspires—that means it calls. We in turn are filled with the Spirit, Spirit-driven—that means we are called. Even people who want "out" from religion still want to be "spiritual" (called). The Spirit calls upon us in unexpected ways, knocking us off our horse when we had set out to do other things. The

Spirit gives us our calling, our vocation, our provocation, whether we like it or not. Speaking of a call does not mean that we are hearing voices in our head, as if a Super Entity in the sky is whispering things in our ear while we listen, ears cocked heavenward. The Spirit breathes where it will, which means it is up to us to decide what is being called for or indeed whether there is a call at all.

The Middle Voice. The mark of the call more radically conceived is that the caller of the call disappears into the calling. There is no identifiable entity, no reassuring caller, with a prestigious and intimidating name—like God, the Law, the Leader, the Nation, the Party—doing the calling. There is no superbeing doing miraculous things—like calling to us from outside space and time, an image which, as Tillich says, is "half-blasphemous and mythological."[26] The blasphemy lies in reducing God to a supernatural entity who does magical things, the mythology in the personification. In the spectralization of the Spirit, there is no nameable Caller calling, no Big Names, no eternal authorization, no divine warranty. Thank God! That would relieve us, deprive us, of responsibility, allowing us off the hook. Then I am just following orders. Rather, the call, as Heidegger says, comes in the mode of silence; and it leaves no calling card, gives no special instructions.[27] There is no proof of a caller; there is only the witness given by the response, which to all the world makes the responders look like dancers dancing to music no one else can hear. The call calls for interpretation (hermeneutics), deep discernment (radical) even to say that there is a call at all. In radical theology, the call get itself called in and under the name (of) "God." (There are other names. It does not care what we call it.) In grammar this is called the middle voice, neither a pure agency acting nor a pure passivity suffering, but an auto-mediating, internally connected system auto-productive of certain emergent effects. "It calls," in the impersonal third person, but the calling is not something less than a person. The action is spooky. The Spirit, weakened into a spectral insinuation, is not a stern imperative but the soft and supple sigh of a call.

Messianic Urgency. This accent on an unfinishable futurity, like a Messiah who never shows up, does not diminish the urgency of the moment; it intensifies it. Far from becoming complacent with the present, the call puts the present under the merciless *white light* of the to-come. The disturbance is an infinitival exaction; it exposes every blemish in the present, every insufficiency, every finite failing and falling short of something to-come. The messianic condition of radical theology is not an evasive deferral that puts off action to an indefinite future. It goes back to Walter Benjamin's idea of the weak messianic power, where *we* are the messianic generation; *we* are the ones the dead have been waiting for, *we* who are expected to make right the wrongs that were done to them, *we* to whom the past lays claim.[28] That is why the timing of the event is also a work of mourning, driven by the dangerous memory of the dead. The complacency of the present is endangered by this memory no less than by anticipating an unforeseeable future. In virtue of events, the present is surrounded, endangered, and destabilized on both sides.

Interventiveness. The force of events is not conventional but interventional. Conventions are settled beliefs and practices in which the event has sedimented. Events are eventive, interventive, interruptive. They break in upon us and awaken us from our quotidian slumbers. Events call upon us in a multitude of forms, in art and science, in public and in private life, in matters big and small, in response to which our lives take form and shape. Events do not subsist; events intervene. Events do not subsist; they insist.

Responsibility. Events call upon us. The call does not originate with us, but it does terminate in us, singling us out, putting us in the accusative, as Levinas says (*me voici*). It does not start with us, but it ends with us, landing in our laps, accusatively, irrecusably,[29] like a homily that seems directed just at me, embarrassing me in front of the entire congregation. The weakness of weak theology, the weak force of the event, does not refer to an indecisive and anemic life. Quite the contrary, the weakness of God shifts the burden of a response on to us, puts the weight of the decision squarely on us. There is no strong omnipotent Superbeing who is going to step in and do the heavy lifting for us. As Derrida says, the call is unconditional, but it comes without sovereignty.[30] As Bonhoeffer says, today the tutelage of humankind is over and the time has come for us to assume responsibility for ourselves, to respond to what is calling to us in and under the name of God.[31]

Whether There Will Have Been God

What, then, of God in a theology of the event? The name of God is the name of a call that calls for a response. The call is risky business, not just for us but also for God, since we may or may not respond, while God, the event that is going on in the name of God, can only solicit, not coerce, a response. The thought of the call is an incomplete thought, an unfinished sentence. For a call comes to naught without a response. It can fall on deaf ears, be ignored, refused, distorted, even scorned. The question of the response raises the question of whether and how we respond to what is being called for. That is the measure of how "God" comes to be, how the event that is harbored by the name (of) "God" is to be realized. The question in radical theology is not what we are to call God but what God is calling for, what is being called for in and under the name of God. The truth of God is whether we will make God come true. When it comes to the event, the task of theology, adapting an expression from Gilles Deleuze, is to make itself worthy of the event that is happening to it, the event that is harbored by the name of God.[32] The question of the theologian worthy of the name[33] is not whether God exists but whether what is going on in this name will have been carried out. The question is not, does God exist? but whether and how existence—ours or that of anything else—makes itself worthy of the name of God. The question of God is the question of whether, when all is said and done, *there will have been God.*[34] Does God exist? We don't know yet. It depends on us.

In the name (of) "God" there is a concentration and an intensification of insinuating disturbances and insistent disruptions, all calling for a passage to the limits in which existence would be transformed. The insistence of God lures us beyond the borders of the possible to the impossible, for with God all things are possible.[35] It tempts us, entices us into the twilight zone of the excess, the exorbitance of the exceptional, lures us outside the walls of the conventional, inviting contact with the event the conventions seek to enclose. Abba, lead us into temptation, please. Disturb us, please. The call solicits something decisive from us. For better and for worse—which is why the worst violence is also committed under our best names, like God and love. Derrida and Tillich alike call the call the "unconditional." Kierkegaard imaged it under the fearsome figure of Abraham making his way up Mount Moriah, thinking unthinkable thoughts, "incommensurable with the universal," is how he put it, all in response to a call Abraham said he heard.

III.
THE THEOLOGICAL DIFFERENCE:
THE REDUCTION

If we approach radical theology by distinguishing it from confessional theology, everything turns on how to establish the distance, on how to open the space between the two, which is how the radicalization is achieved. This is the place where confessional theology would speak of its method and where a radical theology would speak of something in the place of a method. Thus far I have been describing this as a process of "weakening," which I will elaborate here, adapting a term from phenomenology, as a "reduction" of confessional theology to radical theology. If by weakening I do not mean diminishment, by reduction I do not mean destruction.

I mean to lead (*ducere*) theology back (*re*) into its own most proper element. In phenomenology, a reduction removes an obstacle, which releases the phenomenon into its proper phenomenality. A reduction removes the misunderstanding and makes possible the understanding. A *re*duction is a genuine *intro*duction. Just so, the theological reduction releases theology from the grip of everything that makes theology ridiculous and dangerous and draws opprobrium down upon its head. It makes a reduction of idolatry and blasphemy, of reification and objectification, of codification and institutionalization, of literalization and mystification. The reduction admits theology into another, more radical order. The reduction admits what happens, the various theological traditions, into the primal order of events, which is what is going on *in* what happens.

The theological reduction is not, as in Husserl, a purely methodological bracketing, an *epochē* that temporarily and provisionally neutralizes the "natural attitude"[36]—add here the "supernatural attitude"—of confessional theology. The reduction is a genuine setting aside of a misunderstanding, really suspending a distortion, actually putting an illusion out of action, and it is meant to have lasting effects, not to serve a temporary, provisional, and merely methodological purpose. The reduction is not a methodological doubt but a real (Lyotardian) incredulity.[37] It is not a neutrality-modification, as Husserl calls it, which leaves the real object still standing, but a positive incredulity, which is bent on weakening the confessional walls within which events are immured. This reduction is like suspending the grip of the ethical in order to release the religious movement of faith in Kierkegaard's *Fear and Trembling*. Nonetheless, the theological reduction is not the destruction of confessional theology, but its de*con*struction, its radicalization, the reinvention of its event. It does not close down confessional theology. It open its doors to a kind of proto-theology, a radical theology of a certain religion, within or without confessional religion, where the obstacles that have made theology increasingly unbelievable have been removed.

The Reductions

As a purely heuristic device, we can think of this weakening or reduction as taking place in six steps, which I identify as follows.

Suspension of the Supernatural Signified. The theological reduction is the weakening or suspension of supernaturalism without embracing a reductionistic naturalism. In phenomenological terms, this involves the bracketing of the "supernatural attitude," which suspends the "supernatural signified." This reduction relieves us of the mystification that religion means magic, supernatural occurrences that hold the laws of physics in abeyance in order to admit all sorts of supernatural beings (deities, demons, and angels) in supernatural scenes (water-walking, dead men walking). Without this reduction, theology is describing a spectacle that can be visualized only in an animated film. It is a cartoon theology, a photoshopped, unbelievable world of digitalized fantasies, like resurrected bodies sitting down to a lakeside breakfast of fish. That churches make ridiculous efforts to try to *explain* (*erklären*) such supposed occurrences theologically rather than understand (*verstehen*) these stories hermeneutically is why they are emptying. But the result of this reduction is not a naturalistic reductionism,[38] which explains it away, which is but the flip side of supernaturalism, which foolishly tries to explain it in the first place. The result of this suspension is to allow events to take place, where events are neither physical nor metaphysical, natural nor supernatural, neither explicable nor inexplicable, neither caused nor uncaused, but situated in an order or element proper to themselves.

The Theopoetic Reduction: weakening the logos of theology without falling into the illogical and irrational, that is, weakening *theology* into *theopoetics.* By suspending both naturalism and supernaturalism, we open up a new genre, a new space, uniquely itself, where the logic of theo-logic yields to a poetics. By suspending the authority of supernaturalism and the ham-fistedness of naturalism, we release the order of poetics, of metaphor and metonym, of parables and narratives, of the parabolic and the paradoxical, of striking sayings and memorable images and figures. In theopoetic terms, the confessional differs from the radical as the prosaic differs from the poetic. Even the "analogical" language Thomistic theology adopts is at best a logical modesty, but still a discursively proper prosaic mode (*modus significandi*), which lacks both the visceral grip and imaginative reach of a poetic.[39] This is the reduction of the ridiculous magic of literalist theology, of the ludicrous cartoons of holy card theology, of the spectacle of Cecil B. DeMille cinematic theology, of the preposterous concoctions of theme park theology.[40] Only thus do we liberate the *true magic* of the work of art, the spell-binding power of painting, sculpture, and architecture, the haunting power of song and dance, which together and separately make contact with some elusive depth in the human heart. In the poetic order we enter a domain of truth prior to logic, where truth is not confounded but expounded in fiction. We cease making theological claims and enter the order of being claimed by something for which we lack the concepts, propositions, and proofs of logic, something that is neither logical nor illogical because it is pre-logical.

The Reduction of Belief: weakening belief without losing a deeper faith. Here the reduction means bracketing propositional beliefs that pick out supernatural facts of the matter, as if the parting of the Red Sea were an exceptional historical episode which calls for our assent. Beliefs belittle revelation, distorting it into a fantastic operation according to which a supernatural being provides extraordinary information otherwise unavailable to reason or the senses. Belief means assenting to propositions for which we lack sufficient evidence, and the willingness to believe unbelievable things becomes the test of confessional faith. Beliefs fuel a violent institutional economy where creedal assertions get defined by institutional authorities, who pronounce the measure of the right beliefs, the orthodox, and denounce the wrong beliefs, the heretic, with all the institutionalized, heresiological violence that such distinctions provoke. The bracketing of belief means to neither believe nor disbelieve. The bracketing of belief is accompanied by a suspension of disbelief (Coleridge), in order to release or clear the way for a deeper faith in the event. Faith does not mean to assent to a proposition but to place our confidence in the event for which we lack propositions, to trust in something of unconditional worth, which calls on us and solicits our unconditional loyalty. Beliefs are undone by doubt. Faith is fired by doubt, which relentlessly exposes the idolatry lurking in every belief, in the name of allowing the incoming of the event.

The Reduction of Religion: weakening "religion" without falling into the merely irreligious. Weakening religion does not mean banning religious bodies or burning religious books and houses of worship. Weakening is directed at the institutionalization and regulation of religious rites and pieties, at the codification of religious beliefs and the regimentation of religious practices, weakening their rigidity and inflexibility. This reduction results not in an irreligious secularism but in a deeper religion of the event, a religion with or without religion, a "religionless" religion. It releases a proto-religion of the call, an Ur-religion not confined to a particular sector of the culture called religion, where we make contact with the deep structure of the culture, of any sector of the culture.[41] It is found wherever and whenever something lays claim to us unconditionally, be it in science or art, ethics or politics, church or everyday life. This reduction does not recognize the distinction between the religious and the secular; it weakens both the transcendental claims of secular reason and the supernatural claims of confessional religion in favor of a sphere or order or element that eludes them both.

The Theistic Reduction: the weakening or suspension of theism without embracing mere atheism. This reduction is directed at the mythology that turns the event into an entity, making the event that is harbored by the name of God into a being, indeed a Supreme Being with whom we can negotiate, who is angered or appeased, who does or, for mysterious reasons of "his" own, fails to do things, an entity whose existence or nonexistence is up for debate, whence the endless and futile contest of the theists and atheists, the history of ontotheology. The mythology is to turn the event into an omniscient omnipotent superhero who can make things out of nothing, resurrect corpses, make our enemies our footstools, and, if "his" wrath is properly appeased, settle the hash of our enemies. The result of this reduction is not a simple atheism, although a certain atheism about this Superbeing is *sine qua non*. This reduction does not spell the end of theology but the beginning of a new and more radical theology, whose work is not to prove the existence and nature of a Supreme Being but to ponder the event that is harbored in the name (of) "God," free from the superstition and the threats of the supernaturalists and the cynical taunts of soulless mechanists.

The Political Reduction: the reduction of an apolitical, otherworldly supernatural salvation theology to a this-worldly, freedom-now, emancipation political theology. This is the reduction to the interventiveness of the event, to the political event, which calls for justice, which causes the disturbance. The disturbance is political; the event is a political disturbance. That implies a reduction of eternity to time, and a further reduction of nostalgic time, dreaming of the past, to prophetic time, dreaming of the justice-to-come, the theopoetic time of the new being, the year of the Jubilee.[42] This is likewise a reduction of nostalgic time to the time of the dangerous memory of suffering, where suffering is not a redemptive instrument used by God to purify the soul but the wounded bodies with whom a suffering God stands in solidarity. This is the reduction of theol*ogy* to theo*praxis*, which is a theo-*poetics* in the most literal sense of God-making (*poiein*), making God happen here and now, making the kingdom of God come true. Political theology is nothing new. The story of Exodus is a political story; the prophets were the political pundits of the day; and the execution of Jesus was a political act. Theology was never *not* political, never not about emancipation, but in radical theology today the political has become thematic, programmatic, front and center. This began in the founding moments of radical thinking, when Tillich and Bonhoeffer took on National Socialism, Tillich at the cost of his job in Germany, Bonhoeffer at the cost of his life. Martin Luther King Jr., Mary Daly, and James Cone, who had all read their Tillich carefully, said that the courage to be meant the courage to be in the face of forces of nonbeing unleashed in racism and sexism. Political theology is the state of the art of radical theology *today*, where younger—Generation X[43]—theologians carry out a

theological critique of the idolatries of the day, White Christian Nationalism, the wave of intolerance of immigrants (the widow, the orphan, and the
stranger), global capitalism, and climate change denial. This reduction releases theology from the apolitical grip of the otherworldly justice that
White Christianity held out to the slaves, and that Male Christianity held
out to women, in order to keep them in check down here on earth. The
interesting thing is that the political reduction is freestanding. Although
it follows from the supernatural reduction, it does not depend on it. Nothing stands in the way of seeking *both* eternal salvation and temporal liberation. The political reduction can be found on either side of the divide
between orthodoxy and heterodoxy. Mary Daly, starting out as a Catholic
theologian, eventually concluded that the oppression of women was intrinsic to Roman Catholic orthodoxy, but Martin Luther King and Bonhoeffer never felt the need to abandon the creedal faith. Nor did James
Cone, who had little patience with theology, whether radical or confessional, if that meant what goes on in an academic seminar instead of what
is advancing liberation outside the academy.[44] What Cone wants to *radically disturb* is not orthodoxy, but political indifference brought on by the
illusion perpetrated by white theology that *salvation* is an otherworldly
matter that can be separated from political *liberation*.

Exempli gratia

The theological *re*duction is an *intro*duction in the most basic sense of
the term, leading us back to and admitting us into the proper sphere or
element of radical theology. It does not diminish but enhances us. It does
not take away anything from us other than our illusions. It employs a
logic of the "not without," the reduction of x but not without gaining access to a more radical x, a proto-x. The reduction is not a destruction but
a de*con*struction, a reinvention, a retrieval, a radicalization of theological phenomena.

   Let us take an example, which is a great deal more than an example,
the case of Jesus of Nazareth. In order to keep the focus on the man of
flesh and blood, and in order to clear away the baggage of a name that has
been degraded and distorted beyond recognition by the Christian right,
let us call him Yeshua, his Aramaic name. Yeshua lived in space and time
and so is properly the object of historical-critical research. To dismiss the
results of this research is a thinly disguised Docetism (if it is disguised at
all).[45] If to reduce does not mean to debunk, the theological reduction does
not reabsorb the Christ into the historical Yeshua and then dismiss the subsequent Christian tradition, the Christianizing of Yeshua, declaring it all

an illusion, a con pulled off by Paul and the later Greco-gentile church. The reduction does not discredit this elevation of Yeshua, but it redescribes it, this time free of the illusions of the supernaturalism and authoritarianism of the creeds. The function of the reduction is to reduce Christo*logy* to Christo*poetics*, where the New Testament is not a con, or an illusion, but a poetics. In the New Testament, Yeshua is *lifted up into theopoetic space*, where, as the Anointed One (Christ), God's chosen one, he leads the most remarkable life and dies the most remarkable death, where they kill him, but he does not stay dead. In the Councils, under the spell of Neoplatonic metaphysics, the theopoetic distinction between the two bodies of Jesus, the real one which lived and died, and the one who lives on and on in theopoetic space, was reified into the metaphysical distinction between the human nature and divine supernature, whose proper places are time and eternity, respectively. But in the theopoetics of the New Testament, whose authors never heard of Neoplatonism or metaphysics, Yeshua serves as an *ikon*, the occasion of an intuition of the event that takes place in the name (of) "God."[46] In the Councils, by contrast, he is turned into an idol, a divine being. That is the misunderstanding, what is being reduced. The New Testament is not a series of propositions which pass along special information about extraordinary beings and facts of the matter to which we would otherwise have no access were it not supernaturally communicated to inspired writers who wrote it all down for us (which requires a continuing support system of supernaturally guided copyists, translators, and printing presses). It is not a scientific *historia* but a hymn of praise, an *eu-angelon*, good news, amen, alleluia, forged by a constellation of discursive resources, springing from the memory and the promise of the life and death of Yeshua, a man shrouded in the fog of history. It is a song to the event that took place in Yeshua. In the New Testament, the kingdom of God is a poem and Yeshua its poet.

The Reduction to Truth

The reduction does not expose Yeshua as a fraud but *expounds the truth* that is taking place in the New Testament. The reduction is not a reduction *of* truth but a reduction *to* truth, which prevents it from being reduced to nonsense. Radical theology is not arguing that confessional theology is a hoax. It is analyzing how it is true, since it is not true in the straightforward propositional-representational sense, a point it shares with works of art. A reduction is a deconstruction, but it is not a "critique" of religion, which is a creature of modernity. A critique is like an exorcism; a deconstruction is like a haunting.[47] A deconstruction is an inflection or deflection but not a critique. When Derrida reads Augustine's *Confessions*, he does not debunk (critique) its Neoplatonic dualism; instead, he rewrites it, reinvents it, inflects it, in terms of his own story; the "confession" becomes a hybrid "circumfession" written by a "little black and very Arab Jew."[48]

A deconstruction is a close reading that exposes fractures and instabilities, which are not faults deserving of criticism but openings to the future. It is at most postcritical: If we accept the historical-critical critique (the writers of the gospels did not speak Aramaic and never laid eyes on Jesus), a deeper, postcritical religion is opened up. The rationalist-secularist critique of religion seeks to expose it as a fraud. Although it is true to say that it is exposed for what it is, what the confessional tradition *is*, is not a fraud. What C. S. Lewis took to be a perfect counterargument—Jesus was either a fraud, mad, or God—is perfectly ridiculous. The New Testament is a poetics, the expression of an event. True, the stories in the Bible are mostly fictions. Most of them never happened. So what? So are paintings, poems, plays, and novels. The reduction does not deprive any of them of their truth. It discovers their truth. It makes a reduction to their truth, their own proper truth.

Simplifying to an extreme, let us say that this truth can be described in three progressively "weaker" (radical, deconstructive) forms:

For *Hegel*, radical theology is a speculative-hermeneutic phenomenology of the forms of the Spirit. The confessional tradition ("religion") bears within itself the truth in the form of a *Vorstellung*, which is a presentation of the absolute truth in a form more conceptual than art but more sensuous than philosophy. That is half right, but I would weaken this Hegelianism by denying Hegel's rationalism, where the truth of religion is measured by the Concept. Religion is a *Vorstellung* of which there is no Concept, not even in German metaphysics, to which the right theological response is the laughter of Kierkegaard's pseudonyms.[49]

For *Tillich*, radical theology is an existential ontology of a *symbol*. A living symbol seizes us in the ground of our being because it embodies in a conditional form something of unconditional import. That is almost right, but I would weaken it with a dash of deconstruction, rendering this ground somewhat more groundless.

For *Derrida*, radical theology, were he forced to speak like that, is not an ontology but a *hauntology*. The truth of religion takes the form not of a Hegelian Spirit but a specter, of a *spook*, not an absolute *Geist* but a ghost, not a Tillichian symbol of the ground of being, but a kind of spectral demi-being. Any given construction is haunted by the ghost of the undeconstructible (the event). That, I think, puts its finger on—as opposed to getting it in its grip, like a concept—the matter at hand, which is the event.

IV.
WHAT DIFFERENCE DOES THIS DIFFERENCE MAKE?

I said above that approaching radical theology by distinguishing it from confessional theology as its inner disturbance was not only the most accessible approach but also the most useful. So now the question is, Of what use is it? What difference does this theological difference make? Why bother with radical theology? What good does it do? Is it merely a negative and critical undertaking of use only in the academy? The short answer, which has been my main interest here, is that radical theology can save religion from itself. The long answer, which I can only sketch here, is that radical theology can also save the secular order from itself. In so doing, it upends the binary opposition of the religious and secular, a signpost of modernity about which I wish to be as "post-" as possible. What good is that? That polar opposition, I think, is particularly destructive today, and its deconstruction is a central plank in any possible political theology. Events are nothing conventional. The reduction to the event is always and already *interventional*, which means *politically* interventive, as I will point out here.

I understand that the language of being "saved" might make you nervous. In general, when someone announces they are going to save you, the safest thing for you is to head for the door. If being "saved" makes you think of Bible-thumpers, gay-bashing, and rural billboards and school boards denouncing the theory of evolution, or if it makes you worry that I am trying to spring a new confessional religion on you and start soliciting donations, then find some other word that does not make you nervous. Words are polyvalent, and deconstruction is not in the business of abolishing words but of reinventing them. The work of saving I have in mind is making democracy safe from the danger of theocracy and religious violence, intervening in the nationalism and authoritarianism with which religion all too frequently confuses itself. These deadly threats, which we thought were put behind us, have reared their ugly heads with a surprising new force, both in the United States and globally.[50]

Saving Religion from Itself. I began by saying that we live in a world in which religion is making itself increasingly unbelievable, and I want to show now that this is dangerous to itself and to everybody else. By starting with the distinction between radical and confessional theology, the idea was to stress that radical theology is not a freestanding speculative discourse but an interested, interventive, and ultimately a political one. I am neither trying to start a new religion—the ones we have are already enough trouble—nor trying to pass radical theology off as a theology simply without a religion or congregation. Then it threatens to be nothing more than hot air, a free-floating academic abstraction, useful for tenure and promotion applications, perhaps, but not much else. Rather than free-standing, it is a way of understanding (*subtilitas intelligendi*) actually existing religious traditions, a way of interpreting (*subtilitas explicandi*) existing theologies and of intervening in them (*subtilitas applicandi*), which is why I think hermeneutics, radical hermeneutics, is so important.[51]

My thesis is that religion today is more in need of being saved than it is equipped to save anyone else, its offers of salvation up to now having so often resulted in disaster for those it purported to save. I propose that by preventing religion from further descending into superstition and super-naturalism, radical theology helps disarm an increasing theocratic threat to the democratic order. So, to take up a Derridean biological trope, I am proposing that both the seminaries and the seminars (universities) need to cultivate an *auto-immunity* to radical theology.[52] They need to suppress their inbred immune-response to the coming of this other into their bodies, be it to the radical (in the seminaries) or to the theology (in the seminars). The presence of the other-in-me can be in fact a fertile and not a fatal condition, promoting good health, good circulation!

But beyond being insinuated into the syllabuses of the seminaries and the seminars, radical theology belongs in everyday life, in the public square, in the *agora*, in social and political public discourse. In the university radical theology has surfaced as a voice in "theory," and it can be found in the "philosophy of religion," but it hits the streets when it is found in the confessional traditions. Radical theology is often found among the "nones," that is, just where religion thinks there is none. That is half my point. The other half, to stay with the pun, is that radical theology is also found in the nuns, especially today's nuns, like Sister Mary Scullion in the "Tradition and Event" essay.[53] Her kind of radical social and political action on behalf of people who are being ground under by a rigged patriarchal and racist system is radical theology in action. It is confessional theology bearing witness to radical theology *in actu exercitu*. To awaken the radical theological core within the confessional tradition is to awaken progressive religious forces and retake the hill of religion back from a reactionary and destructive religious right. Confessional theologians are very often radical theologians in the trenches. Often, when pastors or theologians are excommunicated or fired—I am not thinking of the sexual abuse scandals, where there have not been enough firings!—it is because they have burned through the surface of sedimented beliefs and unbending practices and exposed the underlying radical theological *event*. Confessional theologians are radical theologians in the making, depending on just how daring they are. *Sapere aude!* Dare to think. Absolutely. But also dare to act, *agere aude!* And dare to hope, *sperare aude.*[54]

To think and do and hope for what? The event.

The intervention of radical theology is strategic: Unlike the learned despisers, it is located at the heart of confessional theology. It is the other inside. Situated within, it interrupts the self-destructive effort of orthodoxy to be identical with itself, to be the self-same all the way down, to expel the other from its body, all so many attempts to prevent the event. Radical theology is not a "critique" of confessional religion, deploying outside leverage like a hammer, like the reductionistic critiques of Marx or Freud or the "new atheists." Radical theology is theology *itself* in its radical mode. It is the event that is stirring within theology, which has always been there, eventive and inventive, interventive and interruptive, ever since the Jewish prophets started raising hell with their Jeroboams. Its advice to the confessional traditions is, *nolite foras ire.* The trouble is here at home. Look within and find their own inner core. The best way to deconstruct theology—or anything else—is to write a meticulous history of it, exposing the plurivocity of what pretends to speak with one voice! The deconstruction of the logical is the micrological. Radical theology has always been there, in the roots and in the rafters, in the prophets and the protesters, in the lost gospels and suppressed gospels, in the heretics and the mystics by which orthodoxy is continually disturbed, a disturbance deliciously depicted by Mary-Jane Rubenstein's account of the "*pan*ic" at "*pan*theism."[55] Thank God for the heretics. They keep the event alive, preventing self-enclosure. Orthodoxy contains a heterodoxy that it cannot contain, a restlessness it cannot arrest, orthodoxy itself being one of the multiple heterodoxies that, for historical reasons, acquired hegemonic power. Radical theology takes place as irreducible and originary heterodoxy, as the dissidence of difference, as the disturbance in the history of confessional theology *itself.* If the confessional theologians ask me where I get all this stuff, my answer is, from them, by reading between the lines, with the interlinear, interventive intelligence (*inter* + *legere*) of a micrological reading

That is why, not to make light of a serious situation, I located the place of radical theology on the unemployment line. Every time a confessional theologian is shown the door for showing confessional theology its limits, we should add a pin on the map of radical theology and pin a medal on the theologian. As Pope Francis said about his ultraconservative critics in the United States, it is an honor to be criticized by them.[56] Radical theology is found at work in pastors who look at themselves in the mirror one Sunday morning and tell themselves to stop deceiving themselves. It is found in believers who look at themselves in the mirror one Sunday morning and tell themselves to stop letting themselves be deceived. It is found in progressive religious communities that find themselves in an uneasy and ambiguous place on the boundaries of the confessional corporation, inside/outside, as Derrida puts it.[57]

That means, first, that these pastors and communities are haunted by the suspicion that they no longer believe these beliefs. Slightly paraphrasing Vattimo, they believe that they no longer believe.[58] The beliefs that make up the confessional creed (*credere*) induce incredulity, but that doubt, according to the paralogic of the event, should lead to a deeper faith. Only by allowing the event can confessional communities assemble in good conscience, without requiring the faithful to check their intellectual faculties at the church door, without expecting them to believe their "salvation" depends on appeasing the wrath of an offended superbeing. But by disallowing the inner promptings of these spectral spirits, the confessional powers that be cut off their own circulation, break the circuit, rob religion of its future, deprive it of its truth, and pose a threat to everyone else. They shrink religion down to a condition where it can flourish only among the least educated populace in an increasingly educated, globalized, and wired world, among people who are easily conned by a con man, a demagogue with simplistic, xenophobic, and race-baiting solutions to the complex problems of globalization. They produce a shrunken monster, disallowing what radical theology can do for confessional theology. They prevent the event that can save it from itself, the reinventing, the new being, which is good news to the poor and the imprisoned and the oppressed—but to white Christian nationalists not so much.

Saving the Secular Order. Radical theology is a two-edged sword, cutting through the self-enclosed systems erected by both the religious and secular orders, which are intended to insulate each from the other as the private and the public. Radical theology wants to weaken this distinction—*not*, I hasten to add, by letting the religious right take over the Supreme Court, which is the nightmare we presently face, the threat of theocracy we are alarmed by. Radical theology requires a radical hermeneutics that saves the secular order from its own mythological and half-blasphemous idol, the one it calls "Reason," in caps and in the singular, by weakening it into having "good reasons," depending on the ever-shifting weight of evidence at the time.[59] Radical theology protects the secular order from volatilizing into a desiccated and bloodless *rationalism*—sneering with curled lip at the mention of religion—all the while failing to recognize its own prophetic sources and resources. If the Jewish prophets were ancient social pundits, the "secular" people today expending their every effort on behalf of immigrants, the uninsured, the schools, and the homeless speak with a prophetic voice, but they are disinclined to confess this for fear they will sound like Bible-thumpers, a fear that never menaced Martin Luther King Jr.

Radical theology finds the religious *in* the secular, not only in what religion does not recognize as religious but in what the secular order does not recognize as religious. It unearths a genuine truth-tested religion—in the radical sense of responsiveness to the *event*—in what a lot of self-righteous and self-appointed defenders of religion, the encircled ecclesiastical set, brush off as the profane world. And it finds a lot more religion than the self-encircled secular left would like to think in their own work on behalf of the oppressed. Think of physicians who put themselves in harm's way in order to eradicate the Ebola virus in west Africa, teachers who are underpaid and undervalued who spend their lives working with children in schools that are badly underfunded in order to hold down the taxes on the rich ("suffer the little children"). None of this need go under the name of "religion," a word which we may not be able to save, which may not be worth saving. But the event does not care what you call it. So to shrink religion down to its rites and creeds on the one side, and the secular order down to a dispassionate, public, purely rational and neutral medium, on the other side, is to cut off the circulation of both and produce two shrunken monsters, distorted and diminished. All honor to academic debates, but this is not just an academic debate. This is the all-too-real and lethal disconnect between the intellectual (secular) left and blue-collar (religious) working people today that has given us *die Gift* of Donald Trump.[60] The secular left would do well to hire a few of our unemployed radical theologians—they need the work!—as political consultants, who could give their candidates some advance talking points about what the "kingdom of God" and the "year of the jubilee" really mean for the next time they visit rural America.

This point is made perfectly by the book that cost Tillich his job in Germany in 1933, in which he exposed the barbarism of National Socialism, on the one hand, and the bloodless rationalism of secular Communism, on the other hand, in response to which he proposed a prophetic, religious socialism.[61] In fact, undoing the dichotomy of the religious and the secular is pretty much the legacy, the continuing mandate, the unfinished project, of Tillich's theology of culture, which explains why Tillich is undergoing a revival in radical theology today.[62] Religion and Reason, in the singular and capitalized, are Janus-faced monsters manufactured in modernity. Radical theology, as "weak" theology, weakens both the strong transcendental pretensions of Reason, on the one hand, and the strong supernatural pretensions of Religion, on the other hand. It is the suspension of both the transcendental signified and the supernatural signified. In radical theology, theology and culture, the religious and the secular, faith and reason, do not belong to two separate and opposing camps; they belong to a single circulatory system. Radical theology lies at the heart of what religion calls the secular order, just because it gives it a heart, a beating, restless heart, and a prophetic voice.

This suspension of the authority of Reason and Religion (a couple of Big Others) is carried out in the service not of an anemic skepticism but of a more resolute faith beyond belief and a more ecstatic reason beyond rationalism.[63] So all this talk of saving does not mean that radical theology is the new religion, or that it has the answer that will save us all. I am not saying it is the answer. I am saying it honors the event, which opens and sustains the question that we ourselves are. I am repeating, in a radicalized modality, Luther's *justus et peccator*. We are saved by recognizing the extent to which we are lost, enabled by our disability, circum-cut[64] off from transcendental and supernatural support systems. We are thus forcibly reminded that we do not know who we are, and that *is* who we are, all of us siblings of this same non-knowing. Our quasi-Augustinian confession, confessing there is no big supernatural or transcendental something or other coming over the hill to save us, *is* the saving, the beginning of the saving. What is saving about radical theology is its sense of the messianic urgency to let the kingdom come, to let justice flow like water over the land. What is saving is the open-ended, infinitival hope in a coming god, not by idly waiting, not by standing by, but by understanding that *we* are the messianic age, the ones the dead have been waiting for to make right the wrongs they endured.

Conclusion without Closure

What is radical theology? We don't know; it's not over yet. Let us just say, for the interim, radical theology, in its widest sense, is openness to the event in all its haunting spectrality, openness to the coming of what we cannot see coming, whatever that will have been, *viens, oui, oui*, world without why, Amen.

1

Tradition and Event
Radicalizing the Catholic Principle

A Test Case

In the summer of 2015, the Philadelphia newspapers headlined the story that a woman named Margie Winters, the director of religious education at a local Catholic academy, had been fired on the grounds that she was openly involved in a lesbian marriage. The word was that this had been a secret in plain sight at the academy but that some unhappy parents had complained to the Philadelphia Archdiocese, which forced the hand of the school's administration. The reaction against the move was swift and strong as Winters was loved and respected at the school. The most interesting reaction took the form of an op-ed published in the Philadelphia newspapers and signed by a parent, a layman philanthropist, and Sister Mary Scullion, a well-known Catholic activist in the city and a member of the Religious Sisters of Mercy, which conducts the academy. The signers said that "the Church's truest integrity is at risk when it emphasizes orthodoxy and doctrine without meaningful engagement with human and historic realities." After pointing out that the church must take responsibility for "its many historic blind spots—persecution of heretics, oppression of indigenous peoples in the name of 'mission,' and second-class status for women," they added:

> We are convinced that this is a moment when insistence on doctrinal adherence is clashing with what we believe the Spirit is unfolding in our history—just as it has in the past, with issues like slavery,

the rights of women, and the environment. Many Christian denominations have listened to the movement of the Spirit and moved toward both full inclusion and full embrace of the gifts of our gay and lesbian sisters and brothers. The Church is at its best when it listens to the Spirit speaking in our times and through human experiences.[1]

That response—appealing to the promptings of the Spirit in history unfolding in human experience—seems to me exactly right. A very good piece of Catholic theology had made the local newspapers. Archdiocesan politics aside, this was the right *theological* argument to make. In my view, the church's position on same-sex love is every bit as wrong as the other historic blind spots to which the letter refers, each one of which eventually succumbed to the pressure of history. Time and again the church in modernity starts out on the wrong side of history and eventually, several centuries later, catches up with the times and adds a modest apology for standing in the way of science or justice tucked away in an obscure section of *L'Osservatore Romano*. But the framers of this editorial are not speaking of merely being on the wrong side of history, but on the wrong side of the Spirit! They speak of the Spirit "speaking in our times through human experience," of what "the Spirit is unfolding in our history," so that to discern the signs of the times is to discern the promptings of the Spirit.

Their argument presupposes a view of God as the Spirit working in history, and of the church as the *populus dei*, the people of God, not as the hierarchy, one of the most important pronouncements of Vatican II. The argument is theological, pneumatological, and ecclesiological. For the Catholic theologian it is the prompting of the Spirit—not "Pure Reason," or the law of dialectical materialism, or the "masses"—that rises up in protest against the violence of history. Against colonialization, say, which the church provided with a theological cover with its notorious "doctrine of discovery," authorizing the *conquistadores* to engage in their lethal land grab in the name of God. In this scene the church as the Spirit immanent in history contests the violence of a "Church" contracted to the official teachings of the hierarchy, which was on the wrong side of both the Spirit and history. Against the deep errancy and fallibility of church-as-hierarchy, the unfolding of Spirit-in-history is a movement of auto-correction and reinvention. Against the calcification of dogmatic formulae, which results in simple reproduction, the immanence of the Spirit in history unfolds in a productive repetition. Debates in the church take place not between liberals and conservatives, nor between the church and its members, but between the contingent doctrinal formulations at any given point in history and the ongoing workings of the Spirit unfolding in and as the people of God.

The case is telling. In its defense the church might rejoin that there is nothing in the scriptures to authorize same-sex love and that Paul appears to have condemned it. I would begin by denying that what Paul was condemning back in the first century is what we are talking about today. But the larger point is that in the Catholic tradition it is the tradition that interprets what the scriptures are saying to us at a given moment. The tradition is the *whole* church, not just the uppermost part, the whole body, not just the "head," a figure used by the unknown author of the pseudepigraphic Colossians (1:18–20), which alters the figure introduced by Paul (1 Cor 12:27) and turns Jesus into a king or emperor. The tradition is the workings of the Spirit in the people of God, and the Spirit often finds itself compelled to take a stand against such a heady church, the one that Marguerite Porete called the "Little Church," meaning big in power but little in Spirit. *Sola scriptura* is the Protestants' problem, not ours. Unfortunately, the old theological axiom, where the Spirit is, there is the church (*ubi spiritus, ibi ecclesia*), has a way of being flipped by the powers that be in the church: where the church is, there is the Spirit (*ubi ecclesia, ibi spiritus*), as if the Spirit has written the church a blank check and simply does the bidding of Vatican secretaries.

Or the church might invoke "natural law," which would only make things worse. For one thing, natural law is a Stoic doctrine—to my knowledge Jesus was not a natural law theorist—in which God is thought in terms of nature and nature in terms of necessity; it presupposes a view of God as the necessary immutable order of nature. God or nature (*Deus sive natura*), as Spinoza said. This completely pagan conception stands opposed to the Jewish and Christian, and in particular prophetic tradition, where God is thought not in terms of nature but of history, and the God of history is thought not in terms of necessity but in terms of making all things new, of the new being, of the future, of the transformability of the future. Stoic natural law was the competing alternative and leading opponent of the church in antiquity, where the choice was posed between making oneself commensurable with the inevitable, affirming the necessity of things, on the one hand, and affirming the God who will make all things new, on the other. So, apart from the fact that natural law has been the argument of choice for justifying the oppression of just about everything, the poor and uneducated, women, children, people of color, immigrants, animals, and the environment, it is a completely pagan argument—pitted against the God of history and renewal, against the view of God as Spirit.

So what happened in the Margie Winters case? How did the appeal of the Spirit fare before the powers that be downtown at the offices of the Archdiocese of Philadelphia? We will come back to that, even if I fear my attempt to hold you in suspense is pretty anemic.

The Catholic Principle

The contemporary debate about same-sex love also makes plain that one has a much easier time addressing such problems if one does not have to deal with a doctrine of *sola scriptura*. Even so, the irony is that the Protestant denominations are way ahead of the Catholics in affirming the dignity of women, same-sex love, and the priesthood of the people, but that is only because the Catholic hierarchy is so adept at snatching defeat from the jaws of victory. The underlying theological presuppositions are all on the Catholic side. The old debate between the Protestants and the Catholics is settled even before it gets off the ground. The Protestant notion of *sola scriptura* represents a misunderstanding on every level. It originates in a factual misunderstanding of the history of the composition of the scriptures, as if they represent eyewitness journalistic reports; in a theoretical misunderstanding of the nature of a written text, which is why it has produced the bizarre result of biblical inerrantism by which, believe it or not, we are still plagued today; and finally in a theological misunderstanding of the Spirit, as if the workings of the Spirit could be contracted to and measured by a book, which is at least as much of a mistake as thinking it is confined to the upper one-tenth of one percent that make up the Catholic hierarchy. The scriptures are not the foundation of the tradition. They are the effect of the tradition. They were produced by the tradition when, at a certain point in time, the Greek-speaking followers of the "way"—we did not yet even have the word "Christianity"—decided they had better start writing things down.

Chronologically, the scriptures are a relatively late formation. The very fact that the various communities chose to write down the sayings and stories that had been orally transmitted—the tradition up to that point— tells us that a great deal of time had been spent waiting for the return of Jesus and the conviction had set in that it might very well prove to be a long wait. Their importance is not chronological—as if they are there at the beginning and reporting back to us latecomers—but kairological. Their composition was the right thing to do at the right time. Right for what? For the *tradition*, for the history of the people of God, in order to allow it to be preserved and transmitted. They serve the life of the tradition; indeed, they are the tradition at work preserving itself. The scriptures are a gift, but they are the gift of tradition, of the operations of memory and expectation that define a tradition, and a tradition is an ongoing process of auto-correction. The scriptures do not compete with tradition as an opposing or even as a separate principle, as if there were two. They insert themselves *within* tradition, as a part of the tradition; they are the tradition *in actu exercitu*. They are still more evidence that tradition is first, last, and always. If the works of Thomas Aquinas were placed on the high altar at the opening Mass of Vatican I, they would have been well advised to put a good account of tradition, like Gadamer's *Truth and Method*, on the high altar of Vatican II. (It had just come out!)[2]

But do not misunderstand me. While I am pressing the case for tradition, I have not come to engage in a chauvinistic reassurance of the superiority of Catholicism over Protestantism, each of which I think has come up with its own way to give the Spirit in the world a good deal of dispiriting grief. As we can see from my opening test case, the results of pressing the case for the tradition cause considerable discomfort to the powers that be on both sides of that divide, not only for the hapless defenders of biblical inerrancy but also for the hapless defenders of hierarchical inerrancy, for inerrancy of any sort, the very idea of which drives a Cartesian stake into the heart of any living tradition, Christian or otherwise. Under the pressure of history, that is, of the Spirit in history, I think the fifth volume of the collected works of Hans Küng will eventually prove to be the right response to the idolatrous and patriarchal violence of infallibility.[3]

Hence, in a show of ecumenism, and to prove that I have nothing provincial and merely denominational in mind, I turn now to what Paul Tillich called the "Protestant Principle."[4]

By a principle he does not mean an abstract general proposition, but a concrete and existential driving force in history.[5] He did not mean the myopic principles of *sola fide* or *sola scriptura*; no such list of solo performances will do. Any list of *solae* would need to be extended indefinitely and any such solitude would end up being very much disturbed. He meant a spirit which, while inspired by historical Protestantism, makes both a wider sweep and a deeper cut and indeed submits the historical Protestant churches to its judgment. This Principle is a function of a prior distinction Tillich drew between the conditional and unconditional. By the unconditional he meant, on the object-side, some substantive matter—let's say, in German, a *Sache*, a thing that matters—something that lays claim to us unconditionally, without compromise, leaving us no room to negotiate the terms of the deal, no way to talk it down. On the subject-side, the unconditional means what we affirm unconditionally, what matters to us unconditionally. This is a matter for which we are willing to live or die, as a very youthful Kierkegaard said in his *Journals*; a matter of ultimate "concern," an English word that would have translated the German *Sorge*, which is the Being of Dasein in Heidegger's *Being and Time*, a book Tillich knew very well. This issues in Tillich's famous description of religion in terms of being seized by a matter of ultimate concern, a definition remarkable for its failure to mention incense, candles, clergy, hierarchy, and dogmas.

Accordingly, the enlarged Protestant Principle is reconfigured as follows. First, *semper reformanda*, which Tillich explains by saying that the church must live in a permanent state of protest, of permanent self-critique, on the grounds that the historical church is a conditioned response to an unconditional demand. Accordingly, the demands placed upon the church—be it Roman, Protestant, or Orthodox—are never met, structurally, in principle. Second, *justus et peccator*: Human subjects always fall short of what is demanded of us (*peccator*), so we are called out by something for which we are never the match, structurally, in principle, guilty, not because of what we did but because of what we are. But we are saved (*justus*) by confessing just how far short we have fallen, saved by this loss, saved not exactly by our faith but by our doubt, by our postmodern incredulity, by our doubt-filled faith (or faith-filled doubt) in something that has seized us unconditionally. For our purposes, Tillich presupposes the challenge of God in terms of the challenge of the unconditional.[6]

Tillich opposes the Protestant Principle to what he calls the "Catholic substance." By substance he does not mean the *substantia* of Greco-medieval metaphysical theology, which shows up in the Catholic theology of "transubstantiation," but the historical faith that had been handed down through the ages, the Christian legacy. He does not mean *substantia*, *natura*, or *essentia*—he means history. The inherited historical tradition, the theology and sacraments and liturgies which have been handed down, which stand in need of constant critique. The substance can only be passed down by passing under the principle of protest. There are not two different principles, one Protestant and one Catholic, but one Principle and a substance, a form and a substance. The Catholic substance is the tradition, the historically transmitted faith, upon which the Protestant Principle is the critical reflection.

So it is significant that Tillich does not speak of a Catholic "Principle." It is as if there is a kind of pre-reflective, precritical naïveté in the substance, which does not rise to the level of a reflective Principle of protest and criticism. I think Tillich is mistaken about that. The substance is the tradition, and the tradition is the promptings of the Spirit in history, and that implies, if not a reflective critical operation, another let us say auto-corrective operation, one embedded in history—which we see when we speak of the "force of history," or of being on the "right side of history." That does indeed represent a principle—a principle of historical process. The stirrings of the unconditional always take place under historical conditions. Just as Luther said that the Bible interprets itself, referring to the dialectic between the whole and the part, so does the tradition interpret itself, by the ongoing process of self-correction and reinvention—which being a work of history is far from inerrant. So there is a Catholic Principle, which is the historical principle, and this historical principle is the hermeneutical principle. Indeed, the neglect of the historical hermeneutical principle is lethal on both sides: It leads Protestantism astray into an ahistorical biblical inerrantism, even as it leads Catholicism astray into an ahistorical doctrine of infallibility which confers unconditional status on a conditional-historical doctrinal formulation. A pope or a paper pope! An inerrant book or an inerrant institution! Pick your poison—or your idolatry!

Like Tillich, let us say that while taking its point of departure from historical Catholicism, the Catholic Principle is not restricted to denominational Catholicism, but indeed submits both historical Catholicism and historical Protestantism under its judgment. I want now to propose that the opposite of the Catholic Principle in this wider and deeper sense is not the historical Reformation but, more important, the Gnostic principle.[7] It is the decision made early on in the tradition to insist that Jesus was a man of flesh and blood, a historical agent, datable and locatable. He was a dark-skinned, Aramaic-speaking Jewish Galilean peasant—enough to get him banned from entering the United States by the Christian Right—a healer and an exorcist, who lived in the first century and was crucified during the reign of Tiberius; he was not a phantom or apparition of a pure spirit. The Catholic Principle appropriately broadened and deepened is the principle of historicality and temporality, materiality and carnality. It is wider and deeper than the words of Scriptures or the datable-locatable declarations of the hierarchy; it is polyvalent, polymorphic, polyglottal. It is the very *Sache* of Christianity, which is Spirit in the world, and—like it or not—the Protestant Principle of protest and critique has been at work in it all along. It has always and already, *semper*, stood in need of being reformed, and it has always and already been reforming, reconfiguring—for better and for worse—under the historical-temporal-carnal-material pressure exerted by the Spirit.

Radicalizing the Catholic Principle

Radicalizing the Catholic principle means both radicalizing the Spirit and radicalizing hermeneutics. Radicalizing the Spirit means that on the Catholic principle, the world is the *sacramentum mundi*, and the Spirit is entirely sacramental and mundane, not an immaterial being outside the space and time of the world. The Spirit is a thoroughly historical one, not an immaterial substance or what the Scholastics called a *substantia separata*; the Spirit is neither a substance nor separate. The Spirit is not an immaterial being in the sky but a being down on earth, a Spirit-in-the-world, as in "being-in-the-world" (*in-der-Welt-sein*), carrying all the force of the Heideggerian hyphens. The Spirit is the breath of the body of the world, the respiration and inspiration of this body. The Spirit inspires by calling, by forcing air through the lungs of the world and calling for the coming of the Kingdom, for the Kingdom to come.

As the Spirit is the people of God, to say that "the Spirit lives" is to say that real people live who are moved by the memory and the promise of Jesus, not that an immaterial Super-Being in the sky is hovering over them and overseeing the traffic down on earth by means of earthly plenipotentiaries in Vatican offices. What exists are real people, a collective, gathered together by the call that is getting itself called in the memory and the promise of Yeshua, while the distinctions drawn in Christian Neoplatonism between time and eternity, and between material and immaterial substances, are fictions, conceptual artifacts. The living Spirit is the living-breathing Spirit, literally. Make no mistake, I mean breathing, with lungs, with real air. On the Catholic principle, I am insisting, the challenge of God is to keep the future open, and to count on the past to give us the courage for the future, to have hope in the future because we have hope in the past. Tillich called this the courage to be; let us simply add, the courage for what may be, not *être* but *peut-être*.

The radicalization of hermeneutics means that interpretation goes all the way down, to the roots, *radix*. There are no uninterpreted facts of the matter. Underlying an interpretation is not a pure fact but another interpretation, no less datable and locatable. The hermeneutical principle is a principle because it has reformative force, exciting an ongoing process of reformation, of transformation, of auto-reformation, whether we like it or not. The tradition alters under our feet, whether we resist these changes, like the conservatives, or embrace them, like the progressives. According to the Catholic (historical-hermeneutical) Principle, every historical event is a conditional expression of the unconditional Spirit-in-history. It is in fact disingenuous to speak of "the" tradition or "the" church because on closer inspection history discloses to us multiple traditions and many churches, which we cluster together in a kind of grand intellectual shorthand when we speak of them in the singular.

The radical hermeneutical point can be summarized by saying that a tradition does not have a meaning or an essence; it has a history. The substance of the Catholic Principle is hermeneutical and historical. If we ask, "What is the meaning or the essence of the church?" the answer is that we cannot say. It has not ended yet. We can only speak of the "meaning," "essence," or "definition" of things that were never alive to begin with, like a triangle, or are dead and gone, like a dead language. Then we are free to compile a list of all its usages without fear that someone will come along and coin a new metaphor or create a new genre or change the language game or initiate a paradigm shift—and cause a shift that reverberates throughout the system and alters its course.

The church, like any tradition, does not *have* a history; it *is* a history. It is the real people coursing through time who breathe with this Spirit, inhaling and exhaling its motifs and stories, beliefs and practices. Always a "pilgrim church," the church is a historical and conditioned response to something that calls to us unconditionally, which I characterize as the memory and the promise of Yeshua, using his ancient Aramaic name. This defamiliarization relieves us of some of the baggage of a name that has been freighted, overwrought, and overdetermined with dogma and violence. It reminds us of a man of flesh and blood, of his carnality and materiality, temporality and historicality—dark-skinned, Aramaic-speaking, Jewish— which are the signature marks of the Catholic Principle radically understood. In general I think that heresies are innovations of the Spirit that the hierarchy fears, but I do think that Docetism is a genuinely damnable idea because it denies the historicality, the carnality of the Spirit by claiming that Yeshua's material presence in history was an illusion. The idea that the body of Jesus is a phantom, that he only appeared to be a man, appeared to suffer and die, while in reality he is an immaterial being, which we want to be someday, is lethal.

The Kingdom of God

The name of Yeshua is not the name of an essence but of an event. Consequently, the challenge of God for anyone who has confidence in this tradition, is keyed in a special way to Yeshua, to what he said and did, to his life and death, which, to use the language of the unknown author of the Letter to the Colossians (1:15), serves as an icon of God. As we have all learned from Jean-Luc Marion, an icon is to be distinguished from an idol, because an idol traps us with its glitter while an icon yields to an excess, draws us beyond itself, and leaves us pointing in the direction of something to which it itself points, while leaving us in the accusative. An icon is something conditional—it is subject to the constraints of history, of its concrete hermeneutical situation—but it comes about in response to the call of something unconditional, something that calls us, something that challenges us. The challenge of God is the challenge God poses to us, that puts us on the spot, puts us in the accusative. The challenge of God is unconditional; it is the challenge of the unconditional—which breaks in on us under contingent, historical conditional circumstances. As an icon, Yeshua is a bit of space and time where the challenge of God breaks in, or breaks out, where the space-time continuum of history is bent or curved by the event that is breaking in or breaking out.

The challenge of God, in all its materiality, distinctly defined and vividly embodied by Yeshua, can be felt when Mark has Yeshua announce his mission by saying that he comes to bring "the gospel of God," the good news of God, the *evangelion tou theou*. He announces that the *kairos* has been fulfilled, which means the "kingdom of God" (*basileia tou theou*) is near, that we should have a new heart, *metanoia*, and put our trust (*pistis*) in the good news (Mark 1:14). If the gospel of Mark is the "gospel of Yeshua the Anointed" (Mark 1:1), the gospel of Yeshua is the "gospel of God," which I take as both a subjective and objective genitive. So we have a multilayered icon, a complex, multiplex event: a text coming from a community, later on emblematized under the name of "Mark," transcribing a memory, handed down by an oral tradition about Yeshua, who in turn announces the "kingdom of God," which itself is an icon or emblem of God. Everything that Yeshua says about God is tied to this expression, the "kingdom of God," which means what life would be like if God ruled, not the world; if God ruled, not Caesar. If so, the challenge of God in what Yeshua said was challenging indeed, and first and foremost it was a challenge to Rome. The expression appears to be almost ironic—since Yeshua was and lived among the humblest of people—and the irony did not go unnoticed by the people who run the kingdom, the real one, the *Imperium Romanum*. We can surmise that Yeshua had a silver tongue, which very likely contributed to his demise at the hands of the Romans. It would not have been beyond him to get in the face of the Romans by posing a threatening possibility to them, the threat of an alternative to Caesar, that the day was near at hand when the rule of the God of the Jews would be established.

When Luke has Yeshua announce his ministry, he uses a citation from Isaiah. Yeshua has been anointed—he is the *Christos*—to bring good news to the poor, to announce to the prisoners that they will be released, to the blind that they will recover their sight, to the oppressed that they will go free, and to proclaim the year of the Jubilee, the year that follows seven times seven, in which all debts are forgiven and the people are able to make a new start, a new beginning. That is how it will look when God rules, not

Caesar. You will notice the materiality and carnality of this list, the poor, the imprisoned, the blind, the oppressed, which is pretty much the same list we find in Matthew 25. So when we press Yeshua about God, he deflects us to the kingdom of God, and when we press him about the kingdom of God, he deflects our attention again, to things like leaven, dinner parties, and treasures buried in a field. So there is a constant deflection—from God to the kingdom, from the kingdom to mustard seeds—not metaphysics.

While Matthew has Yeshua speak more often of the kingdom of heaven, probably out of respect for the name of God, the kingdom of God described by Yeshua seems very terrestrial, and while James Joyce speaks of Yeshua as a "heavenman," Yeshua seems to me very much an earthman. That is as it should be according to the Catholic principle, which is the principle of carnality, materiality, and terrestriality, as opposed to the Docetic principle, which is very heavenly, immaterialistic, and otherworldly.

Did the kingdom come just as Yeshua said it would? Not at all. The challenging thing is that the opposite happened—Yeshua lost and Rome won. Pilate put down this alternative kingdom, swiftly and violently. The Pilate portrayed by the author of the fourth gospel is trying to make "the Jews" look bad and bloody Roman procurators look good. Yeshua, one of "the Jews," would have been appalled by a gospel that, ironically, has earned the nickname of the "gospel of love!" Rome's rule was as firm as ever. So Yeshua's discourse was at best prophetic. Instead of describing a fact of the matter or predicting the future course of events, Yeshua was offering us hope, making us a promise—that is what God means, which means, this is what God means to do. Our challenge is to put our confidence (*pistis*) in that promise, even if it does not happen. The future is better, even when it is not, which is why it is our hope, why we must have confidence in God.

This, I think, is exactly the challenge of God faced by Paul. It all ended in death for Yeshua, and not just death but an execution, and not just execution but a literally excruciating and—in an honor/shame society—a particularly ignominious execution, one that left no doubt about who was ruling. The kingdom was not near, not yet, not now. That was certainly what Paul had concluded, for the longest time. Until he didn't. Until one day, or maybe over the course of many months and years, it hit him; he had a breakthrough. In the only firsthand account we have of this event in his own words—not the romanticized account written many decades later in Acts, no road to Damascus, no voices, no unhorsing, for which we can thank the imagination of the Renaissance painter Tintoretto—he describes an insight (*apocalypsis*, Gal 1:12), a flash of intuition, that God had—to the utter consternation of the world, of Romans, Greeks, and

Jews alike—*revealed himself in the defeat*. The ignominy and the humiliation of the crucifixion bore in fact the mark of God, which is a contradiction of everything that anyone in antiquity had meant by God. The mark of the divine is upon the defeat and the shame. The challenge of God for Paul is to swallow *that*, to accept that unlike the gods of the nations, who triumph over their enemies, the divinity of God of Israel is attested in the humiliating defeat of God's Anointed One.

There could hardly be a greater challenge than that, a greater challenge to our expectations about what we think God is supposed to be. Paul brings his insight to a head in the 1 Corinthians 1 in which the "logic" of this wrenching reversal of our expectations of God is identified in what is, for my money, the most brilliant and explosive account of God, of the challenge posed by God, to be found in the New Testament. There he speaks of the "*logos*" of the cross—of the shame and humiliation, of the death and defeat—which confounded the Greeks, who wanted *sophia*, and the Jews, *us* Jews, including Paul himself, lest we think anachronistically that there were any "Christians" around to oppose to the "Jews," who wanted signs and miracles. Paul puts the challenge of God in the most pointed terms possible. He tells the Christians at Corinth that God has made the wisdom of this world foolish. God's foolishness is wiser than human wisdom; God's weakness is stronger than human strength; and surprisingly, God has chosen them—those at Corinth who put their trust in God's Anointed One—who are not well born, not well educated, not well off. Indeed, he says that God has chosen *ta me onta*, the nothings and nobodies of the world—invoking the very language of being that would have shocked the lovers of Greek wisdom at Corinth—to confound the powers that be, the people of substance (*ousia*), who think they are something, who think they are somebody.

If Yeshua is the *ikon* of what we know about God, the challenge of God is to see God in the poor and oppressed, the hungry and the imprisoned, who await the year of the Jubilee (in the Synoptics), to see God in foolishness, weakness, and nothingness, in defeat and humiliation (in Paul). Of course, this is all in keeping with the *promise* posed by Yeshua's announcement of his ministry. It is not an act of sadomasochistic identification with pain and suffering, and not a simple rejection of every sense of wisdom and strength. So in 1 Corinthians 2 Paul promises the Corinthians that God's day is coming, that the rulers of this world will come to rue the day that they did not listen to Paul, that God will show their worldly wisdom to be foolish and their worldly strength to be weak, and that the real power and wisdom belong to God. That is the apocalyptic part of Paul's *apocalypsis*. But what happened? The same thing. The Romans also killed Paul, and shortly thereafter leveled the Temple, and the people of God were dispersed. Of course, we might say be tempted to say that three centuries later, God's kingdom was finally established—by Constantine. But for a lot of us—not just Stanley Hauerwas![8]—this was less a matter of the Roman *imperium* converting to Christianity and more a matter of Christianity converting to the Roman *imperium*. This was rather more a betrayal of the kingdom than its fulfillment, and it provided the basis of what we call today the "Roman" church. Can you imagine the effect such a phrase would have had on Yeshua? Could any word have struck more fear in his heart?[9]

So Yeshua was proven wrong, and so was Paul. The establishment of the rule of God was not near. The rule of Rome continued even when "Christians" sat on the throne. And it would be very hard to say that over the centuries anything very much like the rule of God ever came about. What Paul called the "powers and the principalities," what we call the greedy, the hateful, the malevolent, continue to do evil and get away with it, and the good continue to do good and to get persecuted for it. As biblical historian James L. Kugel once said, the track record of God in history in intervening on behalf of the good and rectifying evil is so bad we have to wonder why the theologians keep bringing it up.[10]

The Challenge of God

As you have no doubt guessed—there was not much suspense about this—Margie Winters did not get her job back.[11] The appeal of the Spirit fell on deaf ears down at the archdiocesan offices, although President Obama did invite her to the papal reception at the White House in September 2015. Her firing was a betrayal of the Spirit, a departure from the Catholic Principle, and a failure to rise to the challenge of God. Still, the kingdom comes—in the loss, the defeat, in the powerlessness. That's the challenge, the same challenge Paul faced. The kingdom comes whenever people like Margie Winters and Sister Mary Scullion and their colleagues speak out on behalf of what "the Spirit is unfolding in our time," and plead for "listen[ing] to the Spirit speaking in our times and through human experiences," which is a felicitous way to formulate the Catholic Principle, indeed, a felicitous way to radicalize it—only to lose. It's an old story. When the people of God speak out, as these women did, they risk being hauled before the power of the church—like Yeshua brought before the power of Pontius Pilate. The comparison is as apt as it is ironic. The people who express the promptings of the Spirit are judged by the powers that be, the long robes, the men of substance (*ousia*) and authority (*exousia*), sitting in big offices. The Spirit, the spirit of the people, rises up in dignity against the powers and the principalities—of the Roman Church.

The power of the "Churchmen" is organized, not in the image of Yeshua, who was poor and without power, one of *ta me onta*, but of Diocletian, a Roman emperor who persecuted the Christians and became famous for reorganizing the administrative structure of the *Imperium Romanum*— from the "*Pontifex Maximus*" down to the "*dioecesis*"—the very empire which had put Yeshua to death. In this unhappy scene, as in so many others, captured iconically in "The Legend of the Grand Inquisitor," ask yourself: Who stands in the place of Yeshua and who stands in the place of the Roman Procurator? Who stands on the side of divine weakness and who stands on the side of worldly Roman power? What more tragic farce than thinking that the kingdom of God needs to be bureaucratically administered by imperial Roman rule! A church more like Rome than Yeshua, which has tragically confused a historically contingent and conditional form of ancient imperial bureaucracy with the unconditional call for the coming of the kingdom, is exposed for what it is, and exposed by nothing less than the Catholic Principle.

The year of the Jubilee has not arrived. Indeed, this is not a year that is going to have an actual date, one that will go down in history as the year God's rule finally showed up and all things were made new. But if the year of the Jubilee is clearly not a matter of calendar time, what then? There are (at least) two ways to deal with this challenge—the Docetic way and the Catholic way. The Docetic way is to say that the year of Jubilee is a heavenly year, that it does not belong to time at all, where time is treated as an ephemeral shadow, but to what the Neoplatonic philosophers thought to be a timeless One called "eternity." Luke has Yeshua say that the year of the Jubilee is the *pleroma*, the fulfillment of time, but in the Docetic way fulfillment means eradication, that transient time and corruptible flesh will be wiped away. This is most pronounced in that late gospel so idiosyncratic that we often just call it the "fourth" gospel. There the kingdom of God is not a form of life but a form of afterlife, and its central narrative is a cynical story (unknown to rest of the New Testament) of Jesus waiting for Lazarus to die in order to put on a show of divine power (John 11: 4–5).[12] Then the kingdom of God is volatilized into a kingdom of heavenly, incorruptible, docetic bodies flitting about in a timeless eternity doing God knows what. To such mythology, the best religious and theological response, as Tillich said, is atheism.

The Catholic way is to remain faithful to the carnality and materiality, to the temporality and historicality of the kingdom; to mustard seeds not metaphysics; to Yeshua the earthman, not the heavenman. The challenge is to be faithful to this in the face of the evidence, which is that the year of the Jubilee seems very far away indeed, farther than ever. In the Catholic way, the challenge of the God of Yeshua, of the God whose *ikon* was Yeshua, who announces good news for the poor and the coming of the year of the Jubilee, has to do not with predicting the future but with offering us a promise. The year of the Jubilee belongs neither to the timelessness of eternity nor to the chronological time of the calendar but to the theopoetic time of a *promise*. Our challenge is to put our trust and confidence (*pistis*) in God's promise, a trust that is distorted when *pistis* becomes an epistemology of belief, corrupted into a modernist creedal belief, a form of life contracted into a propositional assertion.

Then Protestants pound on their Bible, and popes decree infallibly.

Then the kingdom of God recedes. Then Yeshua weeps over Jerusalem.

The challenge of God comes down to this—that this primal trust is for all the world the foolishness that Paul describes in 1 Corinthians 1. Judged by the standards of the world, the genuine wisdom of God is foolishness, and the genuine power of God is weakness. In God's kingdom, offense is met with forgiveness not retaliation, and hatred with love not a counterattack. Such weakness and folly are a *skandalon*, a stumbling block. They are not part of a long-term winning strategy, or a case of deferred heavenly gratification, or a way the weak have come up with to outwit the strong and take them by surprise, which is pretty much Nietzsche's critique of Christian *ressentiment*. They are not a way to show that the children of the light are ultimately quicker on their feet than the children of darkness, which is a Gnostic mythology. The genuine wisdom and power of God is that the strength is found in the weakness, and the wisdom in the folly— of mercy, love, and forgiveness, where there is every chance, maybe even a likelihood, that the wicked will prosper, and the merciful will lose.

As Margie Winters can tell you, the challenge of God is that God is not about winning. The kingdom of God is a form of life, not of afterlife, and not a secret way to win. The year of the Jubilee is not a world-historical event. It reaches such sporadic and fragile fulfillment as time allows. It is temporal not eternal, and its temporality is neither that of calendar time nor of an apocalyptic time that triumphantly crushes evil. It has the temporality of the *kairos*, belonging to the moment, even little quotidian kairological moments, what Richard Kearney calls "microeschatologies."[13] The kingdom of God arrives not by transcending time but letting the shoots of grace spring up in the crevices of time, by letting being be broken up and disjoined by time. Unhappily, the kingdom happens, grace emerges, when people like Margie Winters lose.

The challenge of God is to recognize that the name of God is not the name of a supreme being (*ens supremum*), nor of being itself (*ipsum esse*), nor of the ground of Being, nor of a hyper-being (*hyperousios*), but of a promise. The challenge of God lies not in the ontological eminence or the ontological depth of being but in the unconditionality of the challenge to make the kingdom of God come true. The operative distinctions are not ontotheological—beings and Being, time and eternity, matter and spirit, body and soul—but theopoetical: conditional and unconditional, call and response. The challenge is, otherwise than being, the name of a promise, of an unconditional call, of a solicitation issuing not from a Super-being but from the bowels of the earth, to use an earthy image, or from the spirit-in-the-world, to use a more edifying one. From time to time, in time, Spirit breaks in upon us as if from without, and from time to time breaks out among the people of God, who are filled with this spirit. This all takes place according to the Catholic Principle, the unfolding of the Spirit in carnality and mortality, in temporality and historicality, in materiality and terrestriality.

I conclude with the same words invoked by the authors of the op-ed in the Philadelphia newspaper, a citation from Pope Francis, a man poised precariously and with great uneasiness between occupying the place of *Pontifex Maximus* and affirming the kingdom of God, "If the Christian is a restorationist, a legalist, if he wants everything clear and safe, then he will find nothing. Tradition and memory of the past must help us to have the courage to open up new areas to God."

2

Proclaiming the Year of the Jubilee
Thoughts on a Spectral Life

When Jesus announced his ministry, he said he was anointed by the Spirit to bring good news to the poor and proclaim the year of the Jubilee (Luke 4:16).

That is a haunting thought.

Why haunting? Why not just inspiring, beautiful, holy? Nothing's simple with you.

I am not saying it's not inspiring, beautiful, and holy. I am just saying that it has a kind of spectral quality about it. In theology, everything is haunted.

By what?

If I knew what, it would not be a specter. By something, I know not what.

Let's just say by "it," with all the anonymity of "it." It's vague, but "it" is "there."

Then why call it theology? "It" could be anything.

That's very true. But in theology it goes under—unless it is coming under—the name (of) "God," of the rule of "God," the year of God's favor.

But what's so spectral about that? Where's the specter?

Jesus proclaimed the year of the Jubilee a long time ago, and for all the world it still hasn't happened, but nobody has given up on it. Don't you find that strange? It's like 50 is a lucky number. We never get to 50, but they still keep saying it. We do the math, we keep counting, and we never get to 50. I'd say that's a very spooky kind of mathe-matics. It is always coming, but it never quite shows up; it keeps getting postponed. Maybe next year. So in my view I'd say we're haunted by its coming, by its prospect, by the specter of its prospect.

Very fancy! And you? I suppose you fancy yourself an expert in this field?

Let's start again. I am giving you the wrong impression. Specters pay us unexpected visitations; they do not come by invitation. This is less something that I propose than something to which we are all already exposed. Specters do not wait on our permission. We are always and already haunted, like it or not. The specter spooks; it spooks, under one name or another, under many names; and we are all subject to it. So it is not a question of being an expert but of experiencing spooks.

You have chosen a very strange profession.

It has chosen me. It never consulted me.

What has chosen you?

It. An insistent, incessant "it." It gives me no peace.

So what do you make of this saying of Jesus? What's going on here?

If it spooks, if it's all spooked, the whole thing—thought, being, God—the one big question I have is how to live with it, with "it," with whatever's spooking things. How to proclaim the year of the Jubilee even though it never comes? How to lead a spectral life?

It Spooks Thought

The Modern Philosophers, the Men of Reason, of the Enlightenment, thought they could save us. They thought their Thought could save us. (Hint: When I capitalize words, I am using "scare quotes" to spook them, or to suggest that "it spooks" them. I could, like the Germans, capitalize almost everything, but that would be impractical.)

Karl Marx, one of the greatest of them, said that the Critique of religion is the first and most fundamental form of Critique, the very paradigm of Critique, after which other forms of critique are to be modeled. That is because religion distorts economic phenomena and supports economic op-pression precisely by mystifying reality with its otherworldly ghosts—a ruse that capitalism also perpetrates in its own way (like the "invisible hand" or the phantasmatic "commodity"). To do Critique, then, is to demystify, to replace mystification with reality, to dispel illusions with the cold truth, to get rid of the ghosts of religion and replace them with hard economic real-ity. To critique is to exorcise. Criticism is exorcism. Derrida wrote a book about Marx and, in the "spirit of a certain Marxism,"[1] said exactly the op-posite: Thinking is not Critique but spooking; not *exorcism* but *haunting.*

When someone offers us a Critique, furrow your brow and suspect something shadowy is going on. I am going to call deconstruction, Derrida's frame of mind, "postmodern," even though I know better. Derrida scorned this word on the grounds of its excessive mediatization—including all the specters of virtual reality and the internet—and of its periodization, its tendency to draw neat lines between historical periods. But, as I used to say to him, I am sure you are right about that, but still, it is a very good way to draw a crowd. Deconstruction is a way of thinking but deconstruction is not Critique. Instead of replacing mystification (ghosts) with reality (presence), it displaces reality with specters. It shows that it spooks the whole thing, Modernity and Critique included. Deconstruction does not dispel ghosts; it offers them hospitality.[2] Derrida gets spooked whenever anyone starts speaking of Critique and has recourse to Reality or Being or Truth in a table-pounding way, without adding on one of his own famous grammatological ghosts—"if there is any" (*s'il y en a*) or "perhaps" (*peut-être*) or "as if it were possible" (*comme si c'était possible*), which modalize, modify, and attenuate these pretenders in the game of thrones of Thought. Derrida suspects every position is spooked by one of these appositions, every ontology displaced by a hauntology. He worried about the mystification baked into what poses as Reality, about all the powerful, intimidating authority of Truth and Being. Talking about Being is never far from talking like the Powers That Be, which really scares the hell out of us, especially when the police of truth come knocking at our door (or hacking our computers).

Marx's concept of Critique is paradigmatic of Modernism and Secularism. It goes about its business by arguing that *x* is "nothing other than" *y*, nothing but a disguised or distorted form of *y*, for which critical thinking steps forth to supply the undisguised, unvarnished, undistorted truth. (Hint: Whenever you hear the words "nothing other than," head for the door, you may be next—that's deconstruction in a nutshell.) Religion, on this accounting, had been dragged before the executioner several times over in modernity. Religion is nothing other than the distortion of economic relations (Marx); nothing other than the desire for our mommy (Freud); nothing other than the will-to-power (Nietzsche). In short, nothing other than an illusion for which Marx and Freud thought they had the Truth—but not Nietzsche, who thought that Truth too was nothing other than an illusion. That is why Nietzsche's critique of religion is on the way toward becoming postmodern. Nietzsche's "death of God" unexpectedly reopened the door for religion; but that's another and a complicated story I have addressed elsewhere.[3]

If deconstruction were a World Historical Spirit (God forbid), I would say it has come into the world to spook the modernist-Enlightenment types.

But the funny thing is that it also spooks the secular deconstructors. They are scared stiff that deconstruction opens the door to the return of (the ghosts) of religion, which from time immemorial has tried to scare the hell out of us (literally) by means of very powerful Sacred Spooks and very Holy Ghosts. That didn't scare Derrida, who liked to think against the grain. If intellectuals these days are all that spooked by religion, Derrida mused, maybe, just perhaps, there is something interesting going on there, and maybe "religion," if there is such a thing, does not mean just one thing. What is it? What is *the* "it" that's so spooky in religion. What is the "it" that spooks? Maybe it's important? Perhaps.

Take the case of Marx himself. The amusing thing is that Marx chased away or busted one ghost too many, the very one he most needed and relied on, which we see in the opening line of the *Communist Manifesto*.[4] There Marx famously said that all of Europe is "haunted" by the "specter" (*Gespenst*) of "Communism." Communism, he and Engels said to Europe, is coming to get you. Now, in this book, after the collapse of the Soviet Union, Derrida is saying to us, do not think that Marx is dead. Marx was trying to spook old Europe with a spook of a vintage "messianic" variety. Everything in Marx turns on calling for the coming of the "messianic" specter of radical justice. So it turns out that, like any Jewish prophet worthy of the name,[5] Marx too was proclaiming good news for the poor and the year of the Jubilee! Marx had a lucky number! What is more scandalous than that? Marx—who, we recall, descended from a long line of rabbis—at the weeping wall praying for the year of the Jubilee? Is this a general rule? Whenever anybody has anything important to say or to do or to make, even and especially if this is supposedly a purely "secular" matter, there's a spook afoot, and maybe even a "religious" one. It's spooking them. There is spooking going on. Perhaps.

Or take the case of the Enlightenment itself. Much as the Men of Reason deny it, if we listen very closely to the cool dulcet tones of Reason in the Enlightenment, we can hear a call, a command, a solicitation, an injunction, a little ghost or maybe a big one whispering in its ear: *sapere aude*, have the courage to think, the courage to ask any question, which sounds like a theologian speaking of the courage to be, to be encouraged by Being itself. Behind all this Big Brave Talk about Critique, a little ghost, a quiet prayer! There it is! I knew it. An invisible spirit was encouraging the Men [*sic*] of the Enlightenment to have courage, to have the heart, *cor*, to use their head, as it took a great deal of courage to question a murderous church and king. So however postmodern you may feel in the morning, do not be ungrateful to the Enlightenment as the day wears on. Behind their veneer of cool rational macho talking heads lies the passion of a whole body at prayer. We Men of the Enlightenment, Kant said, have come of age; we are the adulthood of humankind[6]—but they are all praying like school children for the courage to think. Just like old Marx they were all praying like mad, but they will not admit it. They are praying for "emancipation," which it turns out is not a "metanarrative" but a *prayer*. Emancipation is a *promise*, not a program, Derrida says,[7] which is why Derrida says it is the last thing about which he would have "incredulity." The only courage they lacked was the courage to admit that they are praying for courage. They were terrified of being called "spirit-seers," fearful of what Kierkegaard called the comic incommensurability of the body of a grown man at prayer, sunk to his knees, eyes closed, praying, and weeping—like an old woman, they feared.

Now take the case of the ongoing debate about religion. In modernism, the supernaturalism of religion is challenged by the naturalism of its critics; fideism, the access of faith to a higher reality, is contested on the grounds of the rationality of scientism and materialism. But the two sides share the same presuppositions. "-Isms" aplenty, a war of "-Isms," two sides of the same coin, competing versions of the same thing, two varieties of the same Real-ism—two versions of what Derrida (following Heidegger) called the "metaphysics of presence." Each side competes for the high ground of Presence, of what is really real, declaring the other side an illusion, or—the nuclear option—"nihilism." In this corner, the *ens realissimum*, the really real and really Big Being, where the material world is finite, created, and mixed with a dose of unreality. That emboldens John Milbank to denounce materialists as nihilists (in the name of "peace," of course), because without God matter is nothing at all.[8] Only when matter is sustained by God can matter's reality be maintained; that's the True Materialism. In the other corner, no less big and mean, materialists making matter the only thing that matters, the only reality, while religion is the tragic illusion of thinking that real life begins only after you are six feet under. In short, nihilism again.

One has God on its side; the other has the material universe, two very Big Deals. One looks up unctuously to Heaven; the other squints through its telescopes at the heavens. Each side thinks it has reality on its side and the other side is bedeviled by nihilism, so they each want to drive the devil out of the other. This is what Kant called in his cool transcendental terms an "antinomy," meaning a debate that drives the rest of us crazy and will conclude (without conclusion) only when an expanding universe puts an infinite distance between the parties to the debate so that (mercifully) they can no longer hear each other shouting. Sometimes I wonder even if entropic dissipation, which brings the universe itself to an end (perhaps!), will be enough to shut them up. We should be sure to bury the combatants in separate cemeteries lest their ghosts continue their hostilities even after death and disturb the rest of everyone around them.

But do not be mistaken. Deconstruction (if there is such a thing!) has not come into the world to mount a new postmodern defense of religion, to offer a postmodern apologetics, which is what I like to call "postmodernism light."[9] It is acutely conscious that God and religion have been our best alibi for oppression, exclusion, and murder. Its distrust of religion, which is without limit, goes back, I would venture to say, to the bit of indigestible two-worlds dualism religion has swallowed, the residual Gnosticism of Christian Neoplatonism it unfortunately ingested back when it was getting its intellectual sea legs, which all came to a head in Augustine's *City of God*. This soft Gnosticism[10] transformed purely spectral phenomena into pure spiritual entities, mistakenly reifying them as inhabitants of a realm of Immaterial Being. It allowed Greek philosophical distinctions between eternity and time, the supersensible and the sensible, soul and body to command the interpretation of the Kingdom of God. The Christian Neoplatonists realized that there was something odd about the year of the Jubilee, that its time was out of joint, but instead of meditating on its spectral annularity, its strange and messianic mathematics, instead of appreciating that it belongs to another more haunting, haunted temporality, it abolished its temporality altogether. It turned the year of the Jubilee into the timelessness of eternity. By thus confusing the Kingdom of God with a metaphysical realm beyond space and time, it turned the call for the Kingdom into an economic chase here on earth after celestial rewards in the hereafter, where we are assured we will flit about in maintenance-free bodies doing God knows what for all eternity. That dualism deserves all the abuse, suspicion, and incredulity it gets, and I will come back to it at the end.

In the postmodern style of thinking, religion is not refuted with a table-pounding argument, not bombed into oblivion. Instead, such dualism is dealt with more peacefully, with a yawn, with what Jean-François Lyotard very precisely called, and no doubt after much research, "incredulity."[11] Such religion is unbelievable. We don't believe it and there is no need to discredit it as it is making itself unbelievable all by itself, with every billboard it puts up attacking the theory of evolution, global warming, the emancipation of women, and same-sex marriage. With each passing day it makes itself more unbelievable with the "dare to think" set, although, as Lacan points out, it will probably last forever in the Bible Belt (where they don't dare).[12] The "new atheists" should have spared themselves (and us) the trouble. They are trying to break down a door that is wide open, and besides they are not nearly as good at discrediting religion as is religion itself. Even the believers inside religion, the ones who struggle to believe, who believe that they believe, as Gianni Vattimo says so deftly, do not believe this religion.[13]

So it is not that postmodernism finds nothing objectionable about religion, but that by virtue of its suspicion of Big Reductionistic Stories, it resists saying "Religion"—it resists the insistence of the capital letter—is just one thing, just one Big Diabolical Thing or (the other side of the same coin) just one Big Holy and Celestial Thing. Instead, it thinks, it suspects, that something spooky is going on here, which is both a promise and a threat; we never know about spooks. This is spooky business and the question is, what spooks? So having shown the door to both the Big Strong Men of Reason and the Big Strong Men of Theology, who are out to exorcise each other, it sits down to listen for the spooks, to attend to the multiple, conflicting, and still small voices of religion, if there are such things. It is feeling around for something going on in it, for something playing more quietly in the background, something more elusive, that is not drowned out by the noisy war conducted between the Faithful and the Atheists, something that is complicit with neither secularism's dismissiveness nor religion's anxiety, superstition, and violence, something thought-worthy, something spooky, something oddly, eerily there.

That is what the figure of the specter provides. The specter is neither simply present nor simply absent; it is neither simply living nor simply dead. Specters are neither theists nor atheists, neither black nor white, neither leftists nor rightists. Specters are highly egalitarian; they disturb everybody. The specter leads a shadowy insubstantial life, the demi-life of the living dead, of the undead, a penumbral life, from *paene umbra*, "almost a shadow." Not a full-blown shadow but almost, an exquisite Latin formulation. (Hint: Add the fabulously precise imprecision of "almost" to Derrida's list of spooks.) So to proclaim year of the Jubilee is to say, it's *almost* 50, that it has a special asymptotic annularity, a spectral temporality. The specter makes its presence felt without being actually present, but its apparitions are not mere hallucinations. We do not simply believe or disbelieve specters. We do not know what to believe. We are too uneasy to just believe them but we are too unnerved to suspend our disbelief. These apparitions are not realities but they are not simply illusions. If we try to give the specter respectability in the academy, we could propose offering a course titled spectrology, or spectral hermeneutics, or the phenomenology of the spectral. Its subject matter is not ontology but hauntology; not onto-theology but haunto-theology; not theo-logy but a theo-poetics. We might even propose the creation of a whole department of Penumbralogy. As the curriculum committee would no doubt find all our proposals very elusive, we would, as a last resort, recommend that it be run as an interdisciplinary course and sent over to the Humanities Center where they are always looking for courses on the "wholly other."

We can now distinguish two ways to be critical of religion. The first is (modernist, reductionist) Critique. It has a firm ground external to religion, an external point of leverage (materialism), a secure base from which it launches missiles aimed at the heart of religion, dropping the bombs of Reality upon the villages and towns of religious illusion, aiming at the simple destruction of religion. The second lacks all such armaments, any external leverage, has no firm and unshakable ground, and has not even the wherewithal to lay down its head. It engages in a weak and quasi-transcendental scrutiny—deconstruction can be very critical of religion but it is not a Critique of Religion—which takes up residence within religion, like a war correspondent embedded in a military unit from which it makes all its reports. It undertakes a meticulous, internal reading of multiple religious texts, traditions, institutions and practices, engaging in a micrological exposé of the internal tensions that inhabit and constitute the multiple phenomena of religion. It takes the side of religion in such a way as to get inside it and feel about for what is going on *in* religion, for what's spooking it, looking for traces of the events convening there. The aim is not the destruction of religion, but its deconstruction, indeed the exhibition of the auto-deconstruction that is taking place in religion, where the expositor is doing nothing more than expounding what is already exposed, already going on in religion, like the first reporter on the scene.

The aim is not to destroy religion but to "repeat" it, which means to reread it, to reinvent the events that already inhabit and constitute religion, by exhibiting all the ghosts by which these texts, beliefs, traditions, practices, and institutions (am I omitting anything?) are haunted. The aim is to open or reopen religion to its future, to let it tremble with a future it cannot see coming—and also with a past it would rather forget. Whenever anyone says this *is x*, where *x* is some entity, creed, program, proposition, or proof (am I omitting anything?), the hauntological, penumbralogical, micrological reader suspects that a closer study will reveal ghosts in its closet. Whenever someone says "Religion," deconstruction behaves as if it has seen a ghost, asking in wide-eyed disbelief if there is such a thing, just one thing called "Religion," in the singular, in Western Christian Latin. It turns the table on the table-pounders who say, I *am* a believer, say, a Christian (or I am certainly *not*), with the sly suspicion that a closer examination will show that they are haunted by many other competing voices, which they will not allow themselves to confess. Whenever pressed about whether he *is* an atheist, Derrida would say, "I quite rightly pass for one,"[14] that is what they say about me, and they are probably right, but I do not know. I am haunted by many ghosts and they give me no rest. Believers will find no better formula for their belief than that. Whenever anyone says, this is a strictly "secular" matter, the hauntologist suspects it is haunted by the ghosts of "religion," by a little prayer, by an implicit theology or "unavowed theologeme."[15] Just so, whenever people say, this is a strictly "religious" matter, the hauntologists suspect several secular spirits are hidden up their sleeve, which is why his reverence prefers his long robes for official functions.

It Spooks Being

You are forgetting the most ancient and venerable principles of philosophy. Being is; nonbeing altogether is not. Thus spoke Father Parmenides.

Almost.

That's the point! There's no almost here, no shadowy quasi-nothings, or quasi-beings, which are the illusions with which mortals, two-headed, fill their empty heads.

What is eating you?

I am just following Parmenides, the name of the Father of Philosophy and of the Thought of Being.

Well, the name of your Father is making you awfully anxious.

Loosen up.

Parmenides thought that Being could save us. A long line of metaphysicians—I can see Plato and Aristotle, Augustine and Aquinas up at the front—marches loyally behind him. But Being, on our hypothesis, is spooked. But by what?

We all know that ghosts come back from the dead. The French call these events *revenants* (from the Latin *re-venire*, "to come back"). They are the undead, who have come back to pay us a visit because the business of their life is unfinished, and they are demanding that we finish it for them—like the ghost of Hamlet's father, which is the point of departure for Derrida's analysis, or like the ghost of "Christmas past" tormenting miserable old Scrooge. Ghosts have unfinished work, unkept promises, frustrated hopes, dreams gone wrong, unrequited injustice, and they have come back to see that these matters are redressed. That is why Walter Benjamin turned the idea of the messianic inside out and said that *we* are the messianic generation. That gets our attention. Nobody is going to save *us*; *we* are going to have save the dead. We are the ones the dead were waiting for—which is an eerie thought—to make right what was done to them. We are responsible to the dead. So Being, if by Being we mean Presence, the Present, is haunted by the wounds of the past, by what Metz called the "dangerous memory" of the dead,[16] whose death it is up to us to see was not in vain. In this amazing soteriology, that would mean that the death of Jesus did not save us, but that we have to save Jesus, to see that his death was not in vain. Instead of billboards saying "Jesus Saves," we need new ones saying "Save Jesus."

But the reason—if ghosts need or even have a reason—ghosts come back from the dead ultimately has to do with the future. Old Marley wanted Scrooge to avoid making the same old mistake he did; he wanted Scrooge to have a future in what time was left to him. Scrooge after all had an infinite advantage over Marley; he still had time. So this ghost come back from the past had the future on his disembodied mind. The same thing goes for the King who wants Hamlet to make right his murderous usurpation. It is the future that can be different, the future that holds a promise, the future that lures us on—as we proclaim the coming of the Kingdom, or the year of the Jubilee—even as the future is also menaced by the threat that the worst will happen, since, when it comes to ghosts, no one is guaranteeing anything. So the present is exposed to the advents, the *arrivants*, to who or what is coming, as well as to the *revenants*, those are coming back. We live in messianic or spectral time, responsible to both the living and the dead, both the living and the still to come, to the whole community of spooky saints. We live in the space between a memory and a promise.

Being, then, is haunted, broken open, by the past and the future. Being is unhinged by time. If I ever could get up the nerve to write a book titled *Being and Time*, I would defend the thesis that Being is spooked by time and that time is out of joint. It's time that has spooked them all, metaphysicians, theologians, the whole lot. Hamlet said *the* time, Denmark at his time, is out of joint. But the point is general: Time itself is the out-of-jointedness of Being.

> *It's about time you came clean. You are saying time is it. "It" is about time. The "it" is time.*
> *Almost. Be careful. Don't rush to judgment. Take your time.*

Put it this way. "Time," if there is such a thing, is "it," if there is such a thing. And then add what that famous metaphysician Bill Clinton said when he found himself in a tough spot: It all depends on what the meaning of "is" is. Be that as it may, they're all unnerved by time, by the coming to be and passing away of things. To the poetizing of Parmenides' great poem on Being I would oppose a little verse by Robert Frost titled "The Span of Life" that tidily sums up what is unnerving them:

The old dog barks backwards without getting up.
I can remember when he was a pup.[17]

The first line is haunted by the second line, by the temporal shift to "was," which is what really spooks us. Time is what is eating at us; it is consuming us. Time doth make cowards us of all. So when Parmenides said time is not Being but illusion, Plato thought the old man was going too far. Feeling called upon to rise to its defense as best he could without engaging in open patricide, Plato pleaded that it is a copy of being, a little bit false, that's true, but also a little bit true, too, not simply false, and we even need to use the appearances of things in time to ascend up to the true timeless world. Plato was damning time with faint praise, of course, but he was saying to Father Parmenides, please, be reasonable, it is *almost* real, apparently real, and we philosophers have to account for appearances and live with them. Or, as Derrida might have put it, of course the past and future are not simply present, "of course they do not exist—so what?"[18]

Think of the classical metaphysical picture of Being as Presence as a blurry photograph suffering from a double exposure—to a past that will not let us forget it, to a future that will not stop calling upon us. Far from being full and well rounded, solid and plenitudinous all the way through, as Father Parmenides dreamed, the present is destabilized and discontent, porous and permeable, in a word deconstructible. When you're haunted—and when are you not?—the time is out of joint. What passes itself off as present is inwardly disturbed and disjoined. There is no such thing as a well-joined time, a tranquil temporal "now" imitating an eternal restful now.

Whenever a belief or a practice, an institution or a tradition, steps forward claiming the authority of Being, which allows its officers to pass themselves off as the powers-that-be, the idea is to spook it, or show that it is already spooked, that the "it spooks" is already doing its eerie work there. That will not destroy it but give it a future, which too often it does not want—the one percent, for example, can do without the Jubilee Jesus had in mind—because the future is dicey business. Just consider what an unnerving thing, or non-thing, or quasi-thing time is, if it is. The future is the "future present," the future that we can more or less foresee and anticipate, and for which we can reasonably prepare. That is important and requires a lot of hard work, and things may go terribly wrong with our best laid plans. That is because of the "absolute future," the absolutely unforeseeable and unprogrammable future, which takes us by surprise, which blindsides us, for which we cannot prepare. Anyone who calls for the coming of a new day needs the hardiness to say yes to the coming of what they cannot see coming. It may turn out to be a day in which you should never have gotten out of bed. And it gets worse than that. The future is not only the future of the future; it is also the future of the past, what Benjamin and Derrida call the promise of the past, our hope in the past, the coming back again of something simmering from time immemorial, which will also take us by surprise. These joint specters, of the absolute future and the absolute past, see to it that Being, the Presence of the Present, is spooked by time, disjoined by haunting specters taunting it from either side, by both prospective and retrospective specters, from before and after, giving it no rest.

So what old Parmenides called unchanging Being we Penumbralogists say is a blurry double exposure, luring us on, unnerving us, unsettling us, asking us to screw up our courage, just like old Scrooge, who has these two ghosts to deal with. I have not forgotten the *third* one, the ghost of Christmas Present, the very spirit who was speaking to him right there and then while he stood on his bed all atremble. That is what Kierkegaard and Heidegger called the "moment" of decision, which passes through the ordeal of undecidability. The moment in which we are haunted is not the "now" of Platonism and Christian Neoplatonism, which tries to reassure itself that the temporal "now" is a poor imitation or a copy of a pure unchanging now by which it is constantly monitored and kept safe. The calm Neoplatonic now actually does quite a bit of violence against time and the moment. It is a bit weak-kneed and timid; it has no heart for the future, which is chancy, and it prays for this "moment" to pass—instead of giving it a chance. If only being would hold firm, it thinks, in pure, perfect, compact, complete, leak-proof presence, we would not have to deal with the spooks of undecidability; no ghostly spirits could seep through its cracks. We wouldn't have to talk to them! That's another important point about specters. Notice that when it comes to specters, we cannot be content to just be spectators. We cannot just "look at" (*theorein*) specters. We must, like Hamlet and Scrooge, hear them out and engage them in conversation, address them as well as allow ourselves to be addressed by them, finding out what they have on their eerie minds, discovering what they expect us to *do*. Specters expect something. They expect something to change! Specters have high expectations; they shatter the settled and limited horizon of expectations with which we comfort ourselves. When we say, you can only do what is possible, or no one could be expected to do any more, specters expect more.

But what do they expect? Do they expect the impossible? Why are they bothering me? I was sound asleep in my bed. I did not ask for this trouble. Who invited them? Who asked them to come, to disrupt these quiet midnight hours with their disturbing visions and voices, with such uncanny, fetching, dangerous, insolent, insistent solicitations? Am I even awake? Am I dreaming? Was this a nightmare? What does this specter expect of me?

It Spooks God

So according to you, it's all spooked—Thought and Being. But what about God? God is that than which nothing greater can be conceived.
Almost.
God is the ens realissimum, infinite and perfect.
If there is one.
God is our Savior.
If he shows up.
God is what He Is, Who will be what He will be, who will always be faithful to His people.
Maybe, but you cannot count on it.
Surely, if ever anything were "it," God is it. God always was and always will be necessarily—it.
Perhaps. It depends.

Theologians think that God will save us. God rises up as pure Being above all becoming, as the eternal above the temporal, as most really real of all above the shadowy quasi-realities of the created world. God is the Pure Spirit who eludes this game of ghosts by which we are held captive down here below.

But that's just it! If, as we have been saying, nothing is present without being haunted, that nothing has Being unless it trembles with may-being, *peut-être*, that nothing is real unless it is destabilized by the irreal, that goes for God, for God above all, the *ens realissimum*, the most really real of all. God does not get a pass. God does not stand above this fray. God, God above all, is the most spectral phenomenon of all! God is the most really spooky of all, the specter par excellence, the most suspicious, ghostly ghost of all. God is not only a spectral figure but the very figure or paradigm *of* the specter, *ens spectralissimum*, if we could say such a thing in Latin, which I suspect we cannot. It's barbaric Latin, but you see the point: God is that than which there is nothing spookier, nothing more haunting, nothing more haunted. That's why we would be hard put to find a better case of spectral phenomena than religion, which is a concentration, a celebration, a mélange, an elaborate orchestration of ghosts, even and especially very holy ones, which is why Marx put religion at the top of his (hit) list; knocking out religion would be one of his greatest hits.

Just look at the historical record: God is that than which there is nothing more perfectly present or even omnipresent—yet is nowhere to be found; nothing is more prestigious than the "word of God"—yet what is more biting than the silence of God when evil surrounds us on every side?

Nothing is more luminous that the light of God—yet nothing more hidden; nothing more saving—yet nothing more likely to leave us in the lurch time and again; nothing more powerful—yet seeming never to lift a finger on our behalf when we need help the most.

Just go down the list of divine names and every time you'll find a ghost. I think we need a new list.

Is God it? Is God there? Not there? Was that God, in that moment—or, as Nietzsche somewhat cynically suggests, a bit of undigested beef disturbing our sleep? Was that the ghost of the King, Hamlet keeps asking himself, or a hallucination? This spectral undecidability is the insubstantial substance of one of the greatest masterpieces in the history of English literature. But it pales (like a ghost) in comparison with, unless it draws its power from, the divine undecidability whose visitation leaves us shaken to the bones. Was this God or some malicious specter bent on deceiving me, Descartes asks in a fit of epistemological anxiety. Outside epistemology, out on the streets, in actual life, we have a parallel anxiety. Is that God or the Evil One leading me into the worst violence? Is that the living God or something undead stalking me day and night? Who is calling, or what, and how am I to speak of such an elusive spirit? But then again how can I *not*? He or she or it, I know not what, one or many, real or unreal, saving or dangerous, whoever or whatever this is, will not leave me alone. Whoever said God is dead must have been smoking something. God is the most undead of all.

If I were reincarnated as a medieval theologian, as sometimes happens in my dreams, I would launch my career by announcing a *quaestio disputata*, a (highly) disputed question, in which I would defend the thesis that the essence of God lies in God's para-existence, God's spectral persistence, God's purely penumbral presence, in short, that the essence of God lies in God's *insistence*. Back at the friary, I would daily pray, at matins and at vespers, for God to rid me of God, for God to send the God of Pure Being, Pure Light, and Pure Truth packing. God give me purity but not now, in fact, now that I think about it, not ever! I prefer impure thoughts.

This strange and uncanny somewhat, this insistent and unsettling specter, this anonymous disturbance, this "it" that comes and goes under the name (of) "God" has pursued me down the long corridors of time, all the way back to grade school nuns hovering over us like specters leaving us to wonder if there were real bodies beneath these black veils, all the way up to old age, springing up in the unlikeliest places, breaking through the tiniest crevices of quotidian life, breaking in at moments of high drama, seeping subtly into my daily routine, stealing upon me unawares, looking back at me in the mirror in the morning, hailing me from high atop a frozen mountain peak, calling me to set sail upon the deep, out beyond the horizon, where the land is out of sight, knowing that there I would be alone, unprotected from its insistent, incessant solicitations. Everywhere I turn, high or low, north or south, desert or oasis, I am disquieted by these unsettling visitations, pursued, questioned, accused, exhilarated, caught up short, overcome by the coming over me of something, I know not what.

What does this spirit, this specter of all specters, expect of me? I am addressed, summoned, called upon, called out, *interloqué*, poor me, in the accusative,[19] my cowardly "I" having long fled this scene of accusation.

What was that strange noise that sounded like someone's voice?

"God," they say, and maybe they are right. God, perhaps. The specter of God.

This is a serious case, one for the specialists, the expert hauntologists, ones who have mastered these phenomena and have the latest spectrological equipment, if only I can find a directory of such physicians of the soul. I need the best. It is not simply that there is a hauntological effect here, in the name of God. My situation is much worse than that. I am being disturbed by the very paradigm of the specter, not only the spookiest specter of all, but the very figure of the specter. Whatever this is that has gotten inside my head, inhabited my heart, gotten under my skin, I have to deal with it. I have somehow drifted unawares into dangerous and uncharted waters, or wandered across a border into a lawless land, somehow found myself in a perilous place, at the very heart of hauntology. This place is filled with spooks, everywhere I turn.

This uncanny spirit, let us say "God," perhaps, if only to make an infinitely long story short, does not exist. If God existed, if a name and address could be supplied for the impossible, then the impossible would be possible. Were it ("it") either an existent or a nonexistent, then everything would be easier. Then at least there would be a diagnosis and we could look for a cure. But at the moment I do not even know what kind of doctor I should see. If the question of God were a question of existence, I might be able to settle it, to prove it one way or another, to disprove it one way or another, and then I would be able to move on. But the trouble with God, and God is trouble, believe me, infinite trouble, giving me no peace at all, is that God is neither present nor absent, neither simply given nor entirely hidden. God is neither a saturated phenomenon, as Jean-Luc Marion tries to assure us,[20] nor a total illusion, as the cool-handed rationalists, no less assured, tell us, but a strange and fluctuating phenomenon, a soliciting, incessant, insistent apparition, a specter. God is not an entity out there who answers to the name "God," but a call calling to us in a certain uncertain voice, in and under the name (of) "God," delivering an obscure message, leaving us restless for something, I know not what, eliciting a desire not just for this or that, but a desire beyond all desire, for a knowing without knowledge, reducing us to prayer, to praying like mad to an unknown God, where we pray God to rid us of God.

I am haunted by this voice. "God does not exist; God insists." That is what I hear day and night, running through my mind like an annoying jingle I cannot turn off. I wake up with a start in the middle of the night, bolt upright in my bed, pupils dilated, looking all around. I could swear there was a voice in the room. I distinctly heard it say: "You know it, but you will not say it. God does not exist. God insists."[21] But I look under my bed, open all the closets, look out the window into the night, and there is no one to be found. Is this an inspiration, a visitation by a friendly angel in my dreams—or am I just being spooked? Were I a Rationalist philosopher and of a more sound mind instead of a spirit-seer, I would make this assertion my axiom, my first principle, my ground. But that would be a rash and hypocritical undertaking for one as haunted and disturbed as am I, for one awash in tossing seas, in a tiny craft adrift over fifty thousand fathoms, who can offer in evidence only the groundless grounds of something I know not what. God does not exist, I insist on this, but that does not mean—and everything depends upon this—there is nothing to God. Far from it. If there were an easy choice between being or nothing, my life would be simple. I could make a choice with the full assurance that there is at least a fifty percent choice that I am right. I could condense the ambiguity of my life into a proposition, that proposition would in turn represent reality, and it would come accompanied by warranty. There would be a kit that would contain a proof for my proposition, along with an installation disk that includes an error check to make sure the program was properly installed and there were no miscalculations. What could be simpler than that? Then I could take the weekend off and have some peace.

Hegel began his lectures on the philosophy of religion by saying that religion is the Sabbath of life, the domain of eternal truth where all the riddles of the heart are resolved and all our sorrows comforted, a day of rest from the trials and tribulations of life, when the harshness of fate vanishes and everything dissolves into light and love.[22] I love Hegel as much as the next fellow, but I have to ask, what was the great man thinking? What was he on? What was he sniffing? If I were Žižek, I would rub my beard, tug on my t-shirt, and exclaim in my best Slovenian accent, "My God, the truth is exactly the opposite!" Religion is the source of the greatest unrest and lack of peace. Religion, not the unbelievable one which is out to makes its enemies its footstools—in the name of the God of love, of course—but the thoroughly haunted and disturbed religion, the religion *sous rature*, religion crossed out and erased, but not so thoroughly that we cannot still read the writing underneath, still discern the word "religion" beneath the cross. Let us say, to make another infinitely long story short, a religion without religion, which is also too simple, since we cannot simply do "without" anything. Whenever we try to do without something, we will always be haunted by whatever we think we have left behind, whatever we mistakenly think we have left for dead, without appreciating that the dead are never just plain dead. Nothing is ever simply dead. It always comes back to haunt us, above all the living God, who is the undead par excellence, that than which there is nothing spookier. The more we say, God is dead, the more anxious we prove ourselves to be, looking over our shoulder to see who that shadowy figure is who seems to be following us, the more deluded we prove ourselves to be, the more we prove that something is eating at us—in short, the more we show our insensitivity to the spectral effect. Above all with God! The last thing we could ever say is dead, the last thing we can kill off and leave behind for dead, without a flicker or trace of life, is God! God is that than which nothing is more undead. What greater specter than the specter of God?

To get back to Hegel's point, maybe if I were a great German metaphysician back at the University of Berlin, maybe if I had seen the World Historical Spirit on horseback, maybe my religion would be the Sabbath of life. But as for poor me, a poor existing individual, as Kierkegaard liked to say, my religion with/out religion—both with and without, neither with nor without, religion, if there is such a thing—gives me no rest. My religion is restlessness and disquiet; it leaves me in a state of permanent unease, never satisfied with anything other than dissatisfaction. All my religion does, this spectral haunto-theological counterpart to religion, is disturb the peace and violate the Sabbath laws with penumbral violations. In fact, the Sabbath, if there were one, in my religion with/out religion would not be one day set aside for rest but the restless industry of everyday life, perpetual unrest around the clock, 24/7. What was Hegel thinking?

It Spooks

This all sounds a little crazy to me. Maybe the problem I am having is that I really don't understand what you mean when you say "it spooks."
It's a metaphysical joke.
I fail to see the humor.
It's a riff, a poke in the ribs of Parmenides and Heidegger.
That requires a very strange sense of humor.
You have to be into stuff like this.
You have to be mad.
Perhaps, in a very precise sense. Almost.

The one thing that the long robes most dread hearing is someone say that they are spiritual but not religious. My idea is to give them still more bad news: God, too, is spiritual but not very religious. Actually the news is worse than that. When I say "spiritual," I mean spectral, spooky. It gets still worse. I am not saying that God spooks but that it spooks God. I am not saying that God spooks us, that God is the name of an infinite being who does the spooking and, being infinite, is really good at it. Instead, by saying that God does not exist, I am saying that God is not an agent who does things, like spook, and that God's infinity is of a rather in(de)finite sort. Grammatically, the name (of) "God" is a noun, but grammatologically, in my vocabulary, it not the name of anything nominative or substantive; it is neither a substance nor a subject nor their synthesis.

When I venture to say that God does not exist, I am saying that God is not something present, a pure, perfect, and complete presence, presiding over all, an omni-being who out-knows, out-wits, and generally overwhelms His [*sic*] creatures. I hasten to add, at this point, that I am not saying God is a "he" or a "He." I have spell checked this document, and every time I use the masculine gender for God, I do so on purpose. I am then referring to the testosterone-rich omni-macho creator *ex nihilo* spun out from a highly patrological patro-hierarchical theology so brilliantly put on the run by Catherine Keller.[23] The more insistent, hauntological figure of God, however, the one who is haunting me, appears as best I can make out to be of multiple and fluctuating genders, certainly more than two, at least fifty, sometimes even shading off into neuter anonymous impersonal it-like tones. The "it" of "it spooks" is like the "it" of "it's raining," it's very hard to say what it is. If He started out as a He, He has been in virtue of his transcendence transgendered several times over into innumerable varieties. So what I am saying is very polymorphic and highly apophatic.

So here's the joke. The problem old Parmenides and Heidegger both faced was how to affirm the reality of Being without turning Being into *a* being, a particular, nominative, substantive, subsistent thing. So they both came up with more or less the same solution: Of individual beings we can say that they "are" (or exist), but of "Being itself" we can only say "there is."[24] A particular being is, but there is Being. In German, that would come out "*es gibt das Sein*," literally, "it gives Being," which like the French *il y a* is the idiom for doing what we are doing in English when we say "there is."[25] So, the joke is in the German; instead of saying *es gibt*, we who are spooked by Being say "*es spukt*"; not "it gives" but "it spooks," not "there is Being" but "there is something spooky going on." If you spend enough time hanging out in the Humanities Center you will find this funny, but at the same time you will realize that it is really very serious. I would like to take credit for finding it, but we owe to Derrida who found it in Max Stirner, who said "*es spukt in der ganzen Welt*," the whole world is spooked.[26] This we can use as a general formula for the penumbrality of Being, for the way Being is spooked, with a completely straight face. Almost.

So of God I say the following. God does not exist, but *there is* something going on in and under the name of God, something very spooky. God does not exist, but that does not mean *there is nothing* to God. There is a God-effect, or there are innumerable God-effects, but they are spectral. There is a spectral effect with God. There are spectral effects happening under the name (of) "God." Specters are not particular beings; they do not subsist and they are not agents. Nor are they Being, but there are spooky goings-on (events). Beings have gotten something going on with them called events. In this spookier way of thinking by which I am beset, the name of God is not the name of the First Being of ontotheology, to which Tillich said the proper theological response is atheism, which for Tillich did not spell the end of theology but the beginning.[27] But neither is God the ground of being of Tillich, nor the hyperbeing of mystical theology, to which I reply that the proper theological response is also atheism. I say this, once again with a proviso, that this is not supposed to be the end of theology or of mystical theology, but the beginning of theologizing otherwise. Let us say it is a hauntological theology or a spectro-theology or penumbra-theology, which is, to put it in the most affirmative way possible, at the very least something spectro-apophatic. That just means metaphysics must check its guns at the door when the hauntological marshal is in town.

In saying God does not exist, I am saying there is something going on *in* the name (of) "God," but it belongs to another order, producing effects on another register, neither theistic nor atheistic, neither ontological, me-ontological, nor de-ontological—but hauntological. They are not going on outside space and time but in a special spectral temporality. Treating God like an existent entity is like imagining that a virtual drink is going quench your thirst. God is not an entity, not a matter of spirit or of matter, not a matter of being or nonbeing, not a matter of entities, propositions, and proofs, not a matter of creeds, councils and candles (am I omitting anything?). God is not a Pure Spirit ensconced in an immaterial realm, nor is God Pure Matter, but a specter. God does not exist; God insists. God is neither presence nor absence but insistence. God does not subsist; God insists. God insists with the insistence of a call, like a very holy ghost calling for justice, mercy, compassion, forgiveness, hospitality, love, the year of the Jubilee in a time we cannot calculate but for which we pray and weep. But (there is always a but, which is another nutshell) that in turn means that, spook that God is (spooked as God is), we always risking the worst violence in the name of God's love or justice. Praying God to lead us not into temptation is a bit hypocritical; the name (of) "God" *is* temptation, and to pray is to expose ourselves to temptation, which is why we should take care what we pray for and why the first last and constant prayer is to pray God to rid God of God, as we learn from the mystics. I have a taste for the mystics, for their joys and plaints and pliant strategies for wrestling with the nameless. I love everything about the mystics except for the one thing I do not love, their Neoplatonism. That is my lover's quarrel with them.[28]

Now it is well known that "insistence" is a pathological matter. I admit that. But by admitting that I do not admit that I advocate an obsessive drive that makes us sick and dysfunctional. On the contrary, I am trying to rev up the intensity of life by setting out the prolegomena to a penumbral life, an active salutary spectral life which communicates with the living dead. I am admitting that we are all mortally wounded souls, suffering from an incurable condition called "life." But I regard this as a kind of salutary *pathos* that is the condition of a passionate life, of the intensity of life, of a kind of *élan vital* that pulsates through our bodies and gives us joy even if it keeps us awake half the night. So in speaking of leading a spectral or penumbral life, I do not mean the dispassionate life of a shade one, but one full of passion. If insistence drives us mad, it is with a madness for what is coming, which is highly exhilarating. In spectro-theology we are calling for the year of the Jubilee, for the coming of the Kingdom, which means being mad for justice, mad with loving our enemies, forgiving the unforgivable, being holy fools for the Kingdom. At the same time, I admit that a force this spectral, this uncertain, this insistent, and solicitous, may lead to the worst violence, the worst persecution, and the madness of murder. When it comes to specters we are required to be discerning. So if I am declared mad by the Inquisition or by the Enlightenment, my defense will be that there is more than one madness, that madness does not mean just one thing. There is no such thing as Madness, in the singular. After all, madness is a spectral thing, if ever there were one, just as spooked as anything else and maybe more. So the association of madness and insistence has a perfectly sane explanation. What more rational explanation of a certain madness, a certain folly, than the insistence of God?

The Infinitival

I am surprised that you dared to mention God's infinity. That if anything should put a stop to this craziness. God's infinity means God is complete, whole, and perfect. Why would you even bring that up?

*In my spare time, on my days off, I have been working up a new list
of divine names. Right now I am working on "infinity," which I think
may take a long time to finish.*

By infinity I have in mind not an ontological but a hauntological name;
not a mathematical way of counting but a penumbralogical one; not an infinite being in the nominative, which ontologizes God, but the spectral open-
endedness of the "to-come" in the *infinitival*. As I have been saying, in a
penumbral theology, Being is spooked by time. Being wants to be tight and
well-joined, but time pries it out of joint. Time is the magic potion in penumbralogy, just a touch of which changes the whole solution. With just a
single droplet of time, Being and full presence start to boil over (*ebullitio* was
Meister Eckhart's word in his Latin works) with the open-endedness of the
to-come. The reason this is maddening—if madness has a reason, if there is a
reason in this madness—is that it is like a Messiah who never shows up. Or
if someone whose lucky number is 50 comes along and announces good
news for the poor, shelter for the homeless, and the year of the Jubilee, the
year the one percent are going to have to pay their fair share, someone else
announces the Jubilee has been postponed. Maybe next year. The time is out
of joint. It is coming, to-come. The year of the Jubilee never arrives, structurally. It is an *arrivant*, but it never arrives. If someone proclaims the year of the
Jubilee, and it does not show up, that does not mean it was a bad prediction,
or that we have to crunch the numbers again and see where the calculation
went wrong. It means it is not about mathematics, and prophets are not me-
teorologists. That would be the ham-fisted way the Men of Reason hear this
saying, with no ear or eye for specters, since they are terrified of being labeled
spirit-seers. What Men of Reason miss is that the year of the Jubilee belongs
to hauntological time, not to chronological time. It belongs neither to eternity nor to calendar time; not to the realm of eternal infinite being but to a
spectral and infinitival time to-come. In hauntological time the calculus is
incalculable, which is very strange. You keep counting, but you never get to
50. It is always almost 50, but not yet, and we cannot get that far, even if that
is what we desire, affirm, pray for, and weep over, all day, every day, year after
year. 50 is not a matter of mathematics; it is a matter of hope.

When I say that the maddening thing is that the "to-come" is "structural," that means it is by design, not a design flaw. Structural means that
is the way it was built, its factory condition; it's not a temporary problem
that will go away later on, with more time. The "to-come" refers to an unconditional promise that is never kept, to the in-finity of the un-finished,
of the un-defined and un-definable, to the unconditional open-endedness
of the future, which is the very word for the future in French and German,

where they speak of "the to-come" (*l'avenir, die Zukunft*). The force of the infinitival infinite is that of a broken, hyphenated force, unstably pieced together by a hyphen, deprived of full presence, disjointed, out of joint. The to-come, which makes time out of joint, has come to drive you mad, and it has a maddening makeup. It is a "weak force,"[29] with all the force of a call but without an army to enforce what it calls for. The to-come is like the old line in politics: You campaign in poetry but you govern in prose. We live in the distance between poetry and prose, between the to-come and the situation in which we find ourselves, the space of time called the moment. The to-come is itchy because it is never satisfied with anything. It is always calling, insistently, unconditionally, say, for justice, saying, praying "come" to what is to-come, hoping to making the truth come true, in the world, in the flesh, to give existence to its insistence, to make up what is lacking in the body without flesh of insistence. No, no, this is not the Messiah, or justice, or the year of the Jubilee. No, no, not yet. Maybe next year. Furthermore, it warns us, the whole thing may be a disaster; what looks like a holy ghost must turn out to be wholly ghastly. It may be the worst year of your life. The to-come refers to the coming of what we cannot see coming, which can be nasty business.

(Another hint, a useful methodological tip, a little rule of thumb, one that will help you see the method in my madness: Ontologies consolidate; hauntologies hyphenate. Ontologies confidently speak of democracy or justice, God or the kingdom of Jubilee; hauntologies cautiously speak of a hyphenated democracy-to-come, justice-to-come, kingdom-to-come, a coming God, the Jubilee to come, and so forth. "And so forth," of course, means there are more-to-come, infinitely more. The hyphen is the diacritical mark of spacing and timing, of *différance*, a little reminder that we are woven from the warp of space and the woof of time, that we are warped and woofed by *différance*. Even God cannot pretend indifference to *différance*. The whole world is spooked.)

I said I have a taste for the mystics, whom I love quite madly, above all Meister Eckhart, who said something very pertinent to this little discourse on the "it spooks": God needs us, he said, and the hornets of the Inquisition swarmed all over him. There may be something saving about God, but we in turn have to save God, in just the way Paul said we have to fill up the things that are lacking in the body of Christ. God, being merely infinitival, needs concrete finite bodies, troops on the ground, to conjugate this infinitive. The unconditional to-come is asking us to come to its aid, to fill up what is lacking in its spectral body, soliciting us to gives its spectrality reality. Specters expect us to give their insistence existence, to give their weakness strength. God needs us, and we are the ones God is waiting for. Specters expect everything, the impossible. We are the ones this specter expects and, being infinitival, what it expects knows no limit. The name of this spectral call we call God is the name of a call to which the only testimony is the response, the only evidence is the answer, the only proof is the action. What I call religion, if there is such a thing, is like answering a call we never heard. Everyone in earshot asks, Who are these people talking to? They must be mad.

In my spare time I am also working on a new translation of Augustine's *Confessions*. I have decided to translate his *cor inquietum* as "haunted heart," a heart made restless by the specter of what is to-come. When Augustine hears God calling him through the voices of the children playing the *tolle, lege* game, in my edition I take the liberty of having him open the New Testament to the word "come" (Rev 22:20), which is the penumbral, penultimate verse in the New Testament. It's only fair that I should be given such liberties with the text. I am kept up half the night, my room full of spooks, and I should be able to make a profit on my discomfort. The insistence of God reduces me to tears, to saying, praying "come" in response to an obscure and coming spirit, calling "come" in response to a fetching if elusive call, which is getting itself called in and under the name (of) "God." This specter pays me clandestine visits, sometimes dressed in rags, asking me for a cup of cold water, sometimes coming with an unexpected rapping on my door in the middle of the night, which could be trouble. There's nothing riskier than having commerce with the unknown, the unexpected, the unforeseen, with calling for the coming of what we cannot see coming.

So to make these shady matters as clear as day, let me say this. God does not exist; God spooks. But God is not an infinite being who uses his infinite power to spook us. *Es spukt*, "it spooks," as in "it rains," of uncertain gender, number, and agency. The infinitive "to spook" conjugates into the finite form, third person impersonal, "it spooks," where "it" stands for anything, the whole world; anything and everything is spooked. There is spooking going on everywhere, especially in and under the name (of) "God." Something is getting itself called; something is being called for, asking to be recalled; something insists, in the middle voice. I can neither say God does it nor that this is "nothing other than" my own projection (Feuerbach), that these spooks are all in my head, either of which would finally finitize and decide my infinitival unrest and exorcise this uncertain specter. At the very moment that I can say, *this* is what is spooking me, the spook disappears and is gone forever. At the very moment that I say, this is the living God, or this is my resentment, or my unconscious, or my social environment, or my Mommy, the spook would be completely exorcised, and I would be in the clear, in the black-and-white clarity of being and nonbeing, no longer in the accusative; I would be innocent as the driven snow. The very structure of a specter, and therefore of a call, is that we cannot identify the provenance of the call or make out exactly who or what is calling or being called for, so the responsibility falls on me, in the accusative, which is the decision of the other in me. Otherwise, without this spectrality, I can always say I was just following orders. God, the Law, the Party, the Cause, the Church, my mommy, the nuns, made me do it. Don't blame me. I have an alibi. I just work here. I don't make the rules.

On the Divine Names

> *It sounds to me you are just pulling this out of your hat.*
> *On the contrary, it is pulling at me.*
> *It's all in your head.*
> *It is heading right at my head.*
> *I think you are just making it up.*
> *On the contrary, I have the highest authority for it.*
> *You mean, it is in the Scriptures?*
> *Almost.*

God, I like to say, is not a projection but a projectile headed straight for my head. It is nothing I have imagined. I can even point to text and verse.

God, although in the form of God, did not think existence something to be exploited, but emptied himself of existence, and took the form of insistence, humbling himself and being content with weakness, with the weak force of a call which calls upon us in the form of a slave (Phil 2:6–8). The call rises up from the bodies of *ta me onta*, the nuisances and bodies of the world (1 Cor. 1:1–2), the wretched of the earth, the homeless, the displaced and deported, the least among us, the slum dogs who never become millionaires.

Think of this as the audacity of God—another divine name for my list. The audacity of God is to dare to not exist, to dare to disappear into the world, and to reappear only in spectral form. The audacity of God is to leave the existence to us, which is risky business. God only knows, God may come to regret it (Gen 6:6). That is the most audacious moment in the Christian tradition, which corresponds to the audacity of the God of the Tsim-Tsum, the divine retraction in the Kabbalah. There God entirely disappears in order to make room for the appearance of the world; the divine being shrinks down to an infinitesimally small point in order to let the universe expand out infinitely in every direction. If I were a contemporary physicist, I might be tempted to make something of that, especially one who thinks the process is endless.

The audacity of God is to empty out the robust and intimidating being of the First Being, of the *ens realissimum*, of the Hyperbeing, into the quasi-being, the penumbral being, the fluctuating, uncertain, undecidable para-being of a specter, which leaves everything to us, which calls on us to respond, which puts God in the position that God needs us. God's audacity is to throw the responsibility for God, for God becoming God, on us, which is the height of audacity.

If I am reincarnated as that medieval theologian in my dreams, the other thing I would do is write a treatise on the divine names, a new *de divinis nominibus*, which I would sign Reb Derrisa, a pseudonym I would concoct to throw the hounds of the Inquisition off my scent, hoping they mistake it for the work of some obscure Kabbalahist, by then long dead. In my treatise, I would treat the divine names not as attributes of full-blown presence but as their weaker spectral counterparts. In my version, existence would be weakened into insistence; Spirit into specter; the eternal into the momentary; omnipotence into the weak force of a call; necessity into the perhaps; infinity into the infinitival; divine providence into the risk of an unforeseeable future; perfection into the promise of the world; the all-good into the hope that it works; God's glory into the audacity to not exist; divine transcendence into a way to name the varying intensities which charge the plane of immanence with the anarchic energy of the to-come. Then I would pray for a speedy re-reincarnation somewhere else before the Inquisition decodes the whole thing and tracks me down, as none of this is far from their flames.

What Do Specters Expect?

> *But if the whole thing's spooked, Thought, Being, God, then what*
> *are we to do? Are we not just left paralyzed?*
> *In a hauntology, that's when we're really on the move*
> *But it seems impossible to do anything.*
> *By the impossible everything begins.*
> *If God does not exist, what good is God?*
> *Everything depends on God's inexistence.*

The question is, as JFK would have said, ask not what you can you expect from a specter but what specters expect of you. Ask not what good specters can do, but what kind of life specters expect us to lead. That is why my bumper sticker would read not "Jesus saves" but "Save Jesus," which is up to us.

Let's start with the words of ghosts, which are very special. These uncanny visitors have not just dropped by for an idle chat. They have no time for that; they mean business. Their words are meant as pressing injunctions, exhortations. Specters have great expectations, raised expectations; they expect things to happen. Specters expect change, transformation. They have interrupted their rest and put themselves to considerable trouble—after all it cannot be easy to come back from the dead—because of unfinished business, business they themselves cannot conduct, having been since deprived by death of the necessary credentials, stripped of their worldly papers. These ghostly bodies without flesh lack the material embodiment to affect the bodies of flesh and blood in need of help, and it is with these bodies in need that their business is to be conducted. So the words of ghosts are meant to be transformative, not merely informative; they are not merely passing on a bit of information to correct the historical record of what happened some time ago. Specters expect to transform lives; they do not expect spectators but deeds. They want to touch afflicted bodies, to disturb lives in easy drift, to provoke action in an indifferent world in which they, pure spirits that they are, are ineffective.

Specters insist, but it is we who exist. Specters call, but it is we who must respond. Specters come to us because we are the only ones who can help. They need us; they have been waiting for us.

When Kierkegaard had Johannes Climacus say that the name of God is the name of a deed, he got the whole idea. The name (of) "God" is the name of call to which we are supposed to be the response. Without the response the name is a dead letter. The real death of God is to ignore the call, to let the specter expire, to let it draw its (really) last breath. For all the world, the only thing anyone can see, and the only thing that exists, is the response. The only witness to the call is the response; the rest is spectral, invisible, ghostly.

Specters expect the truth; they expect us to make the truth come true. Truth here does not mean what it means back in the departments of (modern) philosophy, propositions inside our head picking out objects in the world outside our heads. Instead, truth means *facere veritatem*, making the truth, doing the truth, making our lives into a work of truth.

When Meister Eckhart says God needs us, he got the whole idea. Without us, the name of God is a tinkling cymbal, just talk.

When Paul said we are to fill up what is lacking in the body of Christ, he got the whole idea. The earthly body of Jesus had taken its leave of the world, and now it was up to us to heal the sick he left behind and proclaim the year of the Jubilee.

When the author of the Fourth Gospel said the Word must become flesh, he got the whole idea. The disembodied spectrality of the call must be incarnated in the world of flesh and blood. The call must become a response. The word must take the form of transformed flesh.

When Marx said that hitherto philosophers had been content to interpret the world, but now the time had come to change it, he got the whole idea. The idealism of insistence must be transformed into the materialism of existence. But Marx should have been kinder to "interpretation." Interpretation goes all the way down, into action, which is why I like to speak of "radical" hermeneutics. Marx should have understood that there is no such thing as a purely inactive, inoperative interpretation. If it is not engaged in the world, it is not an interpretation but an idle thought, a free-floating fancy. To understand anything at all is to interpret, and to interpret is to have settled into the minute interstices of the concrete world, to have engaged its forces, so as to see what this idea is doing, what it is demanding, what is happening in it, how it is to be played, what disturbance it creates. As they say back in the Humanities Center, there is no such thing as an uninterpreted fact of the matter, no such thing as interpretation that floats above the world in pure weightless inactivity. We do not have an interpretation except in the response to what is addressing us in the concrete situation and calls for action. The call is heard only *in* the response. Without the response, the call remains just a ghost.

When Eckhart has Jesus' "Martha, Martha" mean that Martha had two gifts, both the *vita contemplativa* and *the vita activa*, he got the whole idea.[30] Without the response, the call is like Eckhart's "Mary," languishing at the feet of Jesus, too anemic to act. Martha's hospitality, her preparation for the coming of Jesus, for his most basic and "unmentionable" bodily needs, does not distract her from her unity with Jesus; it constitutes it, providing existence for the insistence of the event that takes place in and under the body of Jesus.

That is what specters expect.

But is this expectation not unrealistic? Is it not impossible? Has it not been utterly undermined with this talk about God's spectral inexistence? If God is not a transcendent, omniscient, omnipotent superbeing in the sky, who can hold back tsunamis before they reach the shore, cure cancer, and come to the aid of the home team in a crucial game; if God cannot help us in our hour of need, answer our prayers, and be there in the first place to answer our prayers—if God is not all that, what good is God? What good is God's inexistence when existence is what we really need? If God cannot separate sheep from the goats, reward his friends and punish his enemies, what good is God? If God merely insists and does not exist, what good can God be? If as we have said God is not an agent/entity and does not "do" anything, what good can He [*sic*] do?

My main response to these questions is another question: If that's the "good news," what's the bad news? My perversity is to think that there is no greater obstacle to the event that stirs within the name of God than to reify that event into an existing being with such superpowers. The name of God is not the name of a superhero, an existing, super-existing Superbeing, swollen with an excess of existence and phallic power, who ultimately—He bides his time and plays His cards smartly—squares all accounts and orders all the disorders that break out down here in our disjointed time. That deserves our unreserved atheistic unbelief, unconditional incredulity. It is the worst paganism. There is nothing that so thoroughly erodes action and distorts life than expecting to be saved and rewarded by a Superbeing, nothing more at odds with the kingdom of God than this cynical economy of rewards and punishment which demeans life into a means to an end, that turns life into a coupon redeemable for an eternal redemption, for an eternal reward, and the love of God into credit in a celestial bank. As Meister Eckhart said, some men love God the way they love their cow, for its milk. The year of the Jubilee is not the reward in the hereafter for sticking it out here below. The year of the Jubilee is the infinitival to-come to be realized in time, always coming, always calling, almost here, never quite. It is not eternal rest but the restlessness of a call for what is coming that intensifies temporal life to the limit.

The spectrality of God is to disappear into the promise of the world and to leave existence to us, not to promise heavenly interventions that will sweep down from the sky and put terrestrial life down below in order; not to stand over the world as a divine accountant keeping track of the credits and debits heaped up by a hapless humankind down below. God is not an infinite immaterial solution to finite material problems. God is the problem of which we are expected to be the solution. God is not the "answer" but the question to which we are to be the response. (I am never going to find bumper stickers like this. I am going to need to find a company that does custom work!) God is not a necessary being but a suggestive possibility, an almost impossible one, of which we are to be the actualization. God is a spirit, a specter, a call, a plea, an exhortation made to us to transform insistence into existence. Nothing perverts God more profoundly than to reify God into an infinite immaterial entity residing in an immaterial realm, who being eternal has a long memory, who does not forget those who have served and those who have offended the divine order; who, having infinite might at His command can right any wrong that He has a mind to correct, just so long as He feels like it. A being of such Big Might is a Big Mystery, remember, so sometimes He does not come through! Chalk off the infant mortality rate in undeveloped countries to The Mystery of Divine Providence. He knows what He's doing, even if we don't, or so they say. Tell that to their parents.

What more perfect mystification of an event, what more perfect perversion of the year of the Jubilee than to make it the year that God will make our enemies our footstool, separate the sheep from the goats, reward his friends with eternal happiness and punish his enemies with insufferable suffering, and perhaps drop by if time permits—after all, He's a busy Man—to shrink an inoperable tumor. What greater perversion than to make the year of the Jubilee the year God inflicts insufferable suffering upon the enemies of God? Such a God would be the envy of Nero—the maximum of pain while being guaranteed the impossibility of death. That would make the sufferings of a Roman crucifixion, lasting but a few mortal hours, small potatoes. Mel Gibson should make a movie about that! As T. J. J. Altizer's Blake asks, What difference is there between this Transcendent Power and Satan?

What more perfect perversion, what more perfect storm, than to enlist the Year of the Jubilee into a Neoplatonic economy that cashes in works of mercy for eternal rewards? That is rather a lot of corruption for people in the business of earning incorruptible bodies! While they were otherwise taken in by Neoplatonism, the mystics saw right through this ruse. That is why they called for a life "without why," without the Eternal Reward in the Sky, and why Marguerite Porete called for bidding adieu to virtue, to cease making the virtues "fat" so that your celestial pension payments will be fatter still. The spectral inexistence of God undermines a life spent trying to heap up eternal rewards, which is the only condition under which the year of the Jubilee is possible.

It Spooks, but Does It Preach?

You will have a hard time selling this in the churches.
How many ways can I say this? This is not about selling anything.

I was once was asked whether I thought this whole thing I was doing with the weakness of God, the inexistent insistence of God, could "preach." It spooks, but does it preach? Can the "it" which "spooks" be preached? I was struck by the expression. To say that something will "preach" means it can touch lives, issue in action. It is a magnificent locution for penumbralogists who love the middle voice. It allows the "it"—something being preached, something getting itself preached, where the agency remains anonymous—to assume the active voice.

My answer is that the spectrality of God is the *only* thing that *can* preach.[31] Otherwise preaching is a sales pitch, and it is trying to pitch celestial snake oil. It is trying to sell the faithful that they can get something eternal for almost nothing (time), when it should be saying that you get nothing for doing everything, that it's not about getting something. Preaching must dare to make its way out into the deep, where the land is no longer in sight, risking the perils of being lost at sea, daring to preach the Kingdom of God without rewards. It must dare to preach of expenditures that have no return; of gifts that do not get reciprocated; of hospitality that puts itself at risk without expecting a heavenly mansion in return. It must dare to preach the insistence of God where God is not a being who packs a punch and can punish his enemies and reward his friends. It must dare preach a God who does not just step in to do the heavy lifting for us, which only mystifies life with supernaturalist fantasies. The insistence of God requires us to assume responsibility for our lives, to respond to what is pressing in upon us and demanding action, to stand up not as an autonomous I but respondents in the accusative, and to do so not because there is celestial money in it for us, not because we will be rewarded in the year of the Jubilee. But because the year of the Jubilee (if there is any) which is both always coming, always to come, is also today, and it presses in upon us here and now, urgently, in the "moment." The to-come is not a distant time in the future; it is the urgency of the moment and it is continually being actualized, intermittently, episodically, here and there, now and then.

My own perversity is to say that the *meaning* of the name (of) "God" *is* what gets done for the least among us, even if (especially if) the name (of) "God" never comes up. Attending to the bodies in need that populate the Scriptures *is* the "body of God," to employ Sallie McFague's excellent expression, with or without the name (of) "God." Lord, when did we see you hungry, thirsty, or imprisoned and come to your aid? That beautiful story (Matt 25) perfectly embodies the spectral life, the spectrality of action, personal and public, ethical and political, because everything in the story depends on the invisibility of God, the inexistence of God, the spectrality of God. In this story, the only thing that exists are these bodies in need and tending to these bodies. But as soon as the veil is lifted, as soon as the anonymity is removed, as soon as the Lord steps forth and is plainly visible, as soon as we get to the punch line of the story, the whole thing is annulled. It turns out that this moving story is framed with the terrifying threat of the coming of the Son of Man on the last day to separate the sheep from the goats, rewarding the former and visiting unspeakable suffering upon those who get out of line. Talk about a "punch" line—it beats the kingdom of God senseless!

Preaching should be a call to make the name of God come true; it should be preached without promising celestial cash rewards, eternal credits for temporal works, without threatening punishment, and without promising timely supernatural interventions to step in just in time when it has all become too much for us; it's about Calvary, not the cavalry.

Comforting the sick and dying should be just that, holding the hand of the afflicted and sitting up with them through the night, without the tasteless assurances of heavenly banquets for people on feeding tubes or whose terminal condition means they are past eating. Comforting the sick and dying already *is* the year of the Jubilee, the life of God in the world, the Kingdom of God, with or without God. It already *is* the word of God made flesh, its realization, enfleshment, incarnation, carnal realization. The existence of God *is* the companionship offered to the dying through the night, God being there wherever two or three gather under the name of God.

The works of mercy are just that, ways of letting the name of God take place in the world, letting the event that stirs within the name of God happen, letting God's insistence acquire mundane existence. God is not eternal; God is momentary, made actual only in the moment, happening only in the moments of mercy and compassion. Otherwise the works of mercy are works of mercenaries with the gleam of eternal rewards in their eye. Serving the wretched of the earth is reduced to a terrific bargain, the best possible way to heap up rewards for the hereafter while still here on earth—and to make a lot of converts in the process.[32] There is no such thing as a free lunch, especially in religion. Works of mercy are a plus-plus, good business, a great deal, a great way to heap up the coin of the realm in the kingdom of rewards and punishments.

Praying in secret is good advice, but please do not pray in secret so as not to forfeit the eternal rewards due to you later on in heaven, as Matthew has Jesus say (Matt 6:6). (No wonder there's a legend that says Matthew was a tax collector!) Prayer is not a matter of delayed gratification. We pray in secret because praying, whether in secret or collectively, is a way to keep ourselves open to a quiet call that is easily drowned out in the booming buzzing boisterousness of life. Praying has nothing to do with rewards at all, here or hereafter. Prayers are not IRAs that we are advised not to cash in before retirement, which incurs a penalty. Prayers are really prayers when we do not know if there is anyone there to hear them or to whom we are praying or for what. By the impossible everything begins.

Marguerite Porete called this perverse economizing on God the "Little Church," a petty and pusillanimous way to treat the year of the Jubilee. To this she opposed the "Big Church," where the Kingdom of God is not a matter of following the celestial money but a magnanimous way of living and loving "without why."[33] For her trouble, the Little Church, which was swollen big with Big Men in long robes who carried a Big Stick, burned her at the stake. In speaking of a "religion without religion," the religion inside religion that struggles to twist free of the constraints imposed by the religion on the outside, I have a parallel distinction in mind. So if the Inquisitors show up at my door I will blame the whole thing on Marguerite. "The mystics made me do it!" is the last thing you will hear me shouting as they drag me away.

My perversity is to think that Mother Teresa's finest moment is found in the doubts she expresses about whether she "believed" any of the teachings of the Church, whether she even "believed" in "God," which is what she called this spectral solicitation emanating from the faces looking back at her on the streets of Calcutta, a solicitation she had been answering all her life. What she never doubts is her *work*, because her work *is* the Kingdom of God; her answer to the call is the only reality enjoyed by that call. In her moments of doubt, of "incredulity toward big stories," I think, the name of God is purified of existence and the sheer insistence of God, the call to make the name of God come true, is disclosed. The sheer purity of that inexistent solicitation shook a very strong woman to the bones, and, while it rattled her "beliefs," it did not lay a glove on her deeper "faith" in the event, under whatever name it addressed her.

Living a Spectral Life

It spooks. It preaches as it spooks by calling for a spectral life.

Everything depends on the spectrality of God, on the inspiration of this spectral spirit, on the promptings of this specter, which expects a transformation of our lives.

Everything depends on the audacity of God, who not thinking existence something to be prized, and being humbly content with spectrality, empties God of God without remainder into the promise of the world, daring to leave existence to us.

Everything depends on us, who must have not only the audacity to think, *sapere aude*, and who must never leave off thinking, which was the specter that inspired the audacity of the Enlightenment, but still more a second audacity, uttering a second yes to what is coming, yes, yes, come, *viens, oui, oui*. That is the audacity to hope in and for the coming of what we cannot see coming, which is a dicey business requiring a high tolerance for risk.

So if someone comes proclaiming the year of the Jubilee, the year that is always coming but never quite comes, that does not call for calculation, that calls for hope. Hope is the air, the ambiance, the element of a spectral life. To live a spectral life is to lead a life of hope. Dare to hope. *Sperare aude*!

3

Derrida and the Trace of Religion

The question of Derrida and religion may be thought of in three stages. When Derrida's work made its first appearance, the common assumption was that he was a secular and atheistic thinker and no friend of religion. Later on, in a fascinating semi-autobiographical text, Derrida surprisingly spoke of "my religion about which nobody understands anything," with the result, he said, that he has been "read less and less well over almost twenty years."[1] That proved to be a touchstone text that set off a widespread reassessment of the question in the broader setting of what has been described as the "theological turn" in continental philosophy. But by the turn of the century, under the impact of Badiou and Žižek, another mood had taken hold among the philosophers, this one aggressively materialistic and atheistic, antagonistic to both postmodernism and religion. I want to address these three stages by arguing that when early on Derrida undertakes a deconstruction of ontotheology, we ought not to be too quick to say that he is not a man of religion, and when later on he speaks of his religion, we must understand this religion is also without religion. Finally, and with all that in mind, I want to assess Derrida's fortunes amid the current renewal of anti-religion.

The Trace (of) "God"

From the start, for all his seeming godlessness, there was the trace of theology in what Derrida was saying, a ghost that constantly haunted him and disturbed his readers. When he wrote that *différance* is neither a word nor a concept, neither sensible nor supersensible, neither this nor that, that sounded like Meister Eckhart and other negative theologians.[2] So early on Derrida faced the accusation, unless it were a congratulation, that this is not the godlessness it seems to be but really a negative theology, and *différance* is its hidden God, the *deus absconditus*. Of course, that was not true, but in deconstruction one learns how not to say "of course" and, of course, how not to say it too easily. One learns not to feel too secure about the difference between an accusation and a congratulation, or even about standard-form distinctions like philosophy and theology, or faith and reason.

But, of course, Derrida is an atheist, and *différance* is assuredly not the God of negative theology, not the *hyperousios,* not the omnipotent creator of heaven and earth. Nothing could be more obvious. One way to put this is to say that *différance* is not transcendent but transcendental, and so it is not a word or a concept, a being or a hyperbeing, just because it is the condition of tracing under which all such "effects" are "constituted," to use the usual language of transcendental philosophy. But then, of course, this is not the business as usual of transcendental thinking. *Différance* is not transcendental consciousness, not a transcendental subject of any sort, but the very difference between conscious and nonconscious, subject and object, and even more to the point, the very space between transcendent and transcendental. Accordingly, *différance* is not God because it is the difference between God and creatures, comparable to the difference between signifiers in linguistics. But *différance* is also not language or transcendental linguisticality, which is why Derrida settled on "trace" and scuttled "signifier." It is also not transcendental for the very good reason that it does not prescribe a fixed set of conditions under which something is made possible. On the contrary, the conditions under which something is made possible in deconstruction are also the conditions under which it is impossible, like a proper name. The very thing that makes a name possible, repeatability, make it impossible for it to be purely proper. Nothing can be purely proper, or purely improper, or properly pure or impure. *Différance* spaces, but then again it does not "do" anything, like spacing, which would require that it be an agent, whereas agents are one of the things constituted in *différance*. That is why Derrida says it is best to think of it in the middle voice, as the condition under which things—anything, subjects or objects, agents or patients, creators or creatures—get themselves spaced (differentiated). Far from the God beyond Being of Christian Neoplatonism, *différance* is more like the *khora* of Plato's *Timaeus*.

So, of course, *différance* is not the hidden God, not even the most hidden of all hidden gods, *but*—there is always a "but" in deconstruction, the necessity for which might be another candidate for its least bad definition—the resources of negative theology, the brilliance of its "detours, locutions, and syntax," the infinite sensitivity to learning how not to speak, the deftness with which it goes about erasing its own traces, are indispensable to something we are describing by constantly saying what it is not. So true is this that Derrida does not trust anything that is not "contaminated with negative theology."[3] The way the negative theologians speak of "God" is exemplary of the way in which everything, whether it is about God or not, whether we are negative theologians or not, should be said—under erasure, saying it and unsaying it, writing it and striking it out, both at once. What we say is a "contingent unity," provisionally stitched together, "forged" (with all of the ambiguity of that word) in a particular context and under determinate conditions, subject to change in the next moment. This contingent unity is—and this is the word that caught on—"deconstructible," that is, recontextualizable, revisable, reformable, and transformable, for better or for worse. Nothing guarantees that the revision will not be a disaster, deconstructibility being the condition of both the best and the worst.

"God" for Derrida is not *différance*, but the effect of *différance*, an effect of the "play of traces." That does not erase God for deconstruction but puts it on the tracks or in the trace of "God." "God" is not an infinite being for Derrida but an inexhaustible example of the sort of thing that *différance* is always doing, or rather, of what was always getting itself done under the conditions of *différance*. For whatever else it is, the name (of) "God" is a name, and a fascinating example, for example, of a proper name, at least in the religions of the Book, where "God" functions as a proper name, of the one and only God, in the upper case. That is the result of capitalizing (on) a common noun, god and the gods, and the matrix of a terrible and endless politics. When he first met Hélène Cixous back in the 1960s, the two young atheistic Jewish immigrants from Algeria began corresponding about her first book, *Le Prénom de Dieu*: Is "God" a first name or a last, a family name or a surname?[4] As a name, it admits of endless recontextualizability, let us say, of endless Midrash, of strange and exotic commentary, which deprives it of its propriety. Indeed, "God" provides the occasion of an infinite repeatability that cannot be contained within the limits of theism or monotheism or even excluded from atheism. Might there not be a "religion" without God, or a God without "theism?" Recontextualizability means you can never say never. You cannot say that "green is or"[5] can never make sense. Maybe even, in virtue of this repeatability, after the death of God, the name of God can be resurrected and live on (*survie*). The name of God is a superlative example of something excessive, *hyper, supra, au-delà*, something that drives language, thought, and practice to their limits, arguably the best example of the play of traces, which in German is itself a play on words (*zum Beispiel*). So there are numerous places in the 1960s and 1970s in which Derrida, atheist that he is, evidently to his devilish delight, enters into this play, like the treatment of the name of God as the trickster in a scatological history in the essay on Artaud,[6] which belongs to the best traditions of a dissonant and dissident midrash by an impudent and heretical rabbi.

However, the most famous and intimidating example of the name of God is precisely to arrest the very play which that name exemplifies and incites, to put that play to rest and to organize everything else around itself as the stable and stabilizing center, the signifier to end all signifiers, the last word and the first, outside the text.[7] That is "God" as a "transcendental signifier," at the sound of which every knee shall bend and every dance shall stop. Enter "theology" as the police of thought sent in to keep the peace, to put down the right to ask any question. That is the example of "God" that comes under attack in *Of Grammatology*, against which all the aphoristic energies of *différance* are lined up, which fills in the meaning of Derrida's "atheism." Against this God deconstruction poses a relentless exposure of the contingencies of our beliefs and practices, of the earthly provenance of things that pass themselves off as having dropped from the sky. The most famous things Derrida had to say about God and classical theology early on revolve around this self-appointed center. All the resources in deconstruction are called on to displace and decenter this pretender to the throne which is trying to confine the energy of *différance*. So Derrida will sometimes identify the "theological" function, as if there were just one, as the very idea of founding, grounding, centering, in a word, "onto-theo-logic," a compound word coined by Kant and made famous by Heidegger, which meant the grounding of all beings on a first and unshakable being. That center is not only the place of God, but the place God holds, which means that God can be replaced by other ontotheological placeholders, like Ego, Spirit, Will-to-Power, Matter, or even the State, the Party or Capital, which Žižek likes to call, following Lacan, the Big Other, anything that keeps the peace (and on which we can make a profit). But Derrida considers that peace the peace of death, eternal rest, *requiescat in pace*. Pure peace is pure death; pure life is pure death. Deconstruction has to do with the endless restless play of traces in which we forge such factical unities as we need to get ourselves through the day, with an acute sense of the contingency of it all, of the open-endedness of the future. That of course is risky business, and it may not end well, but that's life, or rather life/death, this *vita mortalis*, as Augustine called it, in which all the risk and flavor and dangerous joys of life are concentrated.

Of course, Jacques Derrida was an atheist. But deconstruction deals with ghosts and traces, with undecidable fluctuations and crossovers, not with stable categories and well-formed binaries like "theism" and "atheism," and so we do not close the books on religion by repeating this well-known biographical fact. The uniquely grammatological effect would be to warn us that any possible theism is haunted by atheism, even as any possible atheism is haunted by theism, which means that both theism and atheism are unstable categories exposed to an event that they cannot see coming. That is why Derrida warned us about the dogmatic theologians of atheistic metaphysics[8] while saying of himself only, "I quite rightly pass for an atheist,"[9] meaning that this is what they say, and "they" are "right." But when "they" say something "right," that is shorthand and a contraction of something more complex and multifarious, for the unbeliever in him is disturbed by the ghost of faith and so never has any peace. But neither is there any peace for the "believers," who are kept up at night by the ghosts and demons of unbelief. The believers can at best rightly pass for Christians, Jews, or Muslims, while never being identical with themselves. In virtue of everything deconstruction stands for, one cannot say I am, *je suis, c'est moi,* this or that, say, an atheist. Johannes Climacus understood this very well by declining to say he is a Christian; at best he is trying to become one. Whenever we are emboldened to say *je suis,* according to Derrida, we are also inadvertently conceding that we are following (*suivre*) something else,[10] following the trace of something that solicits us, something *je ne sais quoi.*

So what is the upshot for "religion" in all this? Grammatology deals with the energy of the trace. In the sphere of the trace, the trace of a faith, *foi,* or a faith in the trace, is unavoidable. How else could one be related to a trace except by faith? By the same token, what else can faith be except faith in a trace? Deconstruction takes place in and as the space of the trace and therefore of faith. But if religion turns on faith, might there not be a religion that turns on a trace while standing free of the very God sent in to arrest the play of the trace? However unnerving such faith may be to the true believers, as it was, it is no less unnerving to the true unbelievers, which explains why the unbelievers would later on be surprised to hear Derrida talking about his religion. Either way, this faith cannot be contracted to the endless wars between believers and unbelievers, between the opposing *croyances* of the believers and the unbelievers.[11] These are simply opposing "positions," ham-fisted and distracting binary oppositions of what one rightly passes for, both of which beg to be displaced, in virtue of a deeper "affirmation" or faith.

That explains why, from very early on, many of those who knew something about faith and traces in religion and theology were taken by deconstruction,[12] while those who knew little or nothing about such things thought that, of course, deconstruction is a straight out and simple dismissal of religion and theology. But anyone who knows anything about deconstruction, which deals in traces, knows it is not "straight out" or "simple" or a "dismissive" of anything, including "God." Even though the negative theologians were always singing the praises of non-knowing, one thing they knew very well was that we should be infinitely reluctant to use the name of God with any sense of closure. They knew without knowing or putting it this way that the name of God is an effect of the play of traces. It is a name "forged" in the fires of language, time, history, and culture, in gendered and political circumstances, in which something is getting itself said and done, for better and for worse, the problem being we do not know what.

"My Religion, about Which Nobody Understands Anything"

The first quick impression that Derrida created during the heyday of deconstruction in the late 1960s and 1970s, at least among those who based their judgments on academic gossip and what they could gather in conference hotel bars, was one of skeptical relativism and an indecisive apoliticism. But the more considered import of the work that Derrida was doing in those days is best described as disseminative, multiplicative but always affirmative, of which his early interest in James Joyce would be illustrative. He was not saying no; he was saying yes, and repeating it, *oui, oui*. He was interested in something that Joyce called the "chaosmic," in maintaining the precisely calibrated tension between order and chaos that is the condition of novelty, not in spreading chaos pure and simple, nor in restoring order pure and simple. He sought a kind of productive ambiguity not simple confusion, something destabilizing not disabling. He was interested in keeping things open-ended, just sufficiently unstable and mobile to remain exposed to their future. Because giving things a future is the most genuine way of all to preserve a tradition, he once said, with a twinkle in his eye, that he was a genuinely conservative person,[13] even as deconstruction was regarded as poison by conservatives, both cultural and religious. Deconstruction does not destroy things but affirms them by giving them a chance. This chance exposes them to risk, but that risk is their only chance.

One thing Derrida never said in the 1960s and 1970s is that anything is or can be "undeconstructible." The first time he did say such a thing, as far as I can determine, was in 1989, in response to a challenge coming from Drucilla Cornell, on which he took the occasion to respond to this growing distortion of his work. Cornell asked him to address the question of "deconstruction and the possibility of justice" before the audience of the Cardoza Law School, an apt audience, since deconstruction had the look of something like an outlaw and Cornell's "and" had the look of a dare: How can you dare speak in the same breath of this infamous deconstruction *and* justice? To which of course, Derrida famously replied, that deconstruction *is* justice (*et/est*), and that justice in itself, if there is such a thing, is not deconstructible, while the law is deconstructible.[14] The deconstructibility of the law—its revisability, repealability, recontextualizability—depends on the undeconstructibility of justice. The escape hatch in this text, which looks at first like a headlong retreat to Platonism, is the "*s'il y en a*," "if there is such a thing," and of course there *is* not. Then perhaps justice is an inexistent Regulative Idea in the Kantian sense? Not so, because that would require an essentialist ideal of justice, approached asymptotically although never reached empirically. It is just in virtue of *différance* that there can be no universal essences, but only so many effects of the trace, so many provisional inscriptions and temporary formations meant to get us through our works and days, like laws, which are deconstructible.

But if this is neither Plato nor Kant, who or what is it? What "is" justice and what can it mean to say that it is "undeconstructible?" The answer is that justice is an injunction or an imperative, a call or a solicitation. Justice calls, we respond. Justice solicits, we answer. Justice pipes, we dance. Justice happens, opens up in the gap between justice in itself, if there is such a thing, and the law. The gap is structural; it cannot be closed, and that makes justice both possible and impossible. The law is written in the language of universality (repeatability), which is to say that the law is written to begin with, while justice has to do with the singularity of the situation in which justice happens. Justice happens, if it happens, in the singular, in the moment of justice, when justice is called for, when we do our best (or our least worst) to respond to what the singular situation demands. We can never say that a nation or a law or a person or even a deed "is" just. That would represent a kind of freeze-framing and hence injustice and idolatry. The most we can say is that justice happens, if it happens, in the blink of the eye, in the moment of singularity. Justice indeed rules but it can never be contracted to a rule; it must always suspend the rule in order to invent the rule that it follows in an undecidable situation, and justice is urgently needed now even though it never arrives. These "aporias" of justice make justice impossible, but in so doing they provide the only conditions under which justice is possible.[15]

This all sounds familiar to a theologically tuned ear. We have heard these aporias before, when Johannes de Silentio itemized the "problemata" besetting ethics.[16] That the ethical is the universal but the religious is singular makes ethics (like the "law") a "temptation," something we lapse into in order to escape responsibility. So the critics have it only half right: Deconstruction is indeed the exception to the ethical (to the rule, to the universal), but it is not the aesthetic exception, which tries to fly beneath the radar of the law and to avoid decision at any cost, but the religious exception, which passes through the universal in order to endure the ordeal of deciding the undecidable. If we have heard this before, it was not in Plato or Kant. This is father Abraham, and deconstruction is not the aesthete trying to evade the principle of contradiction but the knight of faith. This is more Midrash from Reb Derrisa, another telling of the binding of Isaac (the Akedah), another performance, or per-ver-formance, of the famous story from Genesis. Derrida repeats but alters Kierkegaard's staging (who is repeating Paul's): "Abraham" holds the place of the subject of responsibility; "God" holds the place of the Other (the neighbor or the stranger) who demands justice; and Isaac is left holding the bag, that is, the place of the "other others," whose interests will inevitably be sacrificed. In meeting our responsibility to the Other one in the madness of the moment of decision, that very decision produces an incision, so that when justice happens, justice is also divided against itself. Undecidability is not indecision but the condition of (im)possibility of decision-cum-incision, comparable to the ordeal by which Abraham is tested in Genesis. The "paradox" of Abraham becomes the "paradigm" of ethical singularity.[17]

Justice, then, is neither a Platonic form nor a Kantian ideal but a quasi-Abrahamic call. Justice "is" not, which means that it can only be the object of a "faith" that wants to make it come true. As such, Derrida further dares to call it a desire, a dream, and even a "prayer," which are the stock in trade of a "religion." It is a desire beyond desire,[18] beyond the day-to-day economic desires for things that are plausible and possible, a desire of "the" impossible, which is the only thing we can truly desire,[19] all other desires being unworthy of the name. By "the" impossible, he says, everything begins.[20] We get started by the impossible, are set in motion by it. We desire justice, we dream of justice, of the impossible, which visits itself upon us like a voice that startles us in the night. He is always dreaming of and desiring the impossible, praying and weeping over *the* impossible, which is not a simple logical contradiction but a hope beyond hope, something we love, for which we pray and weep. The impossible—one of the most well known names of God—is a matter for prayer, and now he tells us that he is a man of prayer, that he has been praying all his life, and that if we understood this about him, we would understand everything,[21] and the failure to realize this is the source of all this misunderstanding of his work over the last twenty years. Every night, he says, he kisses his tallith, and he will not take it with him on the road for fear it will be lost or stolen.[22]

Here the religious analogue is Augustine, not (Kierkegaard's) Abraham, and this time he per(ver)forms deconstruction as a religion by restaging the *Confessions*.[23] Once again the reader comes upon a man at prayer, whose back is turned to us as he addresses someone else. The speaker (Augustine/Jackie—he has confessed his real name to us), an immigrant from North Africa (Numidia/Algeria) who has emigrated to the Big Apple (Rome/Paris) to make his career, is praying to "you" (God/Geoffrey, his mother, us, and many others), while their mother (Monica/Georgette) lies dying on the northern shores of the Mediterranean (Ostia/Nice). But how can he be praying if he does not believe in God, if he rightly passes for an atheist? But the real question is, How can he not be praying? How can he be doing anything other than praying? If, as Jean-Louis Chretien says, prayer is a wounded word,[24] whose word is more wounded than someone who does not know to whom he is praying, or if his prayer will be heard, or if there is anyone to pray to? Prayer is a marvelous example of *the* impossible, where the very impossibility of prayer is what sets prayer in motion, requiring us to do what we cannot do, to give what we do not have. That is why every prayer is prefaced by a prayer to be able to pray. Lord, we pray you, teach us how to pray. If he knew to whom he was praying, he would know everything and then he would not need to pray.

Derrida's atheism, then, is no obstacle to his prayer or his faith or his religion, which, to borrow his own expression, is a "religion without religion." That means it "repeats" religion without the dogmas, creeds, rituals, prayer books, candles, and buildings of a concrete and historical religion,[25] whether that be the Jewish one he grew up with, the Christian one by which he was surrounded and harassed as a child, or the lost Islamic one back among his Algerian ancestors. Thus, far from constituting an obstacle to his religion, Derrida's atheism is a crucial ingredient in it, a precious non-knowing and nonbelieving that isolates the very structure of faith. If he believed in the God of the great monotheisms, that would ruin his religion; it would ruin everything. It would arrest the play of the event that takes place in the name of God, of what is stirring there, haunting and soliciting us from time immemorial and from an unforeseeable future. The trace (of) "God" is infinitely precious, even if, especially if, it does not pick out a fact of the matter or correspond to a being out there or up there somewhere. The name of God is the trace of a memory and a promise, a promise that is not undermined but made all the most promissory by the fact that we do not know who is making the promise, that we have absolutely no assurance that it will be kept or that we will be saved. On the contrary, faith is only faith if it lacks every assurance that we are saved, only if we are exposed by it to the worst risk.

Everything happens *by* the impossible. Hospitality is hospitable not when we invite our friends (the "same") to our homes where they are welcome, but when we welcome the unwelcome, when we are visited unexpectedly in the night by the other, by the stranger about whom we have no assurance at all that he has not come to harm us. Forgiveness is forgiveness when we forgive not the forgivable, those who are sorry and make amends, but the unforgivable, the impenitent who reject our offer. Hope is hope when we hope against hope, when hope is lost. Love is love when we love the unlovable (the enemy). Faith is faith when it is impossible to believe. Deconstruction is structured like a religion. Deconstruction retraces the movements of a passion that we call in Christian Latin "religion," repeating the movements of what Augustine called at the very beginning of the *Confessions* our restless heart (*inquietum est cor nostrum*), which is very close to the heart of deconstruction, which has a heart, an "open heart" turned toward the event.[26] The open heart of deconstruction begins by an impossible mourning, by a loss that cannot be repaired, which Benjamin called a weak messianic, weak because the lives of the dead were ruined beyond repair. Deconstruction begins by a hope for the coming or the incoming of the other (*l'invention de l'autre*), of an other we cannot see coming.[27] The religion whose movements are repeated in deconstruction turns on a faith in the future, not the future present (*le futur*) that we can plan for and reasonably expect, a poor and futureless future, but *l'à venir,* the "to-come," the very structure of hope and expectation that the future will always be better. But sometimes it is not. Of course it is not, and that is what demands faith, which is the stuff of things that are seen not and that may visit upon us the worst violence, so that our faith exposes us, structurally and inescapably, to evil, which is what Derrida means by radical evil. That is all to say that faith and hope and love are risky business and not for the faint of heart.

Derrida's religion turns on an underlying faith (*foi*) that cannot be contracted to a determinate belief, a *croyance*, be that "belief" a confessional religion or a professional anti-religion, a theism or an atheism. That is why there is not the least inconsistency between Derrida's religion and his "secularity" (*laïceté*), no more than there is between a tax collector and a knight of faith.[28] The difference that makes a difference in deconstruction is not between religious belief and secular disbelief, theism and atheism, differences that are completely indifferent to faith and of no consequence in deconstruction, but the difference between a structure that is closed to the future and one that is not, one that maintains its exposure to the future and puts itself at risk and one that does not. That is difference between deconstruction and what resists deconstruction. A *croyance* is a circle that threatens to close in upon itself and attempts to keep itself safe from the future, that keeps itself secure on every side, secure in its belief or disbelief from the approach of the other, which shuts down the risky business of faith in what we cannot see coming. Of course, "faith" and "belief" are not two ships passing each other in the night. Deconstruction is not just serving up one more rigid binary of its own. On the contrary, the confessional faiths are constantly being haunted by this deeper, more uncertain and spectral faith, which is why confessional theologians often find themselves in trouble with the powers that be in their own confession. They dig so deeply that they tap into the subversive and underlying *foi* that seeps into their work. Then they find themselves confessing, circum-fessing, that we do not know who we are, or to whom we are praying, or for what, or even if there is anyone to whom to pray, that we do not know what we say or what we pray when we invoke the name of God. Then they also find themselves out of a job.

Make no mistake. Derrida is not talking about a supernatural faith in an eternal destiny offering everlasting redemption. All that, to employ the language of Bultmann, has been "demythologized" in Derrida. But the result is not a "religion within the limits of reason" (of pure reason) but rather what Derrida calls, in a remarkable passage in *Rogues* "an act of messianic faith—irreligious and without messianism," inscribed in "khora."[29] Khora is a Platonic trope drawn from the depths of the *Timaeus* not from the heights of the *agathon* of the *Republic*. Derrida employs it as a nickname for *différance* in order to signify its function as the irreducible medium in which all our beliefs and practices are "inscribed" or "constructed," thereby rendering them deconstructible, and this precisely in virtue of what is undeconstructible, *the* impossible, in which we have a certain faith. This faith is not exactly in "history," which is too reassuring, too teleological, and too metaphysical a name for him,[30] but in the absolute future, in the unforeseeable "to-come" of whatever order or register is under discussion— be it politics, ethics, or the law, be it art, science, or religion. Importantly, the subject matter of the to-come under discussion in *Rogues* is a messianic faith in the future of reason and of democracy, in the "weak force" of reason and democracy (elsewhere it is justice, the gift, forgiveness, hospitality, etc.) which solicits us but have no army to back them up.

On the surface of this khoral plane a "call" arises, "the call for the thinking of the event." The call says "come" ("*viens*"), yes, to the coming (*invention*) of the event (*événement*) and it comes in response to the call that the event first makes upon us like a stranger in the night.[31] Yes, yes, *viens, oui, oui.* The call calls *to* and *from* and *for* the "to-come" (*à venir*). Deconstruction may be seen as the grammar of an infinitive, the grammatology of the infinitival event of the to-come. As an infinitival structure, the pure messianic lacks a (de)finite proper name, as opposed to the concrete messianisms which deal precisely in proper names, with God as a proper name, which pick out a (de)finite entity, a first being. The call "bears every hope" although it remains "without hope." It thus has the same structure as Paul's "hope against hope" (Romans 4:18) while also being separated by an abyss from Paul. Paul thinks that the God of Israel will intervene at just this point of hopelessness, while Derrida entertains no such hope. Derrida's hope is hopeless, meaning he does not think that there is some being out there somewhere who is coming to save us (Žižek's no-Big-Other). Nothing assures us of our safety, so this faith and hope are structurally exposed to the worst violence. His hope is not in a (de)finite entity but in the infinitival "to- come" itself, in the very structure of hope and expectation itself, if there is such a thing, a certain hope in hope as such, not in any entity who can save us, which is not far from Tillich's point that to treat God as an existent entity, a (de)finite being, is to render God finite, a form of atheism! The hope of the concrete messianisms, which is funded by a proper name, turns on what Derrida calls the "teleology" of hopefulness, or what in theology is called the "history of salvation" and even more tellingly "the economy of salvation." This economy or teleology means the good deal promised by the Good News, in which a flickering faith, now through a veil darkly, is redeemable upon delivery at death for unveiled eternal vision. That is a foreseeable salvation underwritten by an identifiable (de)finite God, which thinks "revelation" means it stands free of khora/*différance* and makes contact with some kind of absolute warrantor of hope. Derrida's more austere hope and faith in the weak force of the to-come is foreign to any strong and robust economy of salvation, but it is not foreign to salvation as such, to *salut* as the salutation to the coming of the other. Such faith and hope are foreign to the God (*Dieu*) of the concrete messianisms but not to the event hailed in the name of God, *à Dieu,* that is, *adieu,* "the 'come' or 'go' in peace," in the face of the wholly other (Levinas)—where, as Derrida famously added, every other is wholly other, thereby profoundly transforming Levinas.

We can now see more clearly the difference between the religion of Augustine in the *Confessions* and that of Jackie in "Circumfession." The difference is not, as the confessional "faithful" are inclined to view it, that Augustine is engaged in a true prayer in a serious religion whereas Derrida is an atheist whose prayer is phony and whose religion makes a mockery of a true religion. The difference is not between a true man of prayer and an impostor. The difference is that Augustine knows the name of the one to whom he prays, and he knows the name of what he is praying for, and he enjoys the confidence that the one on the other end cannot fail in the end, whereas Derrida's prayer lacks every such assurance. Augustine's prayers are filled with proper names, whereas Derrida prays an anchorite prayer in a desert khora in a community without community.[32] But the difference is *not* a matter of true prayer and true religion versus a phony prayer in a phony religion. Indeed, one could argue, if one wanted to start another religious war, that Derrida's prayer is more purely prayer, a still more wounded word according to Chrétien's idea of prayer, more wounded than the *Confessions*, since Augustine has all the comforts of the universal, as Johannes Climacus said—the tradition, the community, the liturgy, the "centuries"—whereas Derrida is really hanging on by a prayer.

Derrida thus produces a remarkable portrait of a more radical religion, composing a kind of post-phenomenology of a more radical experience of the to-come, and in particular of the events of faith and hope and prayer for the to-come that undermines the classical distinctions between faith and reason, theism and atheism, religious and secular. He displaces these received distinctions by following the traces of an underlying call or so-licitation by which everything we do is driven, in politics, ethics, and the law, in science, art, and religion, by which everything is solicited, in re-sponse to which they rise up. He shocks the sensibilities of the faithful with his heretical atheistic quasi-Jewish even slightly Arabic Augustinianism, while also managing to scandalize the secularists by exposing himself to the contamination of "faith" and "prayer." He brazenly dines with sinners, outcasts, and lepers on either side of the standard divide, whether they are guilty of the sins of secularism denounced by religion or the contagion of religion denounced by secularism. Depending on the strategic needs of the situation, one might call what he does a religion without religion, a theol-ogy more radical than confessional theology, or an atheology more radical than the business as usual of atheism, all of which reminds us of the les-son of *Glas,* that deconstruction does not answer to any classical bell. It answers only to the ringing of the call for a thinking of the event *to-come.*

The Return of Anti-Religion

With the death of Derrida in 2004, the last of the *soixante-huitaires* was gone and the new millennium was underway, bringing with it a third phase, a reaction against the so-called "theological turn" or the "return to reli-gion." The religious turn had gained a footing with the growing interest in

Levinas and Jean-Luc Marion along with the fascinating texts of Derrida from the 1980s and 1990s we have just discussed. But under the impact of Badiou and Žižek a generation of younger thinkers emerged, seeking a return to the modern and its critique of religion. They have called for a new materialism and a new realism, a restoration of the purity of reason and mathematical science. They affirm the original Copernican Revolution, not the devious one devised by Kant, which effectively undermined science for the subsequent history of continental philosophy. In their hands, "postmodernism" becomes a term of abuse employed in a drive-by shooting of a complex body of work, which unhappily has included Derrida. The theological turn becomes a *reductio ad absurdum* of continental thought: If that is where it leads us, something is seriously wrong. Postmodernism is used as a synonym for undermining truth with fiction, political decision making with an anemic political correctness, and objectivity and certainty with subjectivistic relativism. Interestingly, this attack from a secular left found a friend in theology as well, in the "Radical Orthodoxy" of John Milbank and his circle.[33] Whatever their differences with atheists, confessional theologians are more comfortable with straight up dogmatic certitudes than with Derrida's exquisitely delicate readings of the undecidabilities that interrupt dogmatic thinking at every turn.

Žižek is a good case in point. His taunting of deconstruction in this regard may be charitably read as partly rhetorical, since he credits Derrida with being an emancipatory force early on in his life growing up under the heel of the Party. As I pointed out above, what Žižek is arguing in his recent excursion into "death of God" theology as the death of the Big Other is interestingly close to Derrida's religion without religion, which was pointed out thirty years ago by the theologians.[34] Furthermore, Derrida's conception of a faith inscribed in *khora* that runs deeper than either theism or atheism takes account of the groundless ground beneath us while avoiding Žižek's grim sense of the void. This would all have to be sorted out carefully. But, unfortunately, Žižek's bombastic prose obscures the points on which his views and Derrida's converge and it only serves to whip up widespread antagonism against deconstruction as "boring," to use what he seems to regard as a reliable philosophical category.

A movement of younger thinkers marching under the flag of "speculative realism" has been galvanized by Quentin Meillassoux,[35] a student of Badiou's, who brings two charges against the continental tradition from Kant to the present, and both have a direct bearing on Derrida today. He accuses this tradition of "correlationism," a kind of subjective idealism that reduces the world to a correlate of consciousness, going so far as to claim that thinkers such as Foucault and Derrida are "creationists," who do not think the world existed before human consciousness. Although there are passages in Husserl that might suggest subjective idealism, this cannot be sustained by a careful reading of his texts.[36] The charge is still more perplexing when made against the post-Husserlians, since the history of phenomenology after Husserl was a series of positions that distanced themselves from Husserl on precisely that point. When this kind of objection was made to Derrida, he replied that everything he has to say about the coming of the other "is put forward *in the name of the real*," that nothing is more realist than deconstruction.[37] But if "correlationism" is a red herring, Meillassoux's second charge, "fideism," aimed specifically at the "theological turn," is more on the mark. By fideism, Meillassoux means that postmodern theory has been put to work in a Kantian way, delimiting knowledge and reason in order to make room for classical religious faith. Postmodernism becomes a skepticism about reason that allows theology in the back door. I have argued that this is true of some versions of postmodern theory,[38] but it has no purchase in deconstruction, once you distinguish faith and belief. If anything, deconstruction should be seen as delimiting religious beliefs and certainties, that is, the *croyances* of the confessional religions, in order to make room for a deeper *foi* in the future, which includes the future of reason (*Rogues*) and the hope for a "new Enlightenment." That is why Radical Orthodox theologians criticize Derrida's religion without religion as a modernist religion within the limits of "pure reason!" Once again, the Derridean strategy seems superior to all the alternatives, not to resuscitate the old war between faith and reason, but to excavate the deeper sense of *foi* that keeps both a rationalist reason and confessional beliefs from closing in on themselves while conceding that faith does not ensure our safety.

Of course, if you can't beat them, it is always possible to join them. That is the strategy of a recent work that offers a rereading of Derrida as himself a kind of proto-speculative realist.[39] This has the advantage of offsetting the distortions of deconstruction that circulate through the new materialism, but it comes at a high cost. In a closely argued book, Martin Hägglund contends that since *différance* is spacing-timing, it is perfectly cut to fit materialism. This is carried out by way of an aggressive rereading of Derrida—philosophizing with a hammer, he says—which enforces quite a harsh logic on deconstruction. Deconstruction is said to run in neutral, conducted in a completely "descriptive" mode, having erased every trace of ethical normativity and religious aspiration.[40] Read this way, deconstruction is shrunk down to a series of warnings about the unpredictability of the future and the logic of the double bind, since whatever is done in time is done under conditions that will see to it that it comes undone. Hägglund is insightful about the logical conundrums of deconstruction and there are long stretches in the book which helpfully spell out what Derrida is doing. But the descriptive hypothesis puts him at odds with every major commentator in the literature and, more important, as he is often forced to concede, with Derrida himself.

Hägglund's argument against ethics is that deconstruction is not an ethics of the coming of the other since the other who is coming might well be evil and so cannot be regarded as the "good as such." Consequently, Derrida's texts on the coming of the other are neutral descriptions of the hazards of running into the other. Derrida saw that objection coming and explicitly warned against drawing such a conclusion.[41]

> The openness of the future is worth more; that is the axiom of deconstruction, that on the basis of which it has always set itself in motion and which links it, as with the future itself, to otherness, to the priceless dignity of otherness, that is to say, to justice. . . . Someone might say to you: "Sometimes it is better for this or that not to arrive. Justice demands that one prevent certain events (certain 'arrivants') from arriving. The event is not good in itself, and the future is not unconditionally preferable." Certainly, but one can always show that what one is opposing, when one conditionally prefers that this or that not happen, is something one takes, rightly or wrongly, as blocking the horizon . . . for the absolute coming of the altogether other, for the future.

Deconstruction, Derrida is saying, is the hyperaffirmation of the infinitival "to- come," not the simple affirmation of this or that (de)finite other one. Deconstruction is "against ethics,"[42] but that means it resists proposing a set of norms or prescriptions, including a rule to "always welcome the other," which would be just one more rule relieving us of the need to make a decision in the singular situation. Ethics is for Derrida what it is for Johannes de Silentio, a "temptation," because the recourse to norms and prescriptions is the abdication of "responsibility." True, the other is not the good as such because deconstruction is not the thought of the good but the thought of the event, which is the occasion of responsibility. Deconstruction is the affirmation that the future is always worth more, not as a matter of fact but as a matter of faith and hope. Deconstruction is not less than ethics (descriptive), as Hägglund mistakenly claims, but more than ethics or what Derrida call hyperethics,[43] and it takes place not in a neutral space but in the appellatory, messianic, vocative, charged, and hypervalorized space of the call. Under Hägglund's heavy hand, deconstruction is shrunk down to logical empiricism.

With respect to the question of religion, Hägglund argues that the condition under which religion promises more life—after time, the afterlife—represents the loss of life—death, no more time, no more life, so not only does Derrida deny that God exists (garden-variety atheism) but further that he denies that we can even "desire" that God exist (radical atheism). The argument fails on every level. With regard to classical theology, the argument is circular and simply assumes that there cannot be a sphere of being outside space and time, forcing Hägglund at one point to actually declare *différance* to be a principle of being not of experience. It is true that *différance* has to do with space and time, but for that very reason, if there is an argument against being outside space and time, it is not found in deconstruction. About such a possibility, Derrida says deconstruction has no leverage and it should not have.[44] With regard to the history of religion, Hägglund's argument is remarkably innocent of the many versions of theology and religion which entertain no such idea of life outside space and time. Finally, with regard to Derrida's religion, the argument is at best a missed opportunity. While excavating the conundrums of a mortal life, while seeing that for Derrida life is not undermined but made all the more precious by its mortality, Hägglund fails to see how deeply such "atheism" enters into Derrida's "religion" and how it becomes a moment in the more profound and more profoundly risky faith and hope and "desire beyond desire" described above. Our mortal life is the very stuff of what Derrida calls "my religion about which nobody understands anything," with the result that he is "read less and less well."

Because the ghosts of deconstruction haunt every dogma, be it religious or secular, theistic or atheistic, Derrida's equal opportunity hauntology invites attack from both the left and right, both the secular and religious. If deconstruction started out spooking religion, it has lately been spooking secularism, too, which goes to show it is spooky business, all about the holy and unholy ghosts that haunt our works and days. Deconstruction, we must admit, believes in ghosts.

4

Augustine and Postmodernism

Augustine, it might be said, comes after modernity just because he came before it. He does not observe modernist boundaries between philosophy and theology, reason and faith, thought and passion, fact and value, because these boundaries have yet to be drawn. He wants to think coherently, but he recognizes the limits of human comprehension and would recoil at a "system" in the modern sense. Although it goes too far to say that Augustine is a postmodern *avant la lettre*, it is true that postmodern thinkers find in him the resources for a robust critique of modernity.[1] For postmodern writers, the soul-searching voice of the *Confessions* lays bare a cut and wounded self without pretense to "autonomy" or "pure reason" or "transcendental consciousness"—quite the opposite of the philosophy of the *cogito* launched by Descartes, to whom Augustine is often compared.

The term "postmodernity" has come to be, largely, a shorthand for contemporary "pluralism," an affirmation of cultural diversity, a rainbow mix of aesthetic styles and forms of life in the context of the relentless globalization effected by contemporary information technologies. Postmodern life is "networked" life—the "www" is very postmodern—a multi-culture without a center and with no one overseeing it.[2] The (loosely) corresponding philosophical thesis is that the sun has set on the strong, systematic, methodological, departmentalized, objectivistic, and rule-governed models of thinking that characterized the modern thinking of the Enlightenment, the Cartesian project of the one tree of knowledge nourished by the one (mathematical) method. In its place stands an alternative way of thinking, which draws variously on Heidegger's insistence that understanding is an interpretative act forged by a specific context ("hermeneutics"), Wittgenstein's "language games," and Kuhn's analogy between scientific change and political revolution, where linear progress is replaced by a holistic shift of "paradigms."[3] The postmodern point is that there is no one interpretation to end all interpretations, no one game of all games, no algorithm to regulate scientific change, no method of all methods. Moreover, these multiple forms of life, of thought, are porous and mutually invasive, their borders too unstable to be policed by Kantian critique. Hybrids and heterogeneity are everywhere to be found, for instance in the hermeneutic notion that faith is a kind of seeing-as and reason requires a lot of faith. In postmodernity religion can once again show its head. The "big stories" that try to brush off religion as a distorted desire for our mommy have run their course. Postmodern means postsecular, which gives a new life to premodern thinkers such as Augustine, and even Saint Paul, who are innocent of modernist categories.[4]

But if postmodern thinkers have gotten religion, it is of a rather singular sort. In their readings, Augustine's *Confessions*, and in particular book 10, is expanded beyond a Christian confession, into a plurality of confessional voices. Postmodern writers embrace Augustine's view of a living truth gained only by loving truly rather than the view of the truth as a lifeless set of correct propositions; but they think there are many forms of life and love. That is why it makes sense to begin here with Jean-Luc Marion, whose hypothesis is that, if a "reduction" (in the Husserlian sense) of Augustine's metaphysical theology is carried out with rigor, the result will still be uniquely Christian. Heidegger, Derrida, and Lyotard, in contrast, replay the *Confessions* with odd but arresting results, which engender alternative and more austere voices of *confessio*. Although all these authors resist the Cartesian analogy, what is instructive about the "Augustine and postmodernism" literature can be located in the distance between Marion's "God without being" and these outsider (post-Christian) inquiries into what Derrida calls a religion without religion and without theology.

Jean-Luc Marion: *Interior meo intimo*

Jean-Luc Marion (1946–), arguably both the leading Catholic philosopher and one of the leading Descartes scholars of his generation, enlists the *Confessions* in the project of "overcoming metaphysics," as Heidegger famously framed it, which for Marion means liberating the God of love from "Being."[5] His Augustine does not need to "overcome" metaphysics because, unlike modern readers and translators, Augustine was never a party to metaphysics. Augustine is after metaphysics because he is before it,[6] a formula that encapsulates the play of postmodernity and premodernity.

The *Confessions* does not observe modern boundaries. It is neither "theology," because Augustine is speaking to God and not writing about God, nor "philosophy," except in the literal sense that the true philosopher is someone who loves God. The God to whom Augustine prays is not an "object" constituted by a subject, which is modern (transcendental) idolatry, nor a being, even the highest being, or even the Being of beings, because Being and beings, the ontological difference that structures metaphysics, offers only a still higher idolatry, be it classical (Aristotelian and Thomistic) or Heideggerian.[7] God is God only if God comes to us on God's own (*à partir de soi*),[8] as we learn in mystical theology. God is given (*donné*) in the sphere of pure givenness (*donation, Gegebenheit*), only if every condition, transcendental or metaphysical, is "bracketed" or "reduced," as we learn in phenomenology. Any prior condition compromises the unconditional givenness of God, the "saturated phenomenon"[9] that floods in advance anterior conditions. The place of *confessio* is to have no place except in God, before whom (*coram*) it is placed unconditionally, displaced or dispossessed in itself, which undermines the Cartesian analogy. Instead of a self-positing *ego cogito* ("I think"), Augustine exposes a deposed and exiled self that has become a question unto itself, an "I" who cannot so much as say "I."[10] The "restless heart" (*cor inquietum*) is exactly the opposite of the "unshaken foundation" (*fundamentum inconcussum*). The "subject" *to* which—always in the dative—such unconditional givenness (donation) is given, abolished as a subject, is the "*adonné*," the one who is "given-over-to" (even "addicted" to) such givenness, without preconditions. Inasmuch as I am what I love and I live not of myself but with the life of the living God, the *Confessions* is not even "auto-biography," a category that leaves *autos*, *soi*, "self" uninterrogated. Augustine's story, told from the point of view of God, of the Other, is instead a "hetero-biography."[11]

That the confessing self finds its place only by letting God take its place explains Marion's title: *Au lieu de soi: L'approche de saint Augustin*—"in place of self," "in the self's place," "in the place self finds itself," and also the journey (approach) "to the place of self." Notice the missing article, "self," not "the" self if that suggests something self-constituted. The *Confessions* traverses the distance from the ego (*moi, je*) to the place (*au lieu*) of the genuine self (*soi*), which is God, who is more interior to me than the most inward place in me (*interior meo intimo, Conf.* 3.6.11).[12] As Derrida said, Marion has a gift for titles![13]

When the categories of philosophy, theology, and literature are thus reduced, the unique voice of *confessio* can be heard speaking words of love to the "erotic phenomenon" par excellence, the saturating givenness of the God who has loved us before we loved God, whose love from before being calls us into being. For being—the *sum* ("I am") that Descartes wanted to secure—arises out of love and for the sake of love, whereas being is without love, an anonymous brute presence.[14] The *Confessions* effects an "erotic reduction" from being to love,[15] for the God of love lives without being, without having to "be," not because God does not get as far as being, but because being does not get as far as God.[16] *Au lieu de soi* is based on Marion's 2004 Étienne Gilson Lectures. For Gilson, Aquinas's metaphysics of God as *ipsum esse per se subsistens* ("the self-subsistent act of being") is the central teaching of "Christian philosophy." Marion is pitting himself against the mainstream Thomism of the modern Catholic tradition and against the subsequent Thomistic renderings of Augustine. He goes back to the older tradition of Pseudo-Dionysius the Areopagite and Gregory of Nyssa in the light of a radicalized phenomenology that, Dominique Janicaud complained, forced phenomenology to make a "theological turn."[17] As Marion objects that the *Confessions* is not metaphysics but phenomenology, Janicaud objects that Marion's phenomenology is not phenomenology but metaphysics. Either way, Marion's work is cut out for him, since for most readers Augustine does not attempt to immunize himself against metaphysics quite so purely.

Memoria. The questionability of the self to itself is a function of *memoria*, which is not a particular psychological function of recalling a past present, but a mysterious depth harboring the totality of the self. *Memoria* is the site of the immemorial, of the inaccessibility of a past that has never been present, like Heidegger's "facticity," with which no "intentional act" can catch up,[18] but not like a repository of unconscious drives (Lyotard's reading of Augustine's "late have I loved you": see below). The contact of the self with the immemorial is not through cognition but desire, which is the pressure imposed on the self by this incomprehensible reservoir. Desire is fueled by a memory of I know not what, of some fullness of life of which my life is a share, of some *vita beata* ("happy life") of which I have an irrepressible memory, which I cannot not desire, even as there is no agreement about what makes for happiness.[19] The disagreement is as universal as the desire. The *vita beata* is known (recalled in some way) because it is desired, but desired because it is not known (agreed upon). The issue is not whether, but what we love, which must be true, or truly lovable, because in the *vita beata* we take joy in truth, and only God is truth.

Truth. Loving the *vita beata* belongs to a dynamic unique to the order of desire, where the truth of desire is not theoretical or propositional truth, but the truth that gives joy. True desire is the desire for God, even though one might not know that it is God that one desires. This lack of cognitive clarity is not a defect in knowledge but the excess of the saturated phenomenon of God who dazzles the self.[20] To such truth we can never be neutral: If we do not love it, we hate it because its light falls on our faults. In a proposition I judge something to be true, but the truth of desire is a truth that judges me.[21] While no one would seek a false proposition in a purely cognitive order, there are many who hate the truth in the order of desire. Either I decide to see myself in the dazzling holiness of God, which reveals my shame, or I prefer to linger in the shadows.[22] There are, then, three kinds of truth: the truth of propositions (metaphysics); the truth of unconcealment (Heidegger); and erotic truth, the truth we love or hate. The difficulty this involves is illustrated in Augustine's view that the Manicheans refuse the truth of the Scriptures because of the perversity of their nature. How does Augustine know that they do not desire truly, in good faith, but have simply been led elsewhere by their love? That is why Heidegger objects that, at a crucial point, Augustine invokes a cognitive notion of truth; loving truth means loving the true church, *confessio* means the catholic confession,[23] and the site Marion is locating is the Catholic Church. Why not confess that the very multiplicity of conceptions of the *vita beata* is irreducible, part of the positive excess of the dynamic of desire, which is diminished by restricting it to its Catholic version? True desire desires truly, without arresting its play.

Time. Time poses another vexing issue. Phenomenology is, through and through, a phenomenology of time, whereas Augustine's theology turns on the Platonist distinction between time and eternity, where the soul is divided up,[24] or even "fallen," into time. Heidegger rejects this distinction on the grounds of the originary temporality (*Zeitigung*) of *Dasein*,[25] and he replaces the fall into time with the temporality of the fall—from authentic into inauthentic temporality. But, according to Marion, Augustine is not the Neoplatonist that Heidegger takes him to be, for Augustine distinguishes between *tempora* (the times), living in time as fallen and dispersed (*distensio animi*), and *tempus*—the temporality of the human spirit, which need not succumb to dissipation. In the time of conversion the soul gathers itself up, not by escaping into eternity, which is both impractical and metaphysical, but eschatologically, stretching out to what is ahead (resurrection) by faith (Phil 3:13). By thus tending into (*intentio*) the *eschaton*, the *distensio* of temporality is transformed into authentic confessional time, without pretending to an eternity that befits God alone.[26] Heidegger might be excused if he thought this elegant interpretation would only meet him halfway. For it employs the "factical" experience of time that Heidegger himself has already identified in both Paul and Augustine while remaining prudently reticent about the eschatological itself, which means life after death in a resurrected body that would challenge any phenomenology, embracing the very metaphysical distinction to which Heidegger is objecting.

Creation and donation. For Heidegger, the theology of creation means that theologians cannot raise the question of being because they presuppose that God is the first cause of being. But, for Marion, Heidegger imposes the God of the philosophers upon the Bible, forces the Bible to answer a question it neither asks nor even understands,[27] and misconstrues the confessionality of the *Confessions* as causal thinking. Creation belongs to the sphere not of causality but of *donation*, of emerging "without why" from the spontaneity of divine love. Creatures are so many witnesses to the glory of God; the language of the *Confessions* is liturgical, not cosmological.[28] But the metaphysics and the confessionality of creation are no more inconsistent than "honoring" our parents (*confessio*) is inconsistent with recognizing, when we keep family health records, that they are our cause. Marion himself backs off from excising the causal–cosmological factor completely by calling it derived and secondary.[29] But then, should Heidegger have merely waited until the liturgy was over before making his point? In a purely phenomenological mode, would not the *Confessions* praise the "being given" (*étant donné*) of the world as such, but without separating the giver from the given,[30] hence remaining solely in the element of *donation*? Then why does Augustine seek to identify *whom* he should love? Why have the creatures responded, "We are not what you seek" and "He made us?"[31] Indeed, are not the confession and the *creatio ex nihilo*— "creation out of nothing" itself an innovation of second-century metaphysical theology with no foundation in Genesis—not directly proportional to each other?[32] Does not the creator *ex nihilo* deserve higher praise than the Demiurge of Plato's *Timaeus*, who gives things their form but not their very *being*? Is that not Gilson's point, that the Thomistic notion of God as *ipsum esse subsistens* is indispensable to explaining *creatio ex nihilo*? Without the metaphysics we would be unable to tell the difference between Augustine and the *Timaeus*, or for that matter John Scotus Eriugena, who lavished praise on the power of *natura naturans* to engender the world as *natura naturata*, a "proposition" roundly condemned by the church later on. Might *Au lieu de soi* gain in credibility if it were confessed to be more like what Heidegger called a *Destrucktion*, or a critical "retrieval" (*Wiederholung*) that formally isolates the phenomenological voice of a *confessio* from a companion metaphysical theology by which it is, one is tempted to say, saturated? How far would the pure voice of *confessio* be from Heidegger, Derrida, or Lyotard?

Heidegger: *Terra difficultatis*

One finds a far more austere voice of *confessio* in Martin Heidegger (1889–1976). One might view *Being and Time*[33] as turning on Augustine's *mihi quaestio factus sum* ("I have become a question to myself"; *Conf.* 10.33.50), where the question is the question of Being and the *factus sum* is translated as "facticity." Facticity means not Augustine's theology of creation but the raw experience of finding oneself in the world as "being there" (*Dasein*), a being given that gives no clue as to any whence or whither. Such a self seems even more disarmed, deposed, even more confessional, than Marion's *soi*, because factical life does not have infinite life to fall back on; it lacks a recourse to any deeper center or infinite good. When Marion proposes *donation*, a word suggesting a generous donor, the father of all good gifts, as a French translation of Husserl's and Heidegger's *Gegebenheit*, the dice seem loaded. The German word, like the English cognate, is closer to a simple factical "givenness," which is a much less reassuring rendering than *donation*, suggesting less a beneficent agent/giver than an anonymous *es gibt* ("there is"). Marion's *soi* seems only provisionally decentered in order to be more profoundly re-centered upon God; it loved God late, but not too late. *Dasein*, in contrast, lacks any such center—unless that center is death, which spells the impossibility of any more of *Dasein's* possibilities. Marion's *soi* is a finite created life that is returned by the reduction to its source in the sea of infinite life, as being is returned to God, while *Dasein's* authentic selfhood (*Selbstheit*) seems finally to be swallowed up by death and finitude. Any further "eschatology" is off limits, phenomenologically speaking.

That, at least, is what became of Augustine in *Being and Time* (1927), whose genesis, according to Heidegger[34] owes much to the confrontation with Augustine found in his 1921 lectures on Augustine, which were edited and published only in 1995. These lectures, presenting the first phenomenological reading of the *Confessions*, focused on book 10 and sketched the Augustinian sources of the later dynamics of authenticity and inauthenticity. In the *Confessions*, Heidegger holds, factical life means "trial" (*tentatio*) and insecurity,[35] a struggle in which the self is pulled into the world and away from God, a pull that is summarized in the curiosity of the eyes, the concupiscence of the flesh, and the pride of life.[36] Heidegger would also gloss this same text on concupiscence in *Being and Time*.[37] These are, variously, the three fronts of the "daily war" (*Conf.* 10.31.43–44), the three provinces of the "land of difficulty" (*terra difficultatis*; *Conf.* 10.16.25), the three directions in which factical life flows off (*defluere*). As the soul is scattered about and dissipated by the distractions and curiosities of daily life, so it must gather itself together in the self-containment of continence

(*Conf.* 10.29.40). The field of battle is also linguistic, for the vanity of the self is pleased by words of praise for its virtues, instead of seeking virtue regardless of human opinion. Factical life is not a substance but a movement and a countermovement, constantly falling even as it strains to gather itself together. Life is not a thing but a possibility, a tension, never stable, always uncertain. It does not have a "what" (*quid*), but a "how" (*qualis*). The very being of the self is "being troubled" (*Bekümmerung*)—"care" (*Sorge*) in *Being and Time*—but not in such a way that our troubles (*molestiae*) are contingent obstacles that can be removed. Trouble goes all the way down; being troubled is what factical life is.[38]

Heidegger, who had a lifelong penchant for seeking the primal, the early—later on it would be the "early Greeks"—regards Augustine as a relatively late "Helleno-Christian" figure,[39] already assimilated into "Greek" culture and at some remove from "primal Christian life" (*Urchristentum*) in the New Testament. The *Destruktion*[40] of the *Confessions*, which means ferreting out an authentically Christian experience of life from the overlay of Greek metaphysics, would ultimately require going back to the letters of Paul, the earliest documents in the New Testament, as Heidegger had done in the course he had given the previous semester. He locates the metaphysics in Augustine's use of a Neoplatonic "axiology,"[41] an ascent of the soul from the lowest good to the highest, from *uti* to *frui*[42]—a scale that privileges eternity and rest over time and struggle. This Neoplatonism leads Augustine to say that *vita beata* consists in savoring the highest good and the highest beauty for themselves, in a contemplative act of enjoyment. So where Marion aligns the good beyond being with *agape* in the New Testament, Heidegger sees it as Neoplatonic metaphysics, which is contrasted with the living God of the New Testament, approached in "fear and trembling," just as the self is a land of difficulty, not an immaterial substance. Heidegger is here being guided by Luther's critique of the "theology of glory," an aesthetic theology that treats the wonders of the world as manifestations of God, which is the paganism rampant in medieval metaphysics.[43] Luther contrasts this with the "theology of the cross," in which God is revealed in the destitution of Christ crucified, in weakness and foolishness (1 Cor 1), which scandalizes the world and the philosophers. This distinction, found in Luther's *Heidelberg Disputation*, undertakes a breaking up (*destructio*) of Scholastic theology in order to recover the life of faith in the New Testament.[44] As John van Buren has shown, this *destructio* is almost certainly behind Heidegger's talk of the *Destruktion* of the "history of ontology,"[45] of which Derrida's *déconstruction* is a French translation. Luther himself was glossing the Greek *apolō* ("I will destroy") in the Septuagint translation of Isaiah 19:14, cited by Paul (1 Cor 1:19).

As a critical deposing of the self-positing "subject," Marion complained, *Being and Time* was only a partial success; for, if the Cartesian epistemological subject was displaced, it was replaced with a heroic existential subject, one no less subjectivistic, individualistic, and, to use Marion's term, "autarchical," all earmarks of "modernity."[46] The path of Heidegger's thought confirms this criticism, inasmuch as in his later writings Heidegger dramatically redescribes human existence, moving away from the voluntarist accents of *Being and Time* to a kind of will-less *Gelassenheit* ("composure"), a term Heidegger adopted from Meister Eckhart, whose mystical theology has roots in the very Christian Neoplatonism Heidegger is criticizing in 1921 and from which Marion's own "reduction" draws. But there is still another way to overcome the subject, another voice of confession, which is found in Derrida.

Derrida: *Quid ergo amo, cum deum amo?*

The work of Jacques Derrida differs sharply from that of both Marion and Heidegger. Heidegger was a cultural conservative, wedded to his native German soil and language, who embraced National Socialism. Derrida was a French-speaking Algerian Jew, whose first impression of Latin was of the language used by the Pétain/Vichy regimes to formulate the rule—*numerus clausus*—that got him and the other Jewish children expelled from the lycée.[47] A leftist critic of restrictive immigration policies and of the whole metaphor of blood, brotherhood, and native soil, he once said he had no language of his own,[48] for he did not speak Hebrew, Berber, or Arabic, but what he called "Christian Latin French." But if he shared with Levinas the desire to extricate himself from the "climate" of Heidegger's philosophy, he never denied that Heidegger had posed the overarching project of his generation, that of "overcoming metaphysics," displacing Being and Cartesian subjectivity.

In *Circumfession* (*Circonfession*), composed in 1989 before he had read Heidegger's lectures, Derrida does not write *about* Augustine but instead adopts the very voice of *confessio* and prayer. His mother, Georgette, who lay dying in Nice, where the family had emigrated in 1962, is not his subject but his addressee, thereby restaging the scene of Augustine at the deathbed of Monica. Derrida, who called Augustine "my compatriot," had set out at the age of nineteen from North Africa for the *métropole*—France, Paris, the motherland, the fatherland—to make a career for himself, the way Augustine set out for Rome to make his way up the imperial ladder, both of them getting seasick on the way.[49] The text is thus constructed around a curious analogy: Augustine/Derrida, Monica/Georgette, Ostia/Nice, Numidia/Algeria, Rome/Paris, Latin/French, and God/X. For it is far from clear exactly "to whom" Derrida was speaking/confessing/praying—it was, variously, his mother, his friend and "authorized" expositor Geoffrey Bennington, and himself, all of whom are standing in for someone, no one (himself included) knows whom. These confessions are startling, particularly to a secular and academic audience: "and I wonder if those reading me from up there see my tears, today . . . if they guess that my life was but a long history of prayers."[50] But this confession is accompanied by a counterconfession that he "rightly passes for an atheist."[51] He does not simply say I *am* an atheist ("*je suis*," "*c'est moi*"). As a well-known French intellectual, "Jacques Derrida" has a public "identity." But, more deeply considered, this "identity" is not to be confused with the "self" (*soi*) that so much interests Marion, which is unknown, a question to itself, not "identical with itself."[52] This "I" is not simply one thing, does not speak *una voce*, but constitutes a kind of echo chamber of several voices—several identities, languages, cultures, experiences—which give it no rest. "Deconstruction" is the deconstruction of the very idea of *autos* in the sense of something univocal and undivided, a point whose resonance with Augustine has been fruitfully explored by Robert Dodaro.[53] Just as every believer understands the experience of being haunted from within by a relentless unbeliever and atheist, Derrida—to all the world a secularist intellectual—here confesses that he is disturbed from within by a certain faith.

But Derrida distinguishes faith (*foi*) from "belief" (*croyance*).[54] If one inventories his specific views (*doxa*)—more generous immigration policies, opposition to censorship, and so on—one would not find "believing Jew" among them. By the standards of the local rabbi, "Jacques Derrida" is an atheist. But that would not touch upon the "faith" of Jacques Derrida, the man of prayers and tears, over whom Georgette prayed and wept, afraid to ask directly if her son, *filius istarum lacrymarum* (Aug., *Conf.* 3.12.21), now a world famous "French" philosopher, still "believed in God." Mark C. Taylor's early take on deconstruction and religion—"deconstruction is the hermeneutics of the death of God"[55]—proved too quick, too simple, for if we keep on reading, we meet this quasi-atheistic, quasi-Jewish, quasi-Augustinian who speaks of "my religion":

> That's what my readers won't know about me . . . the changed time of my writing . . . to be read less and less well over almost twenty years, like my religion about which nobody understands anything, any more than my mother who asked other people a while ago, not daring to talk to me about it, if I still believed in God . . . but she must have known that the constancy of God in my life is called by other names, so that I quite rightly pass for an atheist.[56]

But what other names? To whom is he praying? What kind of religion? Whereas in Marion, the *à Dieu*, the turn to God, replaces and re-centers the self in God, its true place, in Derrida it lands us in a nonplace (*non-lieu*), self-interrogating, partitioned in itself.[57] It does not arrest the play but sets it further in motion:

> "*Quid ergo amo, cum Deum meum amo [Conf. 10.11.7]?*" Can I do anything other than translate this question by SA into my language . . . the change of meaning, or rather reference, defining the only difference of the *meum*.[58]

What sort of faith in what sort of God? Derrida organizes *Circumfession* around his Jewishness, around the *circum* itself, the cut around his flesh, called in Christian Latin "circumcision," which is how the assimilated Jews of Algeria referred to *bris* (Yiddish) or *berit milah* (Sephardi). (Derrida's family, immigrants from Portugal to Algeria in the nineteenth century, is Sephardic.) I am the only philosopher to expose my circumcision in public (*in litteris*), he says.[59] Imagine Heidegger reading that!—Derrida once quipped.[60] But the text is no less wound around the wound in the flesh of Georgette. Heidegger, who never mentions Monica, would likely have dismissed Derrida's Augustine as *weiblich*, womanly, teary, decadent. Heidegger's own Augustine was virile, a man tested by the *bellum quotidianum*, a knight of faith, "thrown" into the world (with no mother to speak of), standing courageously "before death" (*coram morte, Sein zum Tode*), never noticing the death of his mother. But Derrida, who had not yet read Heidegger's Augustine lectures,[61] meditates a mortality that is less an exercise in virility than one of coping with flesh laid low, of flowing blood, less interested in breastplates than in the breast that nurtures.

"Circumcision" in this text is both the thing itself, the cut in the flesh, which cost many European Jews their lives, and the figure of being cut down to size, where knowledge gives way to the non-knowledge of faith, where the love of truth means we are severed from the truth and must live on faith. Truth means *facere veritatem*, doing the truth, not truth as correspondence or communicating information.[62] What privately held secret could one pass on to an omniscient God? Truth as avowal, as confession, is more a performance than a predication, more of a per-"ver"-formance than a performance.[63] Lacking Augustine's confidence that the truth we are doing coincides with the truth of the Catholic faith, Derrida's is a more austere truth that will have to speak for itself, without any institutional sponsors, the truth to which the displaced and confessional self testifies in forgiveness and hospitality, echoing with the lamentations of the prophets, who are never far away.[64] Not far either is a certain weakness of God, whose description was begun by Paul in

1 Corinthians 1:27: the power of powerlessness, the "weak force" that meets violence and aggression with forgiveness, that offers the enemy friendship, that offers hospitality to a stranger who may equally be a threat.[65]

The staging of *Circumfession* is "theological." Derrida addresses "G," Geoffrey Bennington, translator and interpreter, who is composing a commentary "on" him, above him, writing on his body, on the corpus of his writings. Typographically, the Bennington text appears above a line dividing each page, with *Circumfession* below it. Bennington occupies the "theological" position, of the omniscient one writing a "Derridabase," a "program," a "generative grammar," or "matrix" of every possible sentence Derrida could ever write.[66] If Bennington succeeds, he will distill Derrida's essence, producing Derrida's "This is my body," "This is my blood." His pen is a syringe drawing Derrida's blood into a bottle labeled "Jacques Derrida" (the name of the book). *Tolle, lege*—pick any sentence you like, and Bennington can derive it. He is trying to rob me of my future, of my event, of my religion, Derrida laments, cutting away the idiomaticity of his writing, of the singularity of his life, trying to close down the open-endedness of the future. Bennington occupies the place of God, the place of SA, *savoir absolu* ("absolute knowledge" in Hegel). So the whole book is a game, a wager, to see if "Jacques" can take Bennington by surprise, outwit his omniscience, which explains the disclosure of autobiographical secrets unknown to Bennington. The whole book is a performative act to see if the "grace" of an event can be given off by the spacing of the two texts.

But the staging permits another nontheological God, or perhaps a weaker theology, one linked to death. Derrida is keeping watch over Georgette, whose approaching death he mourns while celebrating the life of this once very beautiful young woman and mother, to whom he is fiercely attached. As he keeps watch over her death, he watches over his own, over the mortality of us all. He is also speaking to death itself, if it has a self, this mortal life, this living death,[67] with no mention of an infinite life waiting to lift us up from and relieve us of our mortality, as in Marion. Like Marion, Derrida sees that the *Confessions* are hetero-graphical, and, like Heidegger, that they are no less a writing of death; but in Derrida these themes converge. "Circumfession" is an "auto-bio-thanato-hetero-graphical" work, a book of the life and death of the self and of the other (the mother), an *ars moriendi*, in which the author prepares for death by writing his death and the death of the other. Death, he says, is his most faithful and difficult ally. Or God—it is the same thing, death or God, his finitude, the line drawn around his life, the limit.[68]

In the English translation, "G" picks up the play not only of Geoffrey and Georgette, but of "God." (Rather than a Heideggerian longing for the origin and a mourning of its loss, Derrida celebrates the impossible task of translating the idioms of the original language while being admitted to the new field of play of the target language.) His earliest recollection of the name of God is on the lips of his mother who, awash in tears, thanked God, *merci à Dieu*, every time *Jackie* (his birth name—Jacques, we learn, is a pen name) recovered from an illness.[69] Georgette conditioned everything on God, *si Dieu le veut*. The name of God is bathed in prayers and tears, giving voice to a desire beyond desire, to a desire for I know not what, for a *vita beata* I do not understand, for I do not know what I love when I love my God. In Derrida the love or desire driving the *cor inquietum* is not ordered to rest. As in Emmanuel Levinas (another philosopher with whom Derrida was in constant dialogue), desire does not proceed from or express a lack that needs to be satisfied, an emptiness that needs to be filled. Desire is affirmative, a dynamic of "yes, yes" (*oui, oui*). Desire has no "final term"—that would be terminal, death-like—for all the terms in which we express what we desire are caught up in an interminable slippage, an infinite substitutability. We are circum-cut from some once-and-for-all truth, or "final interpretation," deprived of the wherewithal to stop this slippage, to arrest this play:

> Too late, you are less, you, less than yourself, you have spent your life inviting calling promising, hoping sighing dreaming, convoking invoking provoking . . . severed from truth . . . you alone whose life will have been so short, the voyage short, scarcely organized, by you with no lighthouse and no book.[70]

The "too late" (*sero*) is structural and productive, the way no performance of *Hamlet* is definitive. The restless heart is structurally too late for some final "Truth," pure and simple. The hope is to keep the future open, endlessly deconstructible in view of the "undeconstructible," "the impossible." Too late have I loved something, I know not what, that shatters the horizons of knowledge, expectation, and foreseeability, the limits of the possible. The nontheological name of God belongs to a string of such names—such as justice, the gift, or even "democracy"—which are all subjected to the proviso of the "to-come" (*à venir*), which is the work of the "*sans*" ("without"). The *à venir* means the nonfinality of the future itself, not a merely formal "not yet" but the very structure of hope. There are several such words of elemental promise—and threat—among which the name of "God" has from old been exemplary. Where Augustine put more faith in proper names, such as that name at whose sound every knee should bend, or the name of his church that bears his Spirit, there is no one name above every other name that occasions Derrida's genuflection. For Derrida there are no truly proper names; all such names are subject to an irreducible substitution.[71] There are always other names, other traditions, other ways of hailing the possibility of the impossible.[72]

Lyotard: *Sero te amavi*

Jean-François Lyotard (1924–98) is the writer who, while not coining the word "postmodernism," gave it philosophical currency and provided the "definition" of postmodernism—by now standard—as "incredulity toward meta-narratives [*grands récits*]," meaning a disinclination to be persuaded by big, overarching stories that identify where we all came from and where we are all going.[73] Augustine's theology of history in *The City of God* is such a story, one that Lyotard thinks was in essence transcribed into a philosophy of history by Hegel, against which Kierkegaard reacted so famously and furiously. As with the other figures we have been discussing, Lyotard's interests were drawn to the more anguished story of the *Confessions*, to which he dedicated the last years of his life. His book was to be an extended analysis of the *sero te amavi*[74] as a structural delay, deferral, or retardation built into the essence of time and of what phenomenology, too confidently, calls experience of the present.[75] "The cut is primal," says Lyotard, which reminds us of the deferral built into *différance* in Derrida, which "circum-cuts" us off from absolute knowledge, from the single "destination" of a text or an institution or a life.

The structure of the *sero* is made apparent in several ways for Lyotard. First, it means that, for Augustine, we are always too late to say what time means, that we can never catch up, in our reflection on time, with what we already "know" time to be. That in turn implies an irreducible delay between Augustine's life and the narrative (*récit*) of the *Confessions* itself, which tries to gather the *distensio* of his life in time into the unity of this story he is telling,[76] and this gap opens the door to multiple omissions and distortions, a point recently made quite independently by two distinguished Augustinian scholars.[77] But beyond a simple omission or misrepresentation, the *sero* exposes a structural gap described under the figure of "infancy," of which Augustine says that he has no images or memories at all, only the reports of others and his own adult observation of infants.[78] The same thing can be said about the absolute "event" of the "visitation" of "God"—for it was the custom in those days to call this event "God"[79]—in the *Confessions*, for which any possible expression would be structurally too late (a point also made in mystical theology). For Lyotard, however, "infancy"—which is not to be confused with Hannah Arendt's "natality" (which means new beginning)—refers above all to *memoria* understood as the unfathomable unconscious and its libidinal life,[80] hence not conscious memories but unconscious traces and trauma. *Memoria* dupes us and throws the desire for God and sexual desire into an unholy confusion (as in Bernini's famous portrayal of the *Ecstasy of Saint Teresa*), but this is to be said without smugly reducing *memoria* to the libidinal.[81] Lyotard's libidinal *memoria* is almost the perfect opposite of Marion's liturgical "erotic phenomenology," where *memoria* means our inexhaustible memory of God making the heart restless with the love of God. In the infancy-structure of the unconscious, the past was never (consciously) present, is unpresentable, and can never be re-presented, recorded, remembered. We are structurally cut off from the very life we would confess, unable even to say "I" confess with any confidence, unable ever to catch up with time, with the time of the self, or with God. "The cut is primal"—and philosophy and psychoanalysis are as foolish as theology if they think they can take the measure of what is thus incommensurable.[82] This incommensurability is not that of a love without measure (as in Marion), but of an abyss within the self from which we are structurally cut off. Why, then, confess? Not to discover a hidden self, but to reinvent ourselves; not to come up with the big story that cracks the secret of our lives, but to settle for a more tentative and unsettling account, which visits upon us the *dissidio, dissensio, dissipatio, distensio* of our condition,[83] that wrings from us a confession of the question that we are, that elicits an embrace of the events that fortuitously fall our way. Ironically, the interest that Lyotard took in the *Confessions* was itself too late, his book never finished. But that incompleteness invites readers to finish it for themselves, to "link on" as seems propitious to them, constituting something of a paradigmatic postmodern performance, if there were such a thing.

Conclusion

If we think of Descartes (to whom Augustine is so often compared) as the "Father of Modernity," we might think of these postmodern readings as attempts to kill the father, to break up the Cartesian analogy, to get beyond the self-positing *cogito* of the *Meditations* by listening to the many voices of confession in the *Confessions*. We might then conclude that, if Marion's reduction leads us back—with a felicity some find suspicious—to a phenomenologist who is also a recognizable father of the church and confessor, then Heidegger, Derrida, and Lyotard respond to voices more decentered, deposed, and disarming than any Augustine would have acknowledged. The question is, are the latter simply not listening closely enough or are the more severe voices they record really more confessional?[84]

5

On Not Settling for an Abridged Edition of Postmodernism
Radical Hermeneutics as Radical Theology

Note: One of the ways I describe radical theology is as a "religion without religion," an expression I take from Derrida. In a collection titled "Reexamining Deconstruction and Determinate Religion: Toward a Religion with Religion,"[1] a group of philosophers—J. Aaron Simmons and Stephen Minister, in particular, collaborating on a Christian apologetics under the inspiration of Merold Westphal—argues that religion without religion is religion of an abstract ahistorical indeterminate form, whereas confessional religion (with religion) represents a concrete and determinate tradition. It follows for them that radical theology arises from a fear of determinate religious traditions. In my response to this criticism, which has been excerpted from my original essay in that volume and which repays being visited as a whole, I show how the deepest impulses of radical theology arise from Hegel not Kant, from Tillich not Barth, and how the use of Kierkegaard and hermeneutics in radical theology is filtered by Derrida. I have slightly edited this selection in order make it a standalone piece and to eliminate repetition.

The Abridged Version of Postmodernism

The overarching difference between me and my critics in *Reexamining Deconstruction and Determinate Religion* can be framed as a debate between a postmodernism that descends from Hegel and a postmodernism that descends from Kant. We both take our lead from postmodern critiques of modernist rationality, but we strike out on different paths from that common point of departure. The Christian apologists think that post-modernism plays the role of Kant on the contemporary scene, whereas I think it plays the role of Hegel. They think postmodernism is the contemporary way to delimit knowledge in order to make room for Christian faith. I think that is a strategy they have come up with for limiting the exposure of Christian faith to postmodern analysis and that postmodernism interprets religion more holistically and comprehensively by treating religion as a historical form of life. Although we all agree that the only safe way to have faith is to appreciate that faith is not safe, I think it is a good deal more *un*safe than do they.

On the Kantian model adopted in *Reexamining Deconstruction* postmodernism provides a shelter in which believers can keep their faith dry; it is a way to delimit atheism in order to make room for Christians to lay claim to representational truths about Christ and God. On my Hegelian model postmodernism returns without remission any given community of believers to the living-breathing concrete-determinate linguistic-historical form of life to which it belongs, in which its truth is generated, nourished, and expressed. The apologetes think they are being loyal to concrete and determinate life and criticize me for taking flight from the concrete. I think that they are using that as a cover—the best defense (apologetics) is a good offense—to assert their belief that their particular faith is *exclusively true*.[2] I think it is they who are in fact avoiding the full implications of the contingency of the concrete and the circumstantiality of the determinate, which goes all the way down. On their Kantian model, postmodernism stakes out and patrols a space that allows them to claim not merely a unique but a privileged access to the truth. On my Hegelian model, you cannot get away with that, because whatever beliefs one holds are saturated by one's historical condition. The Kantian model results in an apologetics, not a classical-modern but a new postmodern version. The Hegelian model, however, does not issue in apologetics at all but in a theology of the event which feels around for the underlying experiences to which concrete religious traditions give form and figure, nomination and actualization.

On the Kantian model, postmodernism is an epistemology that limits knowledge to make possible a faith in metaphysical-theological realities. But it would be a mistake to conclude, as Simmons does, that the Hegelian model of postmodernism is by contrast metaphysical.[3] Of course, that was true of Hegel himself, but my postmodern Hegelianism is suitably postmetaphysical. The impish Derridean way to put this is that deconstruction is not an ontology but a "hauntology," neither an epistemology nor a metaphysics but a phenomenology, albeit of a post-Husserlian, radical or deconstructive variety. That is because an event is not a metaphysical hypothesis but a phenomenological experience. However, it is not a garden variety experience but a limit experience, an experience *without* experience, having to do with phenomena *without* phenomenality, which Derrida calls an experience of the impossible, whose possibility turns on its impossibility. You can already see what happens if we try to do without "without"— things tend toward full presence. In Hegel, religion is analyzed as the expression of the metaphysical notion of the Absolute Spirit. In its post-metaphysical, post-Hegelian, postmodern mode religion is analyzed as the expression of an event, of some underlying limit experience. The Kantians think that religion without religion is an abstract form of which a concrete confessional religion is a case; I think the concrete confessional tradition is a finite expression of the experience of an infinitival impulse.

On their Kantian model, postmodernism delimits knowledge in order to make room for faith in the God of classical Augustinian metaphysical theology. They crowd under the umbrella of "overcoming onto-theology," but for them that is a highly circumscribed expression; it is limited to getting past "objectifying thinking," say a rationalist proof for the existence of God, so that it remains safe to retain faith without proof in the classical metaphysical theology of Augustine. For them postmodernism means admitting that we are all fallible and finite, with an added corollary about the need for generosity and tolerance toward others. Although that is certainly to be preferred to intolerance, we don't need postmodernism to figure that out. I think that is damage control, an attempt to cut off the exposure of Christian faith to the postmodern critique of metaphysics, which goes much further than the abridged edition of postmodernism they are serving up. We have to read the whole unabridged edition if we want to see its point and not settle for an edited down version cut to fit a preconceived apologetic framework.

While the Kantian model marches under the banner of the concrete and determinate, the analysis takes the form of largely ahistorical arguments that pay no attention to problems of language and historical context (sometimes even launching a propositional calculus). On the Hegelian model, "religion," "faith," and "God" must be returned to their concrete historical matrix in the determinate linguistic and historical traditions of the three monotheisms and, in this case, to the Greco-European traditions of Christianity, which is itself but one way to give word and form to certain underlying events. These expressions cannot be treated as innocently as they are by the Kantians, as if they dropped from the sky. It is a commonplace in the study of religion today that these terms cannot be simply and univocally extended beyond the monotheistic and Greco-European cultures in which they have been born. Outside this framework, these notions either do not exist or belong to a horizon that is profoundly different and does not match up one to one with Greco-European Christianity. In a theology of the event, there are multiple horizons, traditions, languages, and cultural frameworks, among which Christianity is one.

I am not saying that nothing is true, but that we have to use caution when we speak of truth.[4] Each historical tradition has its own vitality, and it is in virtue of this vitality that each framework is true. The vitality of its truth is the truth of its vitality. That means that each tradition, holistically taken, gives word and structure to an enduring form of life. Contrary to Minister's claim, I am not saying these various historical traditions are all different versions of the same thing.[5] These horizons are certainly different, and they embody different forms of life, but they can also be compared and contrasted, and they can even learn from one other. Just because horizons are incommensurable does not mean they cannot be compared. But there is no sense in which one would be *exclusively true*, so that there is a big advantage to being born Christian, as is claimed by the Kantians, no more than one language or culture could be conceived to be exclusively true, even if they are not all saying the same thing. What for one tradition is the "gift of faith" is for another an accident of birth.[6]

On the Kantian model, what is made to pass for "overcoming ontotheology" is really a code word for a saying of Johannes Climacus, that "Existence itself is a system—for God, but it cannot be a system for any existing spirit."[7] That means, just because postmodern analysis severely rocks the boat of classical metaphysics, that does not stop us from believing it anyway as a matter of faith (which is what Kant said to the Newtonians about ethics). That is what nowadays is being criticized by Quentin Meillassoux as "fideism," and on this point at least Meillassoux is right.[8] But on the Hegelian model, "existence," "system," and "God" are all made to tremble by being returned to *différance*, to their historical matrix in their concrete and determinate form of life, to which they give words and cultural form. The underlying events are what need to be examined, so that postmodern analysis reaches much further than the Kantians think and are willing to concede. The Kantian model is defensive and apologetic, a retrenchment in the face of the latest wave of an ongoing series of Copernican revolutions, and it takes the form here of a confessional apologetics. The Kantians want to insulate God from the play of differences and the concreteness of history. God is an infinite center independent of the play of traces for them, and postmodernism is reduced to merely remarking that we are finite. This is a version of the God of the gaps, a constant retrenchment program that is trying to preserve an epistemological gap (Kant's "to make room for") in which a confessional faith may be sheltered. Kant's

purpose too was largely apologetic—he started out with Newtonian physics and the Pietists he grew up with and asked, How can they both be right,
how can I keep them both safe?

The Hegelian model is more robust. It does not start with confessional
faith as a given but puts it into question. It does not ask how it is possible,
but about what is going on in things like faith, and whether there might
be a deeper, more elusive, more uncertain, and unsafe "faith" (*foi*) stirring
restlessly beneath our historical Christian "belief" (*croyance*). In that sense,
we postmodern Hegelians could sneak into the Kantian camp one night
and steal their slogan and say that we have found it necessary to delimit
Christian "belief" (*croyance*) in order to make room for a deeper "faith" (*foi*).
My unabridged version of postmodernism is also more deeply *affirmative*—
of a more radical *faith*. But this faith is a much more restless and obscure
thing, and it can only make those who gather within the protective walls
of an orthodox *croyance* very nervous, wary of a wider wave of critical
analysis of the human condition. The contributors not only ignore this
distinction between *foi* and *croyance* entirely (while still claiming to speak
of deconstruction), but they go on the attack. If anyone speaks of a more
restless faith that takes full stock of the contingency of historical beliefs,
the Kantians say the latter are afraid of the concrete and determinate. But
I think they are in headlong flight from the full implications of the concrete and determinate, from the *contingency* that gives the concrete and
determinate its bite. The contingency of the concrete withdraws the
grounds for claiming privileged access to an exclusive truth—other than
to say, "But you can't prove we're wrong!"

Confessional apologetics is philosophy in an abridged edition, which
starts by assuming contingent beliefs, whose credibility it wants to establish, and is content with a draw, with showing that it cannot be shown to
be refuted. Even if that were true, I would expect more from philosophy.
Simmons and Minister are fond of logic, and in logic this is called the *ar-
gumentum ad ignorantiam*.[9] I counter this with a hauntology, a certain
heretical phenomenology. That is not a metaphysics, and it should not be
confused with the bankrupt Enlightenment project of Richard Dawkins
and Christopher Hitchens. I am interested in unfolding affirmatively the
form of life that unfolds in and as religion, its affirmation of the impossible, the *foi* that is going on in *croyance*, which is why I have sometimes been
mistaken for an orthodox Augustinian myself.[10]

Although I think the Christian faith of these apologetes is whole-hearted,
I think their philosophy is half-hearted. They begin with a firm affirmation of the exclusive truth of the Christian faith, in the Neoplatonic God
beyond time, history, and the play of traces, and, while trying to provide

a generous version of exclusivity (by allowing for some overlapping truths held by multiple faiths), they are content with a standoff. They are happy to filibuster their opponents: Although they have motives inside their community of faith for believing as they do, nobody outside their community can falsify or refute them. That may be so. There are a lot of things we cannot disprove—like angels, demons, and alien abductions. One would hope for more from a philosophical inquiry where everything is on the table. Apologetics produces strictly provincial campfire talk for other (American, mostly Protestant) Christians, of local interest only to fellow [*sic*] Christians, inside stuff, church talk, of little interest to anyone else, as the collapse of mainstream religion in the United States outside of rural America bears witness.

The theology of the event seeks results of a universal and more searching sort, feeling about for the underlying events of life and death, joy and sorrow, love and enmity, hostility and hospitality, that can be proposed to *anybody anywhere* who has an interest in the human condition. It is deeply interested in the concrete communities of faith, not from a desire to defend their right to their private property, but from a desire to get at the underlying experiences to which they give expression. The real difference between me and the Kantians is that they are trying to avoid the implications of the fact that concrete and determinate historicality goes all the way down and I am not. If anybody has "universality" on their side, it is we radical theologians.

One of their main points is that the meaning of belonging to a tradition is to countersign its *truth*, to take its truth seriously. As Simmons says, either one believes what one is saying in church (or synagogue or mosque) or one doesn't.[11] Simmons means that the multiplicity of religious traditions represents a multiplicity of different communities who believe different things and do not agree, and they cannot all be right, based on the principle of the excluded middle. If people didn't believe their religious tradition, they would be nonbelievers, outside the tradition. But you can frame the situation like that—as a logical problem about propositions— only if you think that religious truth is propositional truth and that different religious traditions are defined by different and competing propositional assertions. I treat that as a fundamental category mistake about religious truth. I am not arguing that religious traditions lack truth, but I am arguing that the truth of the religious tradition is not deposited in assertions, in propositional truths (even if you insist that propositions are vain without a corresponding praxis). I think religious truth is found in a more underlying "way" (which is another word for "religion" and was once the name of Christianity before that name caught on). The way is a "world" (a *Welt* in the phenomenological sense), a certain world-disclosure, a form of life, which on my account actualizes the truth of the "event." World-disclosures are multiple, are not tied to privileged access and are misunderstood if they are seen in terms of competing propositional assertions.

Then what about propositional assertions? I think the "way" underlies the assertions that gradually accumulate into a kind of creedal statement in which the way gets reflectively conceptualized in a confessional theology and imaginatively portrayed in its sacred scriptures. But it is a mistake to think that this self-articulation hands the way over to representational truth. These assertions are the way the community clears its head when it tries to spell out its liturgies, songs, and stories. So I do not speak of "beliefs" that make truth-claims, which is a mistaken way of thinking about religion that came to a head in modernity although it has its roots in late Scholasticism, but of being-claimed by the truth of a faith that cuts deeper than beliefs. This arises from a critique of modernism that begins in Hegel's critique of Enlightenment *Verstand.*

If what Simmons calls "C-beliefs" (beliefs he holds as a Christian)[12] are taken as anything more than a contingent community's self-articulation (faith seeking understanding of itself), they are inextricable from privileged access. That is because (among other things) they require historical information—like saying that a young Jewish man back in Galilee two millennia ago is uniquely God incarnate—that would not be accessible before Jesus was born, for example. (So too illiterate Christians in the American Midwest in the nineteenth century cannot know that Vishnu is the supreme deity.) Christocentric thinking like this would mean that when people organize their lives in terms of the deep structure of their understanding of themselves and the world, the vast majority is disadvantaged by the unavailability of information crucial to this task. So the vast majority of humanity is at a disadvantage in matters that could not be more essential—the deep structure of their lives—while Christians have a special advantage.

This question of truth goes to the heart of this difference between me and my critics in *Reexamining Deconstruction*. Simmons wants to be comfortable with his confessional identity as a Pentecostal Christian. I want him to be discomforted, to experience spooky moments—"we're all in this together" moments, we all share a common fate—in which we acknowledge that while our tradition is ours, there are many such traditions, each having its own uniqueness, integrity, vitality, and special "truth," but in such matters as these no one really has privileged access. Privileging our religious tradition is like privileging our parents. They are "special" to us, but we are not making an empirical claim. So too "special revelations."

Everyone's revelation is special; otherwise it would not be accepted as (their) revelation. There are saints and martyrs in many different traditions with very different narratives, some of whom rightly pass for atheists. Religious truth is witnessed, not verified representationally. A great work of art, in literature or painting, is true with a truth that cuts beneath representational or propositional truth.

We do not need postmodernism to learn that we are finite and fallible things and that our knowledge is never adequate. We already knew that. "Fallibilism" is not deconstruction. We need a different conception of truth itself and a fundamentally different kind of analysis of what is going on in religious traditions. Saying we should practice "epistemological humility" and admit our finitude is a pious and innocuous substitute for taking deconstruction seriously.[13] Like Hegel, I think the finite belongs to what he called *Verstand*, and I adapt his idea of the infinite, of infinite depth, infinite responsibility, in a theopoetics of an infinite secret, or more accurately the *infinitival*, since this is not an actually infinite being. I am not trying to stake out critical boundaries for finite beings to observe with all due modesty but trying to meditate an uncontainable, undecidable, infinitival event and affirm the possibility of the impossible.

Nor do we get anywhere by arguing as Simmons does that my position is caught up in a performative contradiction—that my delimitation of propositional truth rests on the propositions I treat as true.[14] That is not a postmodern argument but a favorite of the Habermasians, logicians, and ontotheologicians. It is reactionary objection against radical theory, an argument of last resort among Anglo-American theorists, and testimony to the poverty of formalism, which Derrida derides as a trick, a "puerile weapon".[15] I appreciate the sympathy Minister has to many of my views and also his attempts to clarify the several conceptual problems he raises. I would be happy to sort these things out. I deeply admire contemporary formal logic, but I do not share the confidence of these authors that formal thinking can do service in matters that are profoundly phenomenological.[16] Of course, I think that the *second order* statements I make *about* religious discourse are true propositions. Heidegger—the great critic of "calculative thinking" and "propositional truth" who was trained in late medieval logic—said, at the beginning of "Time and Being," that what follows takes the risk of making assertions *about* something that is *not* a matter of assertions.[17] I am not saying that there are no propositional truths or that I do not make propositional claims. I am saying that treating the New Testament as a body of propositional truths is a category mistake, and that holds also of theological conceptualizations of these narratives. I do not think that narratives like the raising of Lazarus are true with a representational theory of truth.[18] I do not think that this narrative should be understood as representing a state of affairs, as a record of some actual episode in the past. But I certainly hold that this historical-critical claim *about* that story is true, and that there are good reasons for it, which are found in the massive literature of New Testament research. There we can see that the elevation of Jesus of Nazareth, a figure all but lost in the fog of history, into the subject of the Nicene Creed is a largely an imaginative theological construction, as even John Milbank admits,[19] which faith tries to underwrite as the work of the Holy Spirit, while being forced to admit that "faith" in the "Holy Spirit" is of course a *part* of the construction. That is where the force of "reason" is borne in upon confessional "apologetics," which the apologists try to blunt by saying that "reason" cannot see what the eyes of faith can see in these matters. That is why critical and historical work of this sort is usually best done outside the supervision of ecclesiastical institutions where the threat of losing one's job hangs over one's head, where killing the messenger is business as usual.[20] If anybody is on the side of reason, of giving good reasons *all the way down*, enjoying the right to ask any question, it is radical theology, not confessional apologetics.

In radical theology, we are all up to our ears in historicality (the Hegelian point) and the play of traces (the poststructural point). In a radical theology of the event religion is seen as a way to give evocative form to provocative events, to provide nomination and actualization to certain obscure but fertile, latent but underlying experiences or "events" by which our lives are nourished. It concedes the contingency of these beliefs in the name of a deeper faith in something toward which we are always already underway and for which we lack any guarantees. It is not defensive but unprotected, more radically interrogatory, open-ended, and full-throated about our contingent mortal lives. It is more radically confessional, circumfessional, and in that sense more radically Augustinian. In a theology of the event, everything is on the table, including the contingency of the traditions we have inherited. The Simmons claim is to be "as radical as one needs to be,"[21] whereas we post-Hegelians think the real challenge is to be as radical as are the things themselves, which are always slipping away. But thinking is unconditional exposure to what is to be thought, which is risky business. It is not a limited exposure that stays in the water for a bit and then heads for the towels. For the cut in that more radical "circum-fessional" confession, I think these Kantian apologists lack a taste.

Reexamining Deconstruction and Determinate Religion is a missed opportunity. The critique launched there underestimates my most Christian texts, my ongoing meditations on the theology of the Cross in *The Weakness of God*,[22] where my most sustained engagements of religion *with* religion interact with the logic of the *without,* where radical theology emerges as inner disturbance going on *within* confessional theology. Furthermore, by neglecting the distinction between *croyance* and *foi,* between a position taken and a deeper affirmation, between a judgment made (*doxa*) and a deeper, more decisive trust (*pistis*), which is central for me, my critics never notice that the work I do is post-theistic, aimed at undermining the distinction between "theism" and "atheism," with which they are preoccupied, by which they are trapped. For me, theism and atheism are opposed *croyances,* contrasting beliefs, positions posed against each other in a doxological dispute—in this corner Hitchens and Dawkins, in the other corner Reformed Epistemology—one more round of the fun but futile and fruitless debate back in 1948 between Bertrand Russell and Father Frederick Copleston on the BBC. I am focused on the underlying affirmation, an uncertain, troubling, restless, and unsafe faith, that may emerge in either camp, whether one rightly passes for an atheist or rightly passes for a Christian or a Hindu.

Radical Theology: The Unabridged Version of Postmodernism

Although Simmons and Minister say they are trying to help me out, and I would never deny that I need help, I think that, despite their well-intentioned efforts, this fellow they call "Caputo" needs a fresh introduction. I need to do a little rehabbing of the word "without" and its venerable apophatic logic. In so doing, I propose, a genuine continental philosophy of religion will emerge, instead of an alcohol-free by-product of continental philosophy, which seems to be the version of the Protestant Principle on offer in *Reexamining Deconstruction.*

The position taken by Stephen Minister on my work[23] makes for an interesting counterpart to Martin Hägglund's *Radical Atheism* (see my next chapter), in which "Caputo" is staged as a conservative Augustinian theologian who treats Derrida's discourse on the impossible as an argument for the existence of God and of divine omnipotence. I am denounced by Hägglund for being too strong a theologian and by Minister for not being strong enough. I think both these commentators might in part have been misled by the whimsy with which I say certain things. Be that as it may, they and their critiques occupy opposing polar caps and to both I make the same reply. I am not an orthodox confessional theologian, thanks be to God, a theologian if it pleases you, but neither orthodox nor confessional. I decided to use the word "theology"—always qualified as "weak" or "radical"—under the prodding of Charlie Winquist and Jeffrey Robbins because I thought it might unsettle both the (confessional) theologians and the (secular) ethnologists of religion! The "continental philosophy of religion" (one of the academic names for "radical theology") I do is the full-bodied one coming down from Hegel, Tillich, and poststructural theory, not the decaffeinated version coming down from Kant, Barth, and Ricoeur. Weak theology makes for full-strength postmodernism, while strong theology is a bit weak-kneed about putting itself in question.

Confessional theology is a certain "first order" discourse that reports back to the local community of the faithful (Jewish, Muslim, Christian, Hindu, Baha'i, etc.), which has every right to expect that it will be able to "recognize itself." Radical theology, in contrast, is a second order discourse *about* confessional theology in terms of the event. The truth of the event seeks to be nominated and actualized, strives to surface or actualize itself, to unfold, to come true, to become (true). The truth of the event is constantly insisting on existing. Like the Scriptures, it has to be read or interpreted, which is why "radical theology" is just a type of what I have been calling "radical hermeneutics" for many years now. Radical theology, accordingly, is interested in what is going on *in* confessional religion or theology, in its *truth*, in the *event*. So one of my first strategies in responding to Simmons and Minister is to not concede the ground of truth to them. I am playing on my opposition's court, the crowd is against me, but I will not let them boo me for being against truth. Just as Jim Wallis advises the Democrats against conceding the ground of "religion" to the Right, I will not concede the ground of truth to the orthodox of any *doxa*.

Confessional theologians and apologists have a (shrinking) local audience (the faithful, the believers, the card-carriers, the congregation), while radical theology is of universal relevance. Readers should be as interested in what a radical theologian is saying about religion as they are in literature or history, painting, or politics. That is another part of my strategy in this response: I do not concede the ground of universality to the home crowd. That is why, when Minister, inspired by Alain Badiou, advises me to consider the universality of truth, I am nonplussed.[24] I would have said that we radical theologians submit what we have to say to the length and breadth of humankind. The Christian apologetes say they are widening the horizon of apologetics by bringing continental and analytic philosophy into conversation,[25] to which no one can object, but they are ultimately reporting back to their local confessional community whose faith they are trying to conceptually elaborate. As a second order discourse reflecting on confessional theology, radical theology does not require local communities or that its readers be card-carrying Christians, Hindus, Baha'i, or anything else. They may be atheists like Martin Hägglund, not religious at all.

Readers of radical theology just have to be interested in reflecting on the human condition, on the inscrutables of human life and death, and maybe also animal life (since animals and the environment are not Christians, they get very little attention in *Reexamining Deconstruction*), on the moral law within and the starry skies above, as Kant put it (and everything in between). They just need to think there is something to be learned from reflecting on the religious and theological traditions, the way there is in reflecting on literature or any other important human activity. Radical theologians have had a hard time convincing secular thinkers that theology and religion are worth thinking about, because religious and theologically minded people behave so badly every time scientists make a new discovery, or the religion of some chosen people gets unchosen (constitutionally disestablished or just ignored and abandoned). This situation changed dramatically in the last quarter of the twentieth century, thanks in no small part first to Levinas and Derrida and then, at the turn of the century, to Badiou, Agamben, and Žižek, although the latter are uncommonly ungrateful to the former for having shown them the value of thinking about religion and theology, about what Derrida called the "unavowed" theology in everything we do.[26]

I would, however, be the first to confess that the praise I am heaping on radical theology is a bit of a fiction. Because radical theologians are usually not independently wealthy, they have to make a buck as academic publish-or-perishers. As academics, radical theologians do indeed report to promotion and tenure committees, deans, university presses, and other such "normalizing" powers (in the Foucauldian sense), which keep them inside the borders of the academic form of life, borders I have tried to test from time to time (after I got tenure!).[27] But it is also a fiction to think that this distinction between radical and confessional theology is airtight. That is because of what we in the "radical hermeneutical" tradition call the impossibility of pure reflection, the impossibility of the transcendental reduction or of the pure cogito, and it is why the pure messianic is also always another messianism,[28] a point I have been making from the start. Inasmuch as we embrace, we insist upon, the "facticity" of human understanding, its "situatedness"—despite the picture of us drawn by the defenders of the abridged version—there is no pure disengaging of radical theology from the concrete forms of life of which it means to provide a certain second order reflective awareness.

I find it ironic to accuse a radical hermeneut—which means, at bottom, to practice a hermeneutics of facticity—of a distrust of the concrete and factical. That makes one suspect that there is something else going on behind this accusation. My hypothesis is that the rhetoric of the concrete and determinate is a cover. It is made to serve an apologetic argument for privileged access, where a not very subtle trade-off is made between the "uniqueness" of Christianity and its "exclusive" truth (Minister). In the view of us radical hermeneuts, one is *always* reporting to some local community or other—the intellectual, social, gendered, ethnic, linguistic, historical community to which one belongs more deeply than one can say or will ever know. Maybe after you're dead, if anyone still cares about you, they will be able to define exactly what community you were reporting to. So all we can do, the best we can do, is shoot for what Gadamer called hermeneutical universality, with the understanding that this does not result in an agreement on some essence or other; it just means there is nothing we can*not* talk about. Essences are always provisional and local, always *somebody's* essence, always an essence for this time or place, which is why when we hear a case being made for religion *with* religion we have to worry about "*whose* religion?" Essences contribute to tribal conflicts over one's favorite essence, like the "essence of Christianity." The only thing genuinely universal is singularity and the only community is "we're all in this together." So we aim at hermeneutic openness, a hermeneutic hospitality, a potential universal never actualized, according to which for beings of language like ourselves, there is nothing of human import that cannot be put on the table and discussed, nothing that cannot be set forth in terms somehow accessible to the other, that cannot be set forth in words. That hermeneutic hospitality is the principal force behind maintaining the "messianic" openness (or religion "without" religion) of any confessional theology, which otherwise deals in strictly local goods for local consumption.

What I call radical theology is traditionally described in the academy as the "philosophy of religion," a discipline that is enjoying a renaissance today in conjunction with what is often called "the return of religion." Here is where its genealogy from Hegel's *Lectures on the Philosophy of Religion* rather than from Kant's *Religion within the Limits of Reason Alone* is important. Hegel thought that Christianity is the absolute religion toward which all other religions tend. Combating that prejudice is the reason that the ethnographic approach to religion current in the study of religion today is rapidly displacing the philosophical approach to religion in secular departments of religion. From its start with Hegel, the "philosophy" in the "philosophy of religion" tended to mean Western philosophy, and "religion" tended to mean Christianity. Consequently, the "philosophy of religion" has usually been code for the (Western) philosophy of the (Christian) religion, that is, Christian apologetics, which is exactly what is served up in *Reexamining Deconstruction*. So one way that secular universities have found to displace the hegemony that Christianity has traditionally enjoyed in this discipline is just to drop the "philosophy of religion" and leave it to church-related institutions or divinity schools. There it can come out of the closet, drop its pretense to being full-throttle philosophy, and simply concede that it is Christian apologetics, as do these critics. Amazingly, far from trying to dispel these concerns, Christian apologetics is unapologetically embraced; it is what "continental philosophy of religion" is reduced to in *Reexamining Deconstruction*. Faced with undisguised confessionalism like this, it is no wonder the most draconian solution of all available to secular universities is to drop the "department of religion" entirely and make the study of religion a part of the sociology or anthropology department.[29] With friends like this, the philosophy of religion needs no enemies.

But we radical theologians have another idea. While arguing that radical theology has Hegelian credentials, we keep a safe distance from Hegel's idea that Christianity is the consummate religion, religion itself, where religion converges *with* Christian religion, which is what my critics in *Reexamining Deconstruction* share with Hegel. Of course, Hegel went on to say that religion is an imaginative figure (*Vorstellung*) of something that can only be conceptualized in and by Hegelian philosophy—and that is the point at which these Christian apologetes head straight for the door. That was Hegel's attempt to radicalize theology, the move in which we radical theologians recognize a kindred spirit (specter). This radical move was picked up by Tillich, who is the father of radical theology, who helped us clear our heads of supernaturalism and magic. That makes Hegel our grandfather. Old grandfather Hegel was feeling around for what I am calling the truth of the event. But, as I said, I go along only half-heartedly, half-heretically with Hegel.[30] I think religion is an imaginative figure, not of the Absolute Concept, but of the event, which is a phenomenological experience, not a metaphysical absolute. The absolute is what Derrida calls the secret, the absolute secret that there is no secret, none that we know of anyway. When it comes to religion there are only *Vorstellungen*, symbols, works of imaginative genius, and no burning through to an absolute Essence, Concept, Spirit, Will-to-Power, or Divine Special Revelation. So when I speak of the truth of the event, I can just as well speak of its untruth, of its never quite seeing the light of day, of the endlessly altered ways in which this insistence insists on existence.

Thus, notwithstanding his Christocentrism, Hegel made the crucial, I would say defining, move in the formation of a radical theology and of a distinctively continental approach to the philosophy of religion. Hegel upbraided the rationalists of his day for leaving out of consideration the characteristic doctrines of the Christian religion—in particular, the Trinity and the Incarnation—and restricting themselves to the bloodless and barren exercise of the abstract "understanding" (*Verstand*), like proving the existence of God or the immortality of the soul.[31] He would certainly have been no less critical of what passes for the "philosophy of religion" in the textbooks and books of readings assembled by contemporary analytic philosophers and Thomists. In its place, Hegel put the work of "reason" (*Vernunft*), which consisted in the wider work of feeling around for the form of the Spirit that was unfolding in these determinate and particular Christian doctrines. I recommend that we spectralize the Spirit, that we replace "Spirit" with specter, the absolute with the "event," and the Truth of the Spirit with "the truth of the event" (no caps).

That is exactly what I have been recommending in all of my work from *The Weakness of God: A Theology of the Event* to *Cross and Cosmos: A Theology of Difficult Glory*, which are extended meditations on the logic of the Cross, on Jesus as an icon not of God's omnipotence but of God's weakness. (As Catherine Keller shows so nicely, the tradition wanted a more testosterone-rich God than that![32]) There are texts in which I am deeply concerned with "with," with a religion with religion, with a radical religion within confessional religion. The "with" applauded in *Reexamining Deconstruction* is my "within." Religion without religion means the religion that disturbs religion from within. Far from shying away from the concrete and determinate, I want to dig more deeply into it, to feel about by which it is inwardly disturbed. I am like a good Hegelian (of a somewhat heretical stripe) who prefers *Sittlichkeit* to *Moralität* and recommends a meticulous meditation on what is happening in very determinate traditions, like the Christian one, which is the one in which I am least incompetent. That is why Simmons will find in these books, just as in Hegel's lectures on the philosophy of religion, an ongoing discussion of the "C-beliefs" he and his congregation hear in Pentecostal services—even if I think the best sermons are haunted by an uneasy sense of the contingency of what is being preached.

In other words, in this Hegelian schema, the philosophy of religion is distinguished from confessional theology formally, by the point of view—taking religion as imaginative thinking (*Vorstellung*), not a representational thinking[33]—but not materially, as if one could sort out philosophical theses knowable by the use of natural reason, say the existence of God, from theological doctrines that have been supernaturally revealed, say the Incarnation and Trinity. On the contrary, for Hegel, what is most interesting of all are Creation and Incarnation, the Trinity and the Holy Spirit, the concrete, determinate, distinctive, and defining doctrines of Christian life and theology, even as what interests me in *The Weakness of God* and *Cross and Cosmos* is the Crucifixion, which of course also greatly interested Hegel.

The vast majority of my books starting with *The Weakness of God* are given over to reflecting on specific, determinately Christian texts and doctrines and very little or no time at all spent in the rare air of the "pure messianic" or, God forbid, with proofs for the existence of God or the Platonic idea of the "immortality of the soul." My "poetics" of the event is a phenomenology of religion but, once again, a hauntological quasi-phenomenology that questions both the classical idea of "philosophy" and the Western Christian Latin idea of "religion."[34]

As Minister rightly points out to Simmons, radical theology "spooks" confessional theology.[35] To deconstruct is not to destroy but to haunt. Radical theology is a ghost that haunts the confessional theologies from within. Deconstruction is "undead," a trope I borrow from Žižek in order to unnerve Žižek—as if anything could!—about his hasty proclamation that the time for deconstruction is over and that now is the time for, well, in all modesty, Žižek.[36] There is a bit of that in *Reexamining Deconstruction*. The time of indecisive deconstruction is over, my critics tell me, and now is the time to assert the exclusive truth of Christianity (as if that program has not already had quite a run over the last two millennia, as our Jewish and Islamic brothers and sisters can testify). That idea I am here to haunt, like the ghosts who spooked old Scrooge, to whisper in their ears, to visit them in their dreams, and to say, however often you kill it off, by which I mean trying to do without deconstruction and its logic of the "without," it will come back to haunt you. By the logic of the undead, if deconstruction goes, it will come back like a *revenant*.

6

Unprotected Religion
*Radical Theology, Radical Atheism, and the Return
of Anti-Religion*

Radical theology has come of age.[1] It now has its own countermovement—
philosophers marching under the flag of materialism, realism, and anti-
religion and complaining that the theologians are back at their old trick of
appropriating critiques of religion in order to make religion stronger. So this
is an occasion to clear the air and see just how hard and fast the borders are
between religion and anti-religion, realism and antirealism, materialism and
antimaterialism, especially given that deconstruction is an exercise in anxiety
about rigorous borders. Martin Hägglund's *Radical Atheism* is a closely argued contribution to the debate that fits hand in glove with this countermovement, although Hägglund does not mention it.[2] His book is a welcome
refutation of any attempt to reduce Derrida to an antirealist or antimaterial-
ist, especially in the light of Meillassoux's caricature of "correlationism,"
which treats continental philosophers from Kant on as creationists.[3] Given
the historical violence religion has provoked and the reactionary meanness of
the religious right in American politics today, I am no less nervous about
"religion." That makes it all the more important to sort out what I am saying
and what I am not, since my own work on Derrida and religion, as Michael
Naas points out clearly, is no less informed by protecting Derrida's *laïceté*.[4]

Unprotected Religion

Deploying Derrida's analyses of "autoimmunity," Hägglund isolates the logic
of time in Derrida, which is, at it were, the skeletal basis of everything that

goes on in deconstruction. Time, Hägglund argues, is a process of coming to be and passing away such that its "radical finitude" (*RA*, 1) is intrinsic to its constitution and not merely a passing defect from which we can or should seek protection (immunity). The very condition under which time is given ensures that what is given will be taken away. Whatever is present is never "absolutely present" (*RA*, 1); it is always "divided by time," by the "spacing" of time. Its very coming to presence is constituted by its passing away or loss of presence, its passing presence requiring the "trace" to be retained. "Pure" presence—absolute immunity (noncontamination) from passing away—is meaningless and contradictory, since nothing pure could ever be present in the first place. Pure presence is pure death. Presence immunized from spacing and passing away implies the absence of coming to be altogether. Accordingly, desiring a good in a pure or immune condition is a desire divided against itself, desiring a condition under which it would be impossible for that good to be the good that it is. If we remove the condition that consigns a good to perish, we also remove the condition that enables it to be a good. The very condition under which a good is possible—the spacing of time—is also the condition that makes it impossible for that good to be pure. Hence the desire for a pure good would not be idealistic but nihilistic. Purity of presence is not an ideal forever out of reach where reality dictates we must be willing to settle for less. Purity of presence is impossible, nothing at all, and nothing to be desired. Not only are we denied such goods, we cannot and should not desire them. The desire for life is the desire for more life, more time, more mortal time, which Derrida calls "living on" (*sur-vivre*). Survival trades in a time that may, that will, erase the survivor. Survival is not the desire for infinite or immortal life, since immortal life is death. The time of life is "auto-immune," intrinsically exposed and vulnerable, its immunity from perishing disarmed, its desire for immunity broken down.

From this line of argument, to which I think no careful reader of Derrida would take exception, Hägglund takes up Derrida's analyses of phenomenology, ethics, religion, and politics, reaching the conclusion that not only is deconstruction atheistic, it represents a "radical atheism." Garden variety or standard-form atheism admits that we all desire the immortality promised by religion, but it concedes that such a hope is denied to us. This is what Christopher Watkin calls "ascetic" atheism; we deny ourselves the consolations of religion on the grounds of reason and realism, without denying that it would be rather nice to have what religion promises (living forever in a kingdom of pure goodness).[5] Radical atheism, in contrast, denies that we should or even could have such a desire. We can only desire mortal goods and believe in mortal beings; were there such an entity as God, God must also be mortal. Contrary to the "theological turn," deconstruction is "radically"—constitutively and unequivocally—at odds with religion. To this conclusion, any careful reader of Derrida should take exception, as I most certainly do, especially since I am singled out in *Radical Atheism* as the prime culprit responsible for drawing Derrida down the dark corridors where religion does its shady work in this vale of tears.

The exception I take is this. Time and the trace imply no less what Derrida calls "iterability," the constitutive repeatability and recontextualizability—time and time again—of the trace. That means that "religion" is more than one. Religion, "if there is such a thing," just one thing, undivided against itself, " *la*" *religion*, in the singular, the same all the time—that is exactly what deconstruction deconstructs. What we call in "Christian Latin French"[6] *la religion* is a massive globalatinization that splinters in the face of the real multiplicity of actually existing beliefs and practices colonized by this risky word. Is *that* not the first and most obvious result of taking up religion in terms of time and the trace (which accords perfectly with virtually every important study of religion today)? The point of any deconstruction is to de-sediment our most sedimented concepts, to redeploy and reinvent them and so release their inherent play, not to consign them to oblivion with a reductionistic argument. If that is so, as I think any careful reader of Derrida would agree, then the upshot of every analysis from the "dangerous supplement" to autoimmunity is not the radical extermination of religion, as of a dreaded disease or pure evil, but the invention of a contaminated religion, like Damian among the lepers, one that hails (*Salut!*) the coming of a religion to come (*viens*) rather than take sides in the binary war between theism and atheism. Derrida sketches in the dark a certain religion, a religion *without* religion, which turns precisely on this impure, radically finite, and constitutively contaminated condition predicted by the logic of autoimmunity. For Hägglund, "the logic of autoimmunity is radically atheist" (*RA*, 9); for Derrida, it presages a contaminated religion that unhinges a religion of purity, that displaces the *puritas essendi* of the good old God of classical metaphysics and negative theology, that disrupts "a positive infinity that is absolutely in itself" (*RA*, 3) and the corresponding desire for immortal life. But the dualism of Augustinian religion is unfortunately the only "religion" to make an appearance in *Radical Atheism*, a "religion" at whose desedimentation and deconstruction Derrida and I, along with a good many contemporary theologians, have for a long time now been in attendance.

As Clayton Crockett argues in an incisive essay, Hägglund misinterprets my interest in religion, which is not to defend a traditional religion (or confessional theology) in deconstructive terms, but precisely to advance a religion without religion (and hence a radical theology) and has confused me with Jean-Luc Marion.[7] Cast in terms of Derrida's "Faith and Knowledge" essay, a religion without religion turns on a primordial faith (*foi*) in an open-ended but risky promise, not on a confessional belief (*croyance*) in a determinate and assured creedal object, and so draws on the first of the two sources of religion discussed by Derrida (faith) while contaminating the second (the unscathed). Such a faith is deserted and despairing, naked and unsheltered—not unscathed, not safe and sound, not immune from the depths of doubt, error, evil, violence, and death. Unlike Paul, who felt immunized by the blood of the crucified Christ, it does not boast, "O death, where is your sting?" On the contrary, the faith to which Derrida and I subscribe is an impossible faith, arising from the abyss of unfaith, uncertainty, and insecurity, from a prayer that is left without a prayer, sustained by what this same Paul calls a hope against hope in an unforeseeable future. That is why, in "Circumfession," instead of denouncing Augustinian dualism, Derrida engages in an *iteration* of the prayers and tears of Augustine's *Confessions*, subtly inflecting its very title and so boldly engaging in unprotected religion, if I may adapt an expression from those who warn us against sexually transmitted diseases.[8] Such unarmed and vulnerable faith affirms a promise that is not merely fraught with risk but is constituted internally by risk. The risk is intrinsic and structural, not provisional and accidental, not a fault that could in principle be removed at a later point, not a matter of seeing now in part, in a glass darkly, but later on in full (Paul again!). This faith is not a compromise with an ideal faith free from doubt that we just cannot achieve given the weakness of the flesh. This faith is made possible by the very condition that makes it impossible, as Derrida says about all the famous operations of deconstruction. The contamination described by the logic of autoimmunity does not obliterate religion but reinvents it, writing the prescription for an unprotected religion.

Deconstruction has always been the critique of such unscathed immunized purity.[9] It has never changed. "Autoimmunity" was just the last trope Derrida came up with before he died. That is what interests me about deconstruction. That is the point I have defended ever since I first described the project of "radical hermeneutics" in 1987 in terms of facing up squarely to the "difficulty" of factical life, that is, of dealing with the fact that we never make contact with anything safe and secure, pure and unmediated, immune and unscathed.[10] My work with religion is to bring this confession or circumfession to bear upon religion and to show how deconstruction reopens and reinvents religion in a new way—to the considerable displeasure both of secularizing deconstructors and of confessional theology. Radical theology does not deny finitude and contamination; it begins with them.

But Crockett is too generous to say that, while Hägglund misinterprets me, he does not misinterpret Derrida. Although it is true that iterability allows Derrida to be read in the selective way undertaken by Hägglund, this iteration is not nearly as interesting or fruitful as Derrida. It is a torso, a truncated form of deconstruction, not Derrida's doing but Hägglund's, who proceeds at times as if Derrida has nothing to teach him about deconstruction. Hägglund claims (a) that deconstruction reaches an unambiguous result, a decisive refutation of religion (in the singular), and (b) that deconstruction proceeds on a level of neutral, value-free descriptive analysis of the logic of time. These claims, entirely of Hägglund's own devising, are both philologically and philosophically mistaken. They are creatures of everything about modernity that deconstruction sets out to deconstruct, and they are separated by an abyss from both the style and the substance of what Derrida calls deconstruction. Deconstruction is a way of rereading and reinventing religion—or anything else—not of eradicating religion by means of a radical atheism. The atheism attributed to Derrida by Hägglund would be described by Derrida as "absolutely ridiculous."[11] *Radical Atheism* may be a way to philosophize with a hammer (*RA*, ix). Deconstruction is not.

In what follows I first contest what I find contestable in *Radical Atheism*, and then I set out my own interpretation of what deconstruction can do for religion.

Radical Atheism

Let me be clear that I welcome Hägglund's timely presentation of a certain realist-materialist Derrida ("materialist theology" is the order of the day!). He shows that *différance* is not an immaterial spirit but requires a material substance, that the "play of traces" is spacing-timing, and that is all to the good. His mistake is to suppress Derrida's axiomatics of the beyond, of the *super, epekeina, hyper, über, au-delà*,[12] for fear of contamination by Augustinian immaterialism. Derrida himself says that deconstruction has "always come forward in the name of the real, of the irreducible reality of the real—not the real as an attribute of the thing [*res*], objective, present, sense-able or intelligible, but the real as coming or event of the other. . . . In this sense, nothing is more 'realist' than deconstruction."[13] I describe deconstruction not as antirealism but as "*hyper*-realism,"[14] let us say an ultramaterialism, an open-ended materialism, just as Žižek thinks that matter is all, but the all is a non-all, and, as Catherine Malabou describes, a "reasonable materialism" that does not turn life into a cybernetic or neurological program.[15] Derrida, Žižek, Malabou, and I are all "materialists" in the sense that we do not think there are two worlds, one in space and time, the other transcending space and time. So I speak of a "poetics," not a logic; Malabou emphasizes a transformational "plastics"; and Žižek introduces "parallax shifts." But Hägglund mistakenly thinks that defending a certain realism and materialism comes at the cost of Derrida's religion. This conclusion is reached by systematically abridging and/ or altering several crucial notions in deconstruction, which I sketch here and develop at greater length elsewhere (see note 1).

1. *Torsos.* I begin with several elemental concepts in deconstruction that appear only in a truncated form in *Radical Atheism.*

a. *The Unconditional.* Hägglund identifies the "unconditional" with "the spacing of time" (*RA*, 25), the "coming of time" (*RA*, 42), the "exposure to what happens" (*RA*, 43), the vulnerability of the moment to the unforeseeable future—all irreducibly important—but he omits the unconditional claim of the future upon the moment. This claim (appeal, call), which opens up the axiological space that Hägglund wants to close down, is what Derrida calls the "*unconditionals*," nominalized, in italics and in the plural, like the gift, forgiveness, hospitality "—and by definition the list is not exhaustive; it is that of all *the unconditionals*,"[16] or "the unconditional injunction,"[17] "the desire and the thought, the exigency of unconditionality, the very reason and justice of unconditionality," "the demand, the desire, the imperative exigency of unconditionality," "the exigency of an unconditional justice,"[18] "unconditional ethical obligation,"[19] what elicits from us a "desire beyond desire"—for the unconditional gift, or justice, or democracy to come, and so on. Of course, the future is indeed constituted by its unconditional unforeseeability, just as Hägglund says. But it is no less constituted by the promise that the future holds out (and holds back) from us, by the unconditional call that it visits upon us, and that calls for our response.

The difference between the two senses of unconditionality is the difference between existence and nonexistence, being and beyond being, or perhaps better, between being and "perhaps," *être* and *peut-être*, *il y a* and *s'il y en a.* The unconditional exposure to the future is real; it exists; it always exists, always and everywhere, at every moment, whether we like it or not, whether we know it or not. It does not ask for our consent or even, since it can come like a thief in the night (Paul), that we be awake! But (to take but one example) "the unconditional university, the university without condition," which means the unconditional right to ask any question, is irreal; it "*should* be *without condition*," it *should* exist, but it "does not, in fact, exist, as we know only too well."[20] If the unconditional university does not exist, it does insist, that is, it calls in vocative space and awaits our response. It is but a weak and irreal force in a purely vocative and spectral space that is menaced on every side by the all too real "powers" of the "sovereign" nation-state, of market capitalism, of the media, religion, and culture at large.[21] The unconditional university is a weak but unconditional force without sovereignty, a weak force without force, without the wherewithal to enforce itself. "If this unconditionality, in principle and *de jure*, constitutes the invincible force of the university, it has never been in effect. By reason of this abstract and hyperbolic invincibility, by reason of its very impossibility, this unconditionally exposes the weakness or the vulnerability of the university . . . its impotence. . . . It is a stranger to power." It is, like justice in itself, *de jure*, an "invincible force," but it has never existed—which is why its invincibility is "hyperbolic," "impossible," and "weak"—that is the very model of the weakness of God as unconditional without force, invincible without being an agent, of which I make use in *The Weakness of God*.[22]

b. *The "Undeconstructible."* This concept undergoes a parallel abridgment (*RA*, 25, 40–42, 105). What is deconstructible for Derrida is what is constructed in space and time. That means *différance* is not deconstructible for Derrida because, as spacing-timing, it is the condition under which construction takes place, which is the side of this idea that interests Hägglund (*RA*, 143–44). But Derrida first introduced the word "undeconstructible" in reference not to *différance* but to justice in "The Force of Law": "Justice in itself, if such a thing exists, outside or beyond law, is not deconstructible."[23] He said this not because justice is synonymous with *différance*, which it is not, but because justice is never constructed and hence is always calling for construction (in laws) and therefore at the same time for the *de*construction of any law that is, in fact, constructed. Of course, the historical words for justice in the several natural languages are historical constructions and therefore deconstructible, but "justice in itself, if there is such a thing," does not exist and so cannot be deconstructed. It is a promise of an event, a call for an event. Hägglund keeps a good distance from this side of Derrida, because he thinks it makes the undeconstructible into a Kantian ideal or a pure good. But the undeconstructible is not a pure ideal or a pure good. If the difference between the unconditional claim and the conditional is the difference between *peut-être* and *être*, it is not the difference between the ideal and the real. The unconditional is not an ideal essence. Then what is it? An unconditional call or injunction, an unconditional but dangerous demand, a pure promise that cannot be insulated from a pure threat, where "pure" does not means "ideal" but *peut-être*, a pure promise/threat.[24] The undeconstructible is neither a regulative ideal that monitors empirical words in natural languages, nor an essential meaning that animates the body of corporeal words, but a dangerous injunction—like "give" or "go" or "come"—and a dream set off by language, by what is getting itself promised in words like "justice" ("gift," etc.). It is not an "inaccessible Idea" (*RA*, 43), but it is an incessant injunction that gives us no peace.

c. *Desire.* For Derrida, desire is the desire of the impossible. The impossible is precisely what we desire with a "desire beyond desire,"[25] the only thing we can truly love and desire, just because it is impossible.[26] "And deconstruction is mad about and from such justice, mad about and from this desire for justice."[27] Even if democracy does not and never will exist, it is necessary to keep the "democratic desire" alive, "with all one's heart."[28] Desiring the possible is the desire of the future-present and less worthy of the name *desire*. A real desire for Derrida, the event of desire, the desire for the event, always turns on the impossible. But according to Hägglund, the logic of the double bind means "a pure gift is neither thinkable nor desirable as such" (*RA*, 37). Maintaining this view causes Hägglund some difficulty since it is the direct opposite of Derrida's, who says that "one can think, desire, and say *only* the impossible."[29] So Hägglund feels called upon to warn us that Derrida is being "misleading" when he says things like that. Hägglund wants to avoid treating the "pure gift" as a regulative ideal we can never realize and actual gifts as contaminated compromises with our ideals (*RA*, 38). For Derrida, the pure gift means the gift that does not exist because the conditions under which it could exist have been removed. Derrida analyzes the gift in its unconditional and irreal purity in order to isolate its character as a pure demand or pure call (as in his analysis of hospitality and forgiveness), not to construct a transcendental ideal. Derrida is not complaining that he wished he lived in world where we did not have to compromise our ideals. He is trying to explicate the force or dynamics of the gift as driven "by the impossible," *par l'impossible*, the way the gift shatters the circle of exchange.[30] The impossible is not an ideal but an operator, a function, an injunction; it is not an ideal but an ordeal. Gifts are interruptions of economies that give economies a chance, leading up to ever more generous and open-ended economies and ever more open-ended and hospitable narcissisms. The logic of the double bind belongs to the larger poetics of the dynamics of the impossible.

In fact, then, what is misleading is not Derrida's text, which as usual is quite careful, but what Hägglund makes of it, which is to insist that, since Derrida is not making a distinction between a pure transcendental ideal and a contaminated empirical shortfall, there is no gap, no axiological distance, at all between the impossible gift that we desire and actual gifts. For Derrida the pure gift is not pure because it is a pure good or a pure ideal; it is "pure" because it does not exist but calls for existence, as "justice" calls for laws that it also calls to account. It is a pure call, a pure promise, a pure perhaps, a pure demand, a pure injunction, and hence a pure risk. Actual gifts, in contrast, which are the only things that exist, are responses made and risks taken. The distance between the two is irreducible, as irreducible as the distance between *peut-être* and *être*, a call and a response. The distance between "give" (*donne*) and our response is never closed—that would shut the future down!—but only momentarily crossed. The two touch only in the madness of the moment, in the event that tears up the circle of time. The pure irreal gift is a measureless measure of the measurable real gifts given. For Derrida it is precisely the irreducible axiological gap that separates the immeasurable from the measured, the impossible from the possible, that elicits desire and the gift in the first place. So the issue turns on determining exactly the nature of this gap, which Hägglund denies is there at all and Derrida makes the centerpiece of his analysis and carefully explicates in the so-called misleading text. Proceeding on the fiction that deconstruction takes place in a purely descriptive space, that Derrida is simply describing double binds, Hägglund wants to make sure that there would never be a gap or shortfall between the desire for the gift, if there is such a thing, and actual gifts given. That contradicts the central purpose of Derrida's analysis. But Hägglund's duty, as he sees it, is to protect (immunize) Derrida from himself, to "fortify" him with occasional booster shots (*RA*, 11).

The reason Hägglund thinks the text misleading is that in it Derrida invokes Kant's distinction between thinking (ideas of reason) and knowledge (categorical determination of the manifold of intuition). Derrida writes:

> For finally, if the gift is another name of the impossible, we still think it, we name it, we desire it. . . . In this sense one can think, desire, and say only the impossible, according to the measureless measure of the impossible. If one wants to recapture the proper element of thinking, naming, desiring, it is perhaps according to the measureless measure of this limit that it is possible, possible as relation *without* relation to the impossible.[31]

The gift occurs in a gap between our "knowledge" of the possible and our "thought" or "desire" of the impossible:

> This *gap* between, on the one hand, thought, language, and desire and, on the other hand, knowledge, philosophy, science and the order of presence is also a gap between gift and economy.[32]

Crossing this gap has the appearance of a transcendental illusion in Kant's sense, where the cognitive faculty strays beyond the limits of experience lured by an illusory *ens realissimum*, and indeed, Derrida says, it is something like that. The aporia of the gift poses a sort of "quasi-transcendental illusion," where it "is a matter—desire beyond desire—of responding faithfully but also as rigorously as possible both to the injunction or the order of the gift (give [*donne*]), as well as to the injunction or the order of meaning (presence, science, knowledge)."[33]

So Derrida is clear that the gift is not an *ideal* but an *injunction*, and we are caught in the middle of a double injunction, of demands coming at us from both directions—from the impossible and the possible, from a thinking, naming, desiring of the impossible, on the one hand, and from what we know and experience of the possible, of the circle of economy, on the other.[34] The response (not the resolution or "compromise") to the aporia is to take a risk, to enter its destructive circle, expose oneself to the danger, tear up the circle of time—by *giving*, by *going* where you *know* you cannot go, *facere veritatem*, doing the truth rather than knowing it, for the gift is not finally a matter of knowledge:

> Know still what giving wants to say, know how to give, know what you want and want to say when you give, know what you intend to give, know how the gift annuls itself, commit yourself [*engage-toi*] even if commitment is the destruction of the gift by the gift, give economy its chance.[35]

There is no simple outside of the circle, no "transcendental illusion" in the strong sense. There is only the interruption of the circle and the generation of new more ample circles.

d. *The Ultratranscendental.* In this case Hägglund does not truncate the concept but he baldly alters it to his own purposes. He uses the word to mean the ultimacy of the "space-time of the trace," a *ne plus ultra* spatio-temporality, the inescapable horizon "from which nothing can be exempt" (*RA*, 10). Derrida, however, does no such thing. For Derrida it is precisely the name of an exemption. Derrida introduces it against Hjemslev's notion of pure linguistic form to stress that *différance* enjoys an ultratranscendental exemption, that it "cannot, as the condition of all linguistic systems, form a part of the linguistic system and be situated as an object in its field,"[36] and hence arises from a movement "beyond" the transcendental lest it fall "short-of" it. The target of Hägglund's analysis is the transcendentality of space and time in Kant, which makes of them appearances and leaves room for faith in things in themselves; that opens the door to what Meillassoux calls "fideism." So Hägglund uses Derrida's notion of the "ultratranscendental" to close that door, to say that space and time are "ultimate," go all the way down. Derrida has nothing of the sort in mind.

For Derrida "ultratranscendental" has more to do with Mallarmé than any such "materialism."[37] The word does not refer to the ultra-reality of coming to be and passing away in space and time as things in themselves and not mere appearance. It refers to the unformalizable play of linguistic effects we find in writers such as Joyce and Mallarmé, just as the figure of the sister/Antigone in *Glas* represents a quasi-transcendental exception to a rigorous dialectical logic.[38] Hägglund simply alters the sense of "ultra" as "beyond" the formal, as the "exception" to the transcendental rule, and redefines the word ultratranscendental to mean ultratranscendent, the ultimate, unbroken ultra-rule of space and time. Hägglund's ultratranscendental means reality is lodged without remission in spatiotemporal being; the quasi-transcendental condition of experience becomes an ultratranscendent principle that "being is essentially temporal (to be = to happen)" (*RA*, 32). Derrida's "ultratranscendental," however, means the event cannot be contained or subsumed under the universal or transcendental; it is always an excess, a "beyond" (ultra-).[39]

2. *Descriptive and Prescriptive.* The alterations introduced by Hägglund go hand in hand with a decision to treat deconstruction as a strictly descriptive and not prescriptive undertaking, as simply describing the ultra-real, ultratranscendental, ultra-empirical, and unconditional, but never venturing "beyond." This claim is made throughout the text mainly to undercut the ethical and religious (*RA*, 31), which for Hägglund always mean "beyond" in the sense of Augustinian dualism. Deconstruction is an "ultratranscendental description" of our inescapable vulnerability to an unpredictable future, which means "there must be finitude and vulnerability, there must be openness to whatever or whoever comes" (*RA*, 31), and there cannot be any normativity or prescriptiveness about it, no need for an injunction to stay "open" or go "beyond," as we have no other choice anyway. We are open to the coming of the future whether we like it or not, held fast in an unconditional (spatiotemporal) fix.

This is deconstruction *ad usum dauphini*, cut to fit the logic that is driving *Radical Atheism*, and it is at odds with Derrida. Hägglund's radical atheism only requires so much Derrida and no more, after which it covers its ears. What Hägglund leaves out is that, beyond our unavoidable exposure to the future, there lies our "responsibility" to and for the future (and the past), which we *certainly may avoid*. But should we say, then, we "ought" to be responsible to and for the future, and that Derrida's "ethics" is to "prescribe" just that—always and everywhere to stay open to the future? Hägglund thinks not, and again that is correct as far as it goes, for it would be a sad outcome for deconstruction to end up coming up with a new rule. But everything that is interesting about deconstruction turns on the next step, the one Hägglund leaves out, which is the way that Derrida eludes standard form ethical normativity or prescriptiveness. Derrida does not do this the way Hägglund does, by retreating to the descriptive-factual-empirical, but rather by making use of his *own* notion of the ultratranscendental described in *Of Grammatology*, the one Hägglund suppressed, by going-beyond and by passing-through the transcendental, by passing through the universal-prescriptive (ethical) to an ultraprescriptive, an "ultra-responsibility" or "hyper-responsibility" beyond prescriptive universality. Otherwise, Derrida says, if you drop the "passage-through," you will fall "short-of" the transcendental into the empirical or descriptive.[40] That Humean, empiricist shortfall, exactly what Derrida is warning against, is exactly what Hägglund embraces.

If what Derrida is saying sounds familiar, it should, since it repeats according to a dynamics of its own the path to Moriah depicted by Johannes de Silentio: through ethical universality to religious singularity (*hyperbole*, beyond) instead of retreating to the aesthetic (*ellipsis*, shortfall). That famous story was the subject of *The Gift of Death*, one of Derrida's most interesting books, where deconstruction emerges from the inclination of Kierkegaard and Levinas toward each other, about which Hägglund observes Abrahamic silence. While Derrida's topics of choice have changed over the years, the basic structure of his thought has not, which is the passage through the universal to the singular, which is why, *pace* Hägglund, I have never said there is a "religious turn" in any deep or structural sense, just a change of topics, which is why he never cites a text in which I say such a thing.[41]

Hägglund either does not see or simply rejects the way that in Derrida deconstruction is driven by a hyperbolic, open-ended, albeit dangerous, injunction that is structured like a religion, and certainly cannot be accommodated by resurrecting a modernist and empiricist distinction between prescriptive and descriptive, which makes deconstruction look like logical positivism. Hägglund makes much of the fact that whether the *tout autre* unexpectedly knocking at my door is "good" or "bad," an orphan in need or an axe murderer, is structurally unforeseeable and undecidable.[42] From this, Hägglund concludes that the *tout autre* is not the "good" as such, has no claim on us as such.[43] From the *tout autre* "no norms or rules can be derived" (*RA*, 232n4). The *tout autre* is the object of an ethically neutral and purely "descriptive" account. "Hospitality" is a pure descriptor that means we never know who is knocking on the door (*RA*, 105). That is a half-truth, another torso effect, which serves Hägglund's point but blunts Derrida's. Of course, the *tout autre* is not the good as such. Deconstruction is not a theory of the "good" but a theory of "responsibility," of infinite, hyperbolic responsibility. This point could not be more central. The *tout autre* is not good as such but the event as such. Good and bad are the categories of ethics, not of the "hyper-ethics" of responsibility, or the ultraethics "beyond" the ethics, which "passes through" the transcendental or ethical universal.[44]

So of course the other is not the good as such. If it were, everything would be programmed, and we would have a rule to live by. But that does not mean the *tout autre* is something neutral but rather that, as the event as such, the *tout autre* is the occasion of a heightened responsibility, the "beginning of ethics, of the Law as such," "a principle of ethics or more radically of justice." The ultratranscendental constitutes the hyperethical, ethics beyond ethics, the ethicity of ethics, "hyperbolic" ethics, an "increase of responsibility,"[45] which is an ethics beyond duty. Without the *tout autre*, without "the priceless dignity of otherness," "ethics is dormant," in a "dogmatic slumber."[46] When Derrida says such things, Hägglund remarks, we should not be misled by such "positively valorized terms" (*RA*, 105)—which is like Heidegger saying that nothing pejorative is intended in speaking of the leveled-off inauthentic idle gossip of fallen Dasein. As happens often in this book, when Derrida gets to his point, he is chided by Hägglund for straying from Hägglund's point. It is ironic that a notion on which Hägglund leans so heavily in *Radical Atheism* (ultratranscendental) in fact—when we look at what Derrida actually says—exposes the bare-fisted empiricism that Hägglund embraces and Derrida is criticizing.

The account of the *tout autre* is indeed not "normative," not because it is less than normative (*ellipsis*), but because it is more than normative (*hyperbole*). The point of the analysis of the *tout autre* is not to "neutralize" the *tout autre* but to pass through its normative or ethical features, allowing them to break under the pressure of the aporia, in order to intensify the impossible, the passion, the claim, the call, the responsibility, all of which are charges set off upon entering the "beyond" (*ultra, hyper,* etc.). Derrida does not neutralize ethics but destabilizes its transcendental pretensions so as make room for ultratranscendental responsibility to the singularity of the other. The "suspension" of the ethical is not neutralization but Kierkegaardian fear and trembling and Levinasian irrecusability; it suspends the universal-normative under the intensity of the singular responsibility.

From the fact that the future may bring disaster, Hägglund concludes that we cannot think it is "better to be more open than less open to the future" (*RA*, 232n4). Once again, Derrida expressly denies the position Hägglund is advancing. Sometimes, to prevent things from happening is not to prevent the event but the only way to keep the future open. We block those things that would themselves block the future:

> *The openness of the future is worth more*; that is *the axiom* of deconstruction, that on the basis of which it has always set itself in motion and which links it, as with the future itself, to otherness, to *the priceless dignity of otherness*, that is to say, to justice. . . . One can imagine the objection. Someone [let's say, the author of *Radical Atheism*] might say to you: "Sometimes it is better for this or that not to arrive. Justice demands that one prevent certain events (certain *'arrivants'*) from arriving. The event is not good in itself, and the future is not unconditionally preferable." Certainly, but one can always show that what one is opposing, when one conditionally prefers that this or that not happen, is something one takes, rightly or wrongly, as blocking the horizon or simply forming the horizon (the word that means limit) for the absolute coming of the altogether other, for the future.[47]

> The coming of the event is what cannot and should not be prevented; it is another name for the future itself. This does not mean that it is good—good in itself—for everything and anything to arrive; it is not that one should give up trying to prevent certain things from coming to pass (without which there would be no decision, no responsibility, ethics or politics). But one should only ever oppose events that one thinks will block the future or that bring death with them: events that would put an end to the possibility of the event, to the affirmative opening to the coming of the other.[48]

At this point Hägglund's position is so much at odds with Derrida's that he simply admits it and chides Derrida for "giving in" to a bad argument precisely when Derrida should have stuck with the argument Hägglund is making, which reduces deconstruction to the description of double binds, to nothing more than a latter-day form of logical empiricism (*RA*, 231n4). To the long list of distinguished commentators who have misunderstood deconstruction, according to *Radical Atheism*, it seems we have to add Jacques Derrida himself. Derrida has nothing to teach Hägglund. So just whose radical atheism is this?

3. *L'à venir*. Derrida does not speak of *le futur*, nor even *l'avenir*, but of *l'à venir*. *L'à venir* is not a space of time near or far off in the future; it is not the future present. It is not the descriptive-factual not-yet, even an unpredictable not-yet, which is the abridged form it takes in *Radical Atheism*. *L'à venir* is not a stretch of time at all; it is the very structure of the "to-come," which is the structure of a call or claim made upon us and of a certain hope or prayer or promise *sous rature*. It does not and will never

"exist"; it insists, calls, claims, solicits. Deconstruction originates in and belongs to the order of the *viens, oui, oui*, which opens up a scene of risk, of faith and expectation, of what we hope and pray will come, of what could come, what might come, with all the might of the "might be," which means it might be a disaster. The event (*événement*) comes from the "to-come" (*à venir*), and the "to-come" comes from the *viens!*

> The event of the "Come" [*viens*] precedes and calls the event. It would be that starting from which there is [*il y a*] any event, the *venir*, the *à venir* of the event [*événement*] that cannot be thought under the given category of the event.[49]

The event takes place in a scene (time-space, *Zeitspielraum*) opened up by a call, by an invocation (*viens!*), and not the reverse. Deconstruction transpires not in a neutral descriptive space but in the sphere of the future active participle, the *ventura*, what is to come, what promises to come, what we call upon to come, which by coming calls upon us like a thief in the night. The call announces "the desire, the order, the prayer, or the demand" that opens the vocative space of deconstruction.[50] That is why I say deconstruction is structured like a prayer. Derrida has isolated the quasi-phenomenological structure of a certain elemental prayer and loosened it from the God of strong theology and confessional religion. He analyzes a circum-fessional prayer of a heart more cut than confessional theology can concede, reinscribing prayer in a desert khoral space that is outside religion even while religion cannot get outside it. That means the cut is inside religion too, striking it through, marking it with its *sans*, and these marks show up inside religious scrolls from which he tries to "extract" a certain philosophical "function."

The "come" belongs not to an empirical descriptive future but to the time of the promise, what I called in *The Prayers and Tears of Jacques Derrida* a "messianic" time, or what Derrida once called an "apocalyptic" time.[51] The "Come" has already come as a famous prayer, as the last word of the New Testament (*erkhou, veni, viens*). In saying "Come" Derrida was already citing the New Testament, but without realizing it, citationality being a structural feature of every discourse, whether you realize you are citing or not.[52] "Come" calls up what we cannot simply call the "place" but "the advent of what in the apocalyptic in general no longer lets itself be contained simply by philosophy, metaphysics, onto-eschatology." Why not?

> First of all, because "Come," opening the scene, could not become an object, a theme, a representation, or indeed a citation in the current sense, and subsumable under a category, even were it that of coming or event. . . . Nevertheless, I am trying to extract from this, at

the risk of essentially deforming it, the demonstrative function in terms of philosophical discourse.[53]

"Come" is not an object you can describe. You can no more "arraign" (*arraisonner*) "Come" before an "onto-theo-eschatology" (strong theology) than before a "logic of the event"—for example, *Radical Atheism*—"however new they may be and whatever politics they announce." "Come" is "neither a desire nor an order, neither a prayer nor a request," because all the standard-form "grammatical, linguistic, or semantic categories" that would determine "Come" are themselves always already traversed by "Come." The "Come" opens the scene in which these categories—like the distinction in *Radical Atheism* between prescriptive and descriptive—are inscribed.

"This 'Come'—I do not know what it is . . . because the question 'what is' belongs to a space . . . opened up by 'come' come from the other."[54] It does not fit into the grammatical category of a standard form prayer, imperative, or a performative; it is not a constative—let alone a descriptive!—because it opens the scene to which all such categories belong. "Come" is like a prayer—it is neither true nor false, but optative or jussive—but it is a kind of archi-prayer or quasi-prayer before any determinate prayer. Only if we pass through the given category of prayer can we pray this prayer. Still it is not an origin but derivable, or a divided origin, because "Come" comes from the other, to which it comes in response. "Come" comes second, after the first "Come" comes calling. Perhaps one might call this calling a "tonal" difference, a new tone.[55] It does not belong to a descriptive space but opens a vocative space of calling, recalling, being called upon, calling in response. But this quasi-prayerful tone is left hanging without a prayer, belonging to an "apocalypse without apocalypse, *sans vision, sans vérité, sans révélation*,"[56] as much a threat as a promise, a hope against hope, unveiling the apocalypse as such, which for Derrida means the structure of the "chance." The charged scene opened by the "Come" is not that of "good or evil" or of "truth." It is "older" than good or evil or truth and "beyond Being," not to mention being a good deal older than the descriptive and the prescriptive. It belongs to the domain of chance itself, that is, of a promise that is entirely lacking in assurance and destination, traversed throughout by the strange (il)logic of the *sans*. Indeed, that very *destinerrance*—and here is the so-called philosophy of religion I love in Derrida—is even inscribed inside the scroll of Revelation, in the last lines of the last book of the New Testament, when it says "do not seal" these words (Rev 22:10), that is, do not close this book; the future is open, quasi-transcendentally.

4. *Negative Ontological Argument.* *Différance* is a condition of experience, not a metaphysical principle. But Hägglund says that Derrida "repeatedly

argues" (no citations) that *différance* "not only applies to language or experience or any other delimited region of *being* [emphasis added]. Rather it is an *absolutely general condition*, which means there cannot even in principle *be* [emphasis added] anything that is *exempt* [emphasis added] from temporal finitude" (*RA*, 2–3), that "*being is essentially temporal (to be = to happen)*" (*RA*, 32, emphasis added). But if there is a text in which Derrida says he offers an account of absolute, essential being beyond experience, it must have been lost in the mail. The term *différance* is introduced to explain how "language, or any code, any system of referral in general is constituted 'historically' as a weave of differences."[57] What Derrida actually does "repeatedly say" is that deconstruction is an experience of the impossible, which means that *différance* is an "absolutely general condition"—of *experience*! The very "unpredictability" on which Hägglund lays all his emphasis is a feature of experience, requiring an experiential horizon of predictability. Deconstruction is not a theory of absolute being. The ultratranscendental does not mean ultratranscendent.

When Derrida warns us against the "theological prejudices" (dogmatic claims) essential to metaphysics "even when it is a theology of atheism," he is warning us against *Radical Atheism avant la lettre*.[58] Hägglund inflates *différance* into a negative ontological argument, an a priori proof of the nonexistence of God, thereby turning deconstruction into a metaphysics of becoming. Like Derrida, I have no sympathy—only Lyotardian incredulity—for Augustinian metaphysical dualism, but Hägglund is overreaching. He presents *no noncircular arguments against the God of classical metaphysics or the metaphysical idea of eternity*. He simply stipulates everything in advance by "defining" life as "essentially mortal" (*RA*, 1) and being as "essentially temporal" (*RA*, 32), from which it merely follows by definition that "desire" is the desire of perishable goods. Nothing is settled by such decisions other than to stipulate how Hägglund is using these words. To say that nothing "happens" in eternity (*RA*, 32, 45, 122) is analytically true, trivially true, since to happen is defined as to happen in time. Similarly, to say that the desire to "survive" would be ruined by "immortality," or that someone who wants to "survive" does not desire "immortality," is simply true by Hägglund's definition of the terms. It does not settle anything to define desire either as the desire of the imperishable—as does Augustine—or to define it as the desire of the perishable—as does Hägglund—and then to insist that reality abide by one's definitions. Within the framework of immortality, mere survival is of only passing worth; within the framework of survival, immortality is pure death. Those who desire immortality cannot imagine that anyone would be content with survival, and those who desire surviving cannot imagine that immortality would satisfy anyone. Each side thinks that the very terms in which desire is framed by the other destroy what desire "means." To say that "God is death" simply defines the borders of the binary dispute between Augustinian eschatology and radical atheists. Both sides are agreed about this assertion, but they interpret it differently. No one can see God and live, say the Augustinians, but they would rather see God and not live (a merely mortal life) because they think seeing God represents a higher life. Radical atheists would rather live a mortal life and not die any sooner than need be because they think seeing God in another life is an illusion and no life at all. But such completely circular arguments are the hallmark of metaphysics. They accomplish nothing more than to successfully immunize each side against the other, each side treating the other side as a nihilism that denies what is real.

Derrida certainly never claimed, as does Hägglund, that there is an a priori argument against the existence of the God of metaphysics. While Derrida has no faith in such a God, he says that *différance* has "no lever," has "nothing to say," on anything that transcends experience—like saying there is absolutely no such thing.[59] Hägglund, in contrast, agrees with Anselm and Descartes that the existence of God can be settled on a priori grounds, albeit negatively. He simply uses *différance* to stipulate that life is mortal and that being is spatiotemporal, but he offers no noncircular argument that there is no life or being outside space and time. His objection to eternity is that it does not abide by the conditions of space and time. But that is not an objection to eternity; it is the definition of eternity.

Hägglund creates some confusion on this point because occasionally he speaks not of being in general but of being that can be "cognized and experienced . . . thought and desired" (*RA*, 10, 19, 29). If so, then radical atheism is weaker than traditional atheism, not more radical. For classical atheism maintains that God does not exist, regardless of what we desire, whereas radical atheism is defined by our desire, almost as if, by not desiring it, it will go away. But the real does not depend on our desire. Furthermore, such a view succumbs to the intractable difficulty of *dénégation*, this time in terms of desire: *Comment ne pas désirer*? How not to desire God, how to not desire God, how to desire not-God without ending up desiring God after all, without being in denial? To deny we desire God would require that we be sure that we are not by some trick of the unconscious desiring God all the more, that desire be transparent to itself, which, as Hägglund points out, Derrida rejects (*RA*, 57). Hägglund thinks our desire of the imperishable dissimulates a desire of the perishable. Augustine thinks that our desire of perishable things dissimulates a desire of the imperishable. Both claims require an undissimulated understanding of desire, immune to self-deception. The positions are perfectly symmetric and caught in an irresoluble metaphysical antinomy, just as Kant predicts. Derrida avoids every such interminable argument over the "final word." The logic of radical atheism requires stable and transparent concepts of desire, God, and *la religion*, undisturbed by other voices, unhaunted by specters, everything from which Derrida dissociates himself when he says he only "rightly passes for" an atheist and that the multiplicity of voices within him give him no peace.[60] For Derrida, desire is desire when it is fired by the very thing that makes it impossible—not knowing what we desire. We begin, we desire, *par l'impossible*.

In short, Hägglund's stated aim is to "fortify" Derrida's resistance to religion—in the name of autoimmunity! He mines the works of Derrida for a certain logic that supports his own argument, sweeping aside a great deal of careful work on deconstruction that Derrida himself valued as a new way of thinking about ethics and religion. He uses Derrida where he can, corrects Derrida when he cannot, and ignores what he does not need. However one might judge that strategy, at least it makes clear that when push comes to shove this is not a book about Derrida but about Hägglund's independent orchestration of the logic of autoimmunity in the name of his own radical atheism, which is not to be confused with the work of Jacques Derrida.

The Point of View of My Work as an Author

When I wrote *The Prayers and Tears of Jacques Derrida*, I steered around the two prevailing ways to think about Derrida and religion. I loved Mark Taylor's impious deconstruction of classical theology in *Erring*,[61] but I thought Taylor failed to remain on the slash of his "a/theology" and made it look like deconstruction dances gaily on the grave of the dead God, is not responsible to anything, and has no faith.[62] I also loved the pious path of negative theology that followed Derrida wherever he went, which Derrida too admired—its "detours, locutions and syntax"[63]—but I emphasized with him that deconstruction is not negative theology, not even the most negative of negative theologies, which turns on an absolute and silent center.[64] I had made the same point in 1978: When Heidegger uses Meister Eckhart's word *Gelassenheit*, Heidegger is talking about the historico-linguistic happening of *Ereignis*, whereas Eckhart has in mind the wordless, timeless unity of the soul with God.[65] That applies a fortiori to *différance*. Both Heidegger and Derrida repeat certain structures found in negative theology, but both deploy them in order to think radically temporal and mundane operations. So I proposed a third path, both pious and impious, laughing through my tears: neither the death of God nor Christian apophaticism, but the circumfessional path inspired by the impudent figure of an atheistic Jewish Augustine. Deconstruction is structured like a prayer, belongs to the vocative and invocative space and time of prayer, an odd archi-prayer (*viens!*). Deconstruction is praying for the impossible, with a prayer without (*sans*) a prayer, singularly lost and adrift, *destiner-rant*. Unlike Taylor's a/theology, this is structured like a *religion*, and unlike negative theology is only *structured* like a religion, a religion without the God of classical religion, a khoral or an-khoral religion without religion, a post-theistic theology.

Derrida famously said that the "least bad" definition of deconstruction is the "experience of the impossible,"[66] which I used as a way to read what he said about this religion *without* religion. I was not speaking about a being called God, but about what is being called (what's happening) in the "name of God." Like Žižek I agree the therapy is over when you see there is no big Other. The possibility of the impossible is not about a Big Being coming to save us by doing the impossible things that we could not possibly do—this central misunderstanding informs everything Hägglund says about my work (*RA*, 120)—it is about responsibility. Once you "have" a Big Being like that, once you "know" it, you have undermined the experiential structure (the possible/impossible). That is why, like Derrida, I deny that the impossible *is* God, which would collapse the possibility of the impossible into something proper and identifiable. As Derrida said in his commentary on *The Prayers and Tears of Jacques Derrida*:

> If there is a transparent translatability [between "God" and "the impossible"] "the faith" is safe, that is, it becomes a non-faith. At that point, it becomes possible to name [the impossible] . . . because there is some*one* whom you can name and call because you know who it is that you are calling. . . . If I were sure that it was possible for me to replace "the impossible" by "God," then everything would become possible. Faith would become possible, and when faith becomes simply possible, it is not faith anymore.[67]

When Derrida points out the two sources of religion as faith and the desire to keep safe, he proposes an auto-deconstructive formula that brews a religion *without* religion—because faith cannot be what he calls faith if it desires to be safe. Religion without religion is unprotected religion, faith without safety, a mad risk of everything on the impossible. But in classical metaphysical theology God is precisely the possibility of the impossible in a straightforward sense, for whom nothing is impossible (Marion's "impossibility of impossibility"). Classical omnipotence effectively ruins the deconstructive idea of "*the* impossible" and also of Derrida's "God"—which is why I criticize Peter Damian's God who can change past time (*Weakness of. God*, chap. 9). I argue that "God" in Derrida, like justice, can only be a weak force (*force faible*), a dream.[68] But, as Hent de Vries has shown, this is an "exemplary" dream. The becoming possible of the impossible in Derrida is not the name of an Über-being but of an event that goes to the heart of the structure of experience. This structure intensifies the possible to the point of the impossible, constituting the desire, passion, existence, and temporality that are at work *in* religion, *as* a certain religion that deconstruction exposes in all its unsafe, unprotected anarchic energy, with all the "might" of the "might be," not the might of omnipotence. The axiomatics of deconstruction are organized around a poetics of the impossible, of the "becoming possible of the impossible."

I am not arguing that there is a being called "God" somewhere who does or mysteriously declines to do impossible things. Nor do I argue or think that God is the Being of beings, or a hyper-Being beyond Being in the tradition of mystical theology, the "God without Being" of Jean-Luc Marion, a point I have been making ever since I cautioned about confusing *Ereignis* with God.[69] Nor do I, God forbid, attribute any such views to Jacques Derrida, nor, thank God, did Derrida think I was doing any such thing.[70] I am not theologizing deconstruction but deconstructing theology, Christian theology, causing a scandal to the pious and a stumbling block to the theologians, reimagining, reinventing "God," which is why my radical theology is considered radical atheism and a "death of God" by my evangelical friends. In the place of what I call "strong theology," I offer a certain "poetics" of the human condition, not a theo-logic but a "theo-poetics," just as Derrida stresses the necessity of his "grafts of poetry upon philosophy, which are anything but confused."[71] I compare religious beliefs and practices with Wittgenstein's "forms of life," Heideggerian modes of "being-in-the-world," Merleau-Ponty's ways of "singing the world," transpiring on what Deleuze (and Laruelle) would call the "plane of immanence." They have to do with the passion, the intensity, the temporality, and, yes, the mortality of the human condition. Cosmic mercilessness itself (Quentin Meillassoux and Ray Brassier owe a footnote to Pascal) only intensifies the religious condition, just as mortality intensifies the preciousness of life, which is the starting point of my own *Against Ethics*[72] and *Radical Hermeneutics*, where I argued that we make no gains by concealing the "difficulty of life."

In this spirit, Derrida has been my co-conspirator, a conspiracy occurring in two stages.

In the first stage—*The Prayers and Tears of Jacques Derrida*—I mingled the gorgeous prayers and tears of Augustine's *Confessions* with those of a certain "little black and Arab Jew," producing an atheistic Jewish Augustine, who surprises us by saying he has been praying all his life, kissing his

prayer shawl every night, and that nobody, not even his mother or Geoffrey Bennington, knows about his religion, as a result of which, he says, he
has been "read less and less well over almost twenty years."[73] He prays to
an unknown, even nonexistent God, practices an ironic irreligious religion
growing out of rightly passing for an atheist.[74] The religious pulse vibrates
precisely in the "rightly passing for"—in the passion of undecidability—
in the destabilization of both theism and atheism, launching the work of
inventing new parergonal, paratheological post-theistic categories, where
not believing in God does not disqualify the religion but constitutes it.[75]
Deconstruction, like religion, is "brewed from a devilish mix of 'faith and
atheism,' 'radical doubt and faith.'"[76] Everything interesting about deconstruction and religion lies in the way it opens the structure of experience
by rendering the binary war between theism and atheism obsolete.

From the point of view of the local rabbi or pastor, Derrida is an atheist,
and that atheism has always been irreducibly important to me. Without his
atheism, he and I would be lost. I would lose my faith in a religion without
religion. If Derrida had at some time been "converted" like Augustine, returned to the religion of his mother, *The Prayers and Tears of Jacques Derrida*
would have been ruined. Without this atheism we would have to make do
without the without and we would be immured within the walls of religion,
unable to repeat the form of life that religion is, the multiple forms that the
several religious traditions take, without being drawn into their doctrines
and the dogmas, unable to break open their closed confessional circles, unable to put them at risk as so many precarious ways to "do the truth" (Augustine).[77] Derrida's atheism reopens the books of religion, making texts like the
Scriptures and Augustine's *Confessions* available for reading, no longer under
either secular censure or ecclesiastical protection (two alternative forms of
excommunication, immunization and dogma). Like Derrida, I feel around
for the cluster of events that stir within a text like the *Confessions*, repeating
religion without its dualist two-worlds transcendence-operators—body and
soul, time and eternity, this world and the next, etc.—feeling for the pulse or
rhythm of the immanence of life, for the life of immanence, for life/death.[78]

I proposed that the "religion without religion" that in *The Gift of Death*
Derrida attributed to others is performed in the flesh, scarred on the body,
inscribed in the texts of Jacques Derrida himself. *Prayers and Tears* con-
structs the categories and the images, the tropes and the strategies, of such
an ir/religion. I do not assimilate Derrida to Augustine, or conversely, but
I read religious texts as a meditation on our mortal lives, as a certain poetics of the human condition. When I examined the baffling commentary
Hägglund made on my work in *Radical Atheism*, I realized that he had
confused me with an orthodox two-worlds Augustinian who thinks that

a hyperbeing called God can do impossible things while we humans, alas, cannot. That is, as Hägglund says of me in an excellent phrase, the matrix of a systematic misreading of everything I say (*RA*, 120). Like Derrida, I think we have "never loved anything but the impossible,"[79] but that has nothing to do with positing the existence of a higher agent who does things impossible for human beings.

The second stage is *The Weakness of God: A Theology of the Event.*[80] That is a book not about Jacques Derrida but about God, about the "event" that stirs within the name of God, inspired by Derrida's remarks on a coming God who would lack sovereignty.[81] The argument that this book makes against divine omnipotence can be extended analogously against any other divine name, including "goodness," which is the one to which Hägglund next turns in response to my complaints.[82] If I had set out from the point of view of "goodness," I could have named my book *The Radical Evil of God*, meaning the structural possibility of evil inscribed in the name of God (something Boehme and Schelling were pondering on a metaphysical level).[83] I singled out "weakness" because I am interested in the political critique of sovereignty and because the "weakness" of God has a literally crucial purchase in the Christian tradition, in the crucified body of Jesus, in what Johann Baptist Metz calls the "dangerous memory of suffering."[84]

In this book I spoke with undisguised irony of a "weak theology"—like a "minor literature" in the Deleuzian sense, where mystics and heretics snipe at the heels of the majority voices. But I did so with two hands, with a right hand writing a genuine but immanent theology, and with a left-handed Socratic irony, Derridean impishness, and Kierkegaardian humor. I opposed it to Kierkegaard's riff on a theology all powdered and rouged sitting in the window waiting for a Hegelian to stroll by. In *Radical Atheism*, Hägglund missed the irony and misread *The Prayers and Tears of Jacques Derrida* as if I were staking out an orthodox theological position, while not reading *The Weakness of God* at all.[85] Had he done so he would have found a creation story without omnipotence and a Lazarus read in terms of "living on," *survive* (to which *Radical Atheism* is dedicated). I read the Resurrection against itself, took the moral of the narrative to be "more life," life-death, and Jesus to be someone who talks the sisters of Lazarus through their grief and helps them find a way of "living on," bringing them *salut* as salutation not as eternal salvation, consoling Mary and Martha who say they are not interested in eternal life for their brother but more time (see *RA*, 225n39).

Having now reorganized his argument around the divine name of goodness, Hägglund continues to assimilate me to some form of classical transcendence.[86] After all, if Caputo is speaking about "religion"—*la religion!* always in the singular—then he must be a two-worlds Augustinian, which is what "religion" "essentially" "is" in *Radical Atheism*. Conceding now that I bid adieu to divine omnipotence, he turns me into an apologist of the "pure good." So my God is "good" but too weak to do any good. I repeat I am not saying that God is an innocent but weak being, or a good being who means well even if his means are limited. I am not making ontic, ontological, or me-ontological claims about a hyperbeing or hyperperson called God. I take leave of the order of presence, of being and Beings, weak or strong, good or bad, transcendent or immanent, providential or blind, in favor of the *event* of *peut-être*. I am not debating about a being and which predicates the being takes (omnipotence, omniscience, etc.) but about an im/probable, im/possible promise/threat, about the experience of the impossible, for which the name of God is one of our best and favorite names, which is my view and the express view of Jacques Derrida.[87]

My question is, What is happening in the enormous provocation of that name, what is getting itself said and done there, in the middle voice? Taking up Derrida's suggestive notion of a weak force, of an event without sovereignty, I say this event lays claim to us unconditionally but without force, soliciting us, addressing us, haunting us, like a specter. That does not make the event a pure good but a pure risk, a risky injunction, because such solicitations may lead us into the worst evils, as the history of "God" testifies. The event is no more "pure good" than "pure evil," no more "strong" than "weak," because it is nothing entitative or ontological, is neither a being nor an agent, neither a substance nor a subject, neither finite nor infinite, does not subsist and does not "do" things (or fail to do them) for which it could be praised or blamed. As I argue in *The Insistence of God*, God does not exist; God insists.[88] So no matter which of the divine names Hägglund settles on, I have, in fact, the same view. If "omniscience," I will defend the cause of the "blindness of God," or if "necessity," the contingency of God. In fact, my precise proposal is that the event harbored in the name of God is the *peut-être*, "perhaps," not the contingency of God but the name of God harboring the force of contingency, not the might of omnipotence but the subjunctive "might" of might-be. As there is an infinity of divine names, this debate could go for some time!

As opposed to Hägglund, *The Weakness of God* was an argument that the "good, good" of Genesis is to be glossed as "perhaps, let's hope so." The pure good is, at best, a pure risk. In my line of work I am frequently glossing scriptural texts where the notion of the pure good is in play, which I, however, repeat and redescribe as pure risk (*RA*, 120–21; 223–24n21). In my unprotected religion I recklessly expose myself to texts Hägglund seeks to quarantine (the Scriptures), which are dreaming of paradise and the Kingdom of God. But my repetition and redescription of them is obvious, as when I title a chapter "The Beautiful *Risk* of Creation," where I redescribe the benevolence of God in strong theology as the chance for the good that is menaced by evil not only on all sides but even from within. I frame the story of creation within a Talmudic gloss that serves as the epigraph of the chapter (epigraphs are important in deconstruction). God attempted and failed to make the world twenty-six times (so much for omnipotence). But on the next attempt he succeeded and then exclaimed not "good, good," as in Genesis, but "let's hope it works," which signifies, the rabbi says, that "history is branded with the mark of radical uncertainty" (*WG*, 55). God could not foresee what was coming, had no power over it, and realized that everything was at the mercy of chance, so God was keeping the divine fingers crossed. Hägglund reads my citation of the literal words of Genesis[89]—good, good, very good—and then ignores my gloss, my point—which is the "perhaps," *peut-être*.[90] God rolled the dice and took a chance on the good—and by the sixth chapter of Genesis God regrets (not a familiar divine name) the mess he has created and wipes the world out with a flood and starts all over again. Everything in this chapter, and in *The Weakness of God* as a whole, presupposes the structural inhabitation of the good by its constitutive exposure to evil, and the structural chance for good in the most risky situations.[91] Creation launches the promise/threat, the beautiful risk, which landed straightaway in Cain's murder of Abel. I am talking about the chance of an event, not the adventures of a superhero named God.[92]

Radical or structural evil, atheism, or blindness are not objections to my radical theology but constitutive elements within it. That is why, were I ever to edit an anthology of readings in radical or weak theology, I would include Hägglund's own account of "Circumfession," which is perhaps polemically the best response to his criticisms. To conclude that in deconstruction the case for atheism is a case against religion is to absolutize the binarity of theism and atheism and to miss the point of deconstruction, where atheism about the God of theism is not the end of religion but the beginning of a new and post-theistic one. The prayers and tears of this religion offer no protection, keep no one safe, but remind the faithful that faith is structured from within by unfaith. There are stretches of *Radical Atheism* that I admire and with which I agree, although I think its logocentric and self-certain presentation is contrary to the style, the point, the stylus tip of deconstruction, which cannot be isolated from its substance. For any possible "logic" in deconstruction is but one of its styles—it can be called a logic, Derrida says, "up to a certain point"[93]—which is written more *in* fear and trembling than as an attempt to inspire fear and trembling in everyone else.

Like Derrida, and unlike Hägglund, I do not trust any discourse not "contaminated with negative theology;"[94] like Derrida, and unlike

Hägglund, I heed the non-ousiological voices in mystical theology, voices of errancy, of being lost.[95] If strong theology is a handbook for being saved, weak theology is a circum-fession of being lost—"without salvation, resurrection or redemption—neither for oneself nor for the other"[96]—of something salutary without salvation. I am not seeking to be saved by God, but to save God, to save the name of God, *sauf le nom*, "God, for example," praying more for God than to God, praying for the world in a religion without religion. In deconstruction, we are saved from being saved, just as being lost is the only way to start searching. The unavoidability of being lost, the impossibility of being saved, is the condition of possibility of an aporetic soteriology, which meditates the mercilessness and mortality of our condition. If prayer is a wounded word, as Jean-Louis Chrétien argues, there is no more radically wounded word than the prayers and tears of one for whom the very possibility of prayer is lodged in its impossibility.[97]

The atheism of Jacques Derrida is a precious elixir and an irreducible lemma in the dilemma of a religion without religion, without otherworldly transcendence and supernatural dogma. The mortality of our lives clears our head of ethereal otherworldly bodies, exposing the fleshly bodies of an immanent religion, the religiousness of our mortal flesh, of which the crucified flesh of Jesus is emblematic in Christian life. One would be hard put to find a more ardent and profoundly religious dialogue than the haunting conversation between Derrida and Cixous, two Jewish Algerian atheists, musing over their mortality (more poignant than ever after Derrida's death), started over forty years ago when he commented on the manuscript of her first book titled nothing less than *Le Prénom de Dieu*. Theirs is a meditation on faith inhabited by unfaith, on life inhabited by death, a faith in life made more intense by death and unfaith, he believing, on his side, that in the end we die too soon, while she, on her side, had more faith in life. Would that he might believe her, where that subjunctive might (*puissé je*) is all the "might" (*pouvoir*) available, the might of the powerless power of might-be, the being of may-being, the possibility of the impossible:

> As for me, I keep forever reminding her each time, on my side, that we die in the end, too quickly. And I always have to begin again.
>
> For she "because she loves to live" does not believe me. She, on her side, knows well that one dies in the end, too quickly; she knows it and writes about it better than anyone, she has the knowledge of it but she believes none of it. . . .
>
> And I say to myself, on my side: "Would that I might [*puissé-je*] believe her, I wish I might [*puisse*], yes, I wish I might believe her. . . ."[98]

7

Forget Rationality—Is There Religious Truth?

That we are discussing religion in terms of rationality and irrationality means that we are already sailing in modernist waters and have agreed to the terms set for the discussion by modernity. Before modernity we would have distinguished those who love and serve God (modernity's "theists") from the fool who says in his heart, there is no God (modernity's "atheists"). Such a denial was deemed unwise in the extreme, because it cuts us off from God, who is love and truth, and it is excessively foolish to deprive oneself of love and truth. The love of truth is the mark of wisdom, which means, Augustine said, that the only true philosopher is one who loves God. Before modernity we would have distinguished wisdom and foolishness, *sophia* or *sapientia* and its lack, not rationality and irrationality. To be sure, before modernity, there was a robust idea of "reason" (*logos, ratio*). Indeed Aristotle had defined humans as rational animals, but reason was integrated into a fuller, richer, deeper conception of human life which bore the name of wisdom, whose ends reason served.

That is why charging medieval "Scholasticism" with excessive "rationalism" is a bad rap. That is the mark of early modernist Scholasticism, but it has nothing to do with Augustine or Bonaventure or Aquinas. They put *ratio* in the service of explaining their deepest and most profound orientation as human beings, their Christian faith, in order to make their life intelligible to themselves (*fides quaerens intellectum*). Their theological works, like those of medieval Jewish and Islamic theologians, were not "systems" because they made no pretense to being comprehensive. Their works were orderly but reverent reflections on God, whose first, last, and constant mark was incomprehensibility. If you comprehend it, Augustine said, it is not God, who is love itself and truth itself and far beyond our grasp. Their work as theologians was a part of their life of prayer and did not fit what Heidegger, using a term found in Kant, called the "onto-theo-logical." Aquinas called his five proofs "ways" (*viae*) out of respect for the incomprehensibility of God, which did not fit inside what modernity meant by a "rational" argument. *Ratio* itself for Aquinas was the lowest rung in the analogical order of intelligence, the weakest form of intellectual life (*debilitas intellectus*), greatly surpassed by angelic *intellectus*, both of which are themselves participations in the subsistent *intellectus* of God.[1] Reason does not stand in judgment over God. Reason is a finite participation in the life of God. Even the notorious "ontological argument" of Saint An-selm was neither "ontological"—the word was coined only in modernity—nor an "argument" in the modern sense, as Barth, von Balthasar, and Marion have all shown. The argument belongs to a prayer that Anselm di-rects to God, much like Augustine's *Confessions*, whose literary genre, as we will have occasion to note below, is not an "autobiography" but a prayer.

The Eclipse of Truth in Modernity

But in modernity "reason" broke loose from its place in life as a whole and in the order of being and took on a life of its own, an ultimately purely formal and lifeless life, independent of wisdom, truth, love, and God, over all of which it purported to stand in judgment. From the medieval point of view, that was excessively unwise. What the moderns call "reason" is from a medieval point of view foolishness—although it was not in medi-eval terms "mad" because, as Foucault has reminded us, the medievals re-spected the mad as friends of God. They thought that the mad were "touched" by God, that the voices they heard were not subjective noises inside their head but the words of angels whispering in their ears, which is why they did not segregate or institutionalize them. Modernity may well be defined by the eclipse of truth and the invention of the category of "Rationality"—now it is best to capitalize it, because it has grown into a hegemonic force of its own—which famously defined itself against what it excluded as "irrational," among which it included both the mad and "reli-gion." "Religion" was another category invented by modernity—previously there were Christians, Jews, and Muslims, or believers and infidels, but not "religions," which is a category on the maps drawn up by rationalism and colonialism. Indeed modernity is perhaps best defined not by the inven-tion of any one of these categories, not even of Reason itself, but by its invention of the category of the "category," the various chambers within which modernity immured science, ethics, politics, art, and religion.

That makes Kant the preeminent philosopher of the light of the Enlightenment. Philosophy does not do first order creative work in Kant. It does critical work. It stakes out the borders of the various creative work others do—in science, ethics, and art—and then polices them. Philosophy is more like a referee than a player on the field. It is not first order scientific knowledge but a science of science, knowledge of knowledge. Kant's reason is purely formal, purely universalistic. Reason does not have content; it is a system of formal universality. What makes science rational is not its insight into the truth but its power of a priori synthesis; what make ethics ethical is not the good it does or the good it seeks, but its formal universalizability; what makes art artistic is not the beauty of our life but our ability to appreciate its formal perfection. What the medievals called the true, the good, and the beautiful, the very stuff of being, its transcendental properties, is hollowed out by what Kant called Reason. Pure reason is pure form, pure formalism, pure lifelessness, the dissipation of being, the dehydration of the good, the desiccation of the beautiful, and the eclipse of truth.

One of the most remarkable things about Kant is how much focused he is on the formality of knowledge and how little focused he is on truth as a content. He does not define Reason as a faculty of being or truth but as a faculty of principles, of a priori synthesis. If anything, his interest lay in making sure that "knowledge" is denied access to the true world—a move that would have left everyone from Plato to his own modernist predecessors dumbfounded—in order to make room for ethics. That might suggest that ethics has access to the true world. Not quite. Ethics is blind; it answers a command it hears but cannot see. Ethics knows nothing at all. It does not do or make contact with the good. The only thing we can call good, he says, is a good will, a will whose maxims are formally universalizable. Were a will to be moved by what is substantively good, well, that would not be a good will. We do not tell the truth because it is good or God-like, but because it is a formally universalizable duty. Then perhaps art makes contact with the beauty of being? Not so, the paradigm work of art for him is an Arabesque, in whose formal properties we take a properly formal subjective delight but in whose content we remain disinterested. Knowledge does not know the true world; ethics does not do the good; art does not make contact with being's glow. But have we rushed to judgment? We have not mentioned religion. It is even worse with religion, which is nothing more than a chapel built on land owned by ethics. We are free to regard the categorical imperative as the voice of God, but no matter whose voice we might believe it to be, our duty is our duty. That reduces religion to ethics, which is itself reduced to formally universalizable maxims, and excises everything else in religion as superstition. To call this a ham-fisted and parsimonious analysis would be too generous.

In ancient Greece or the Middle Ages that would have been regarded as foolishness. Not irrational, but unwise, foolish. The ancients might have admitted the dexterity of Kant's reasoning, the cleverness of the architectonic, but they would have been appalled by the foolishness and lack of wisdom in the outcome: a philosopher whose intent is to deny us access to the true, the good, and the beautiful, and whose formal function is to police the borders lest anyone seek in the cover of night to sneak across the lines and make contact with their loved ones on the other side. The fool says in his heart, there is only Pure Reason. Or as Shakespeare's Puck says, Lord, what fools these modern rationalists be! Nowadays we would recommend a good psychiatrist, someone who would listen very patiently to the man. He reports the following symptoms. He is convinced he lives in a world of appearances; he marches to a drum beat by an unknown drummer, and he takes every precaution lest he actually love the things he does for fear it would distract him from his duties. The doctor would surely start by asking Kant about his childhood. You were attached to your mother, you say, but your father was very strict. Very interesting; please go on.

To be sure, by the very terms of deconstruction, systems are incapable of closing up entirely, try as they might. They are always marked by crevices, openings, ruptures that allow for escape and for futures that the systems do not foresee or desire. In the case of Kant, such an opening is found in the analysis of the sublime, the representation of the unrepresentable, toward which we experience the ambiguous feeling of a sympathetic antipathy. This famously provided Lyotard with an opening to postmodernism. Lyotard theorized the postmodern as a repetition of the modern, which in Lyotard's account even makes the modern possible, since the "modern" (from the adverb *modo*, meaning what exists now, the latest thing) is both the subject and the constant effect of the suspicion incurred by what is currently present (*modo*). Far be it from me to renounce this opening or to denounce the sublime.

I would only say that *Kant's* sublime, like the third *Critique* as a whole, is the resolution of a problem of Kant's own devising, an attempt to recover from a self-inflicted wound. His sublime proceeds from multiple presuppositions—his representationalism; his preoccupation with the interplay of "faculties"; and the metaphysical dualism between sensible appearances and supersensible things in themselves—all obstacles that Kant has put in his own way in the first place, from which the sublime offers relief. Furthermore, Kant's analysis of the sublime is aimed at assuring the superiority of the supersensible faculty of reason to the imagination and to sensible nature. Human subjectivity is only temporarily and provisionally displaced (as sensibility) by the sublime, but soon recovers its equilibrium (as reason)—whereas for Lyotard the sublime signals the irremediable displacement of the "language games," which is how he has redescribed (repeated) Kant's "faculties."[2] Kant's sublime issues in Romantic longing for the infinite; Lyotard's sublime issues in the infinite affirmation of the new without nostalgia. Kant's analysis is ultimately the issue of what Heidegger called Kant's reduction of the "thing," the human experience of the world in which we live, to the perceptual experience of spatiotemporal-causal objects, the model of which is the scientific object.[3] This analysis collapses when contrasted with far more adequate accounts found in the phenomenological tradition, like being-in-the-world (Heidegger) and incarnation (Merleau-Ponty), and in particular, from my point of view, with the experience of the event. I have not the slightest intention to deny the phenomenon of the sublime, but I do deny the terms in which it is cast by Kant, and I would propose it be recast in terms of the experience of *the* impossible, the possibility of *the* impossible, which has been paradigmatically set forth by Derrida.[4]

Descartes is another good example of what happens to wisdom, God, and truth in modernity. Descartes raises the question of truth and even invokes the ancient link between God and truth, but he does so in terms of the "criterion" of truth. He does not exactly say that God is truth but something less than that, that God is veracious, a truth-teller. As the author of our nature, the veracity of God supplies a warranty for a good product, which we can count on in sorting out statements about ideas that are clear to us from dubious ideas. It would not take long for God to become the subject of one of those statements whose truth value would be on the line. God would have to make an appearance before the court of Reason, which would determine whether belief in God is "warranted," or whether it has "sufficient reason," which meant it would not be long until it was concluded that it was not. The church's attitude toward Galileo and Descartes was reactionary and repressive, but the church was not stupid. It always had a good nose for trouble when it came to its own authority.

From Modern to Postmodern

Among the categories invented in modernity the distinction between public and private enjoys a certain pride of place. This distinction was created above all to solve the problem that religion has always brought with it since the invention of biblical monotheism—strife within religion (the persecution of heretics, the suppression of inquiry) and the strife between religions (religious wars). The solution modernity came up with was to segregate religion from the public order. The public order is a formal, neutral, rational matrix within which various forms of private life can be freely practiced. Religion is reduced to one of our "choices," as Charles Taylor says. By institutionalizing this distinction, modernity reached a political solution to a political problem, religious strife, but not a philosophical one, unless you think philosophy is the love of boxes, the art of depositing things in their proper box. It had decided to suspend the philosophical question, which is the question of religious truth. In premodern times, we say God is truth. In modernity we separate religion from truth and redescribe it as a protected right. It is the right of private individuals to believe anything that can nest inside their heads provided they do not try to force others to believe it or otherwise do violence to people who do not share their beliefs. In modernity, religion is a matter of private conscience; it is formally a protected right even if it is materially a bit mad.

To be sure, modernity had very "good reasons" (as opposed to "Pure Reason") for embarking on such a course. We are all in the debt of the Enlightenment for freeing us from the hegemony of church, king, and superstition, and for putting in their place the rule of civil rights, freedom of religion, and free scientific inquiry. It would be a really foolish thing to go back on that. The separation of church and state is the continuing legacy of the Enlightenment that few people in the NATO world would disavow, although the rising tide of Christian Nationalism makes me wonder about that. We can only be grateful to the Enlightenment for trying to contain the damage done by the idea of the "one true religion," which is the legacy of monotheism and long antedates modernity. But in separating church and state, the Enlightenment was also separating religion and truth, and therein lies the problem that interests me. It behaves like a court that refuses to hear a case. It declines to rule on whether a given religious belief is true or not (the philosophical question) and is content with the political resolution. When the philosophers themselves turn to religion, they duck the question of truth and take up instead the question of "rationality." That is, they debate the formal question and they duck the material one. They do not debate religious truth, the truth of religion, what I will shortly call the "event" that takes place in religion, but religious "beliefs" or propositions and whether they are "justified." They ask whether there is some frame of reference within which one would be (privately) "warranted" in holding such views even if one does not expect others to share them.

That explains the simmering conflict that shows no line of easing off between religious and nonreligious people. Privately, religious people in the monotheistic traditions think that their religion is *true*, even that it is *the* one true religion, that it is the eternal truth revealed to them by God, which authorizes them, when push comes to shove, to follow the authority of God not the state, whose powers are finite, temporal, and fallible. That itself is dangerous, but not unambiguously good or bad. It could lead either to people who bomb abortion clinics or to Martin Luther King, both of whom refused to concede that the state is God or has the last word. Privately, non-religious people view religious people with disdain; religious heads, they think, are filled with primitive superstition and nonsense, and they repre-sent a menace to science and the civic freedoms we are meant to enjoy in a democracy. It does not take much for the lid modernity has put on this pressure cooker to explode. There are of course cooler heads in all these camps who promote dialogue between the religious and the secular, and interfaith dialogue among the different religions, but, after pointing out various things on which they can all agree, they have finally to agree to disagree and let the political solution stand. The problem lies not in sepa-rating church and state, which I endorse, but in separating religion and truth. But the problem with uniting religion and truth is even greater. The whole idea of *the* true religion is the source of all the conflict within and among religions and getting the state involved in deciding which religion is true, in the "establishment" of religion, makes a bad situation incompa-rably worse.

That is the state of the question of religion in modernity, and it is as far as modernity can get us. The resources of modernity in this regard are ex-hausted. It has said everything it has to say, has done all the good it is going to do. My own view is that the time has come to thank the Enlight-enment for its services and move on. We need what Derrida calls a "new Enlightenment" or an "Enlightenment to come,"[5] by which he means not a jettisoning but a continuation of the old one and its work of emancipa-tion but by another means, one that is more critical of what the Enlight-enment called critique, and more enlightened about what the Enlightenment calls the light of reason. We need a more reasonable idea of reason, a less ham-fisted idea of religion, and a more amiable and ambient notion of truth, one that allows the nose of "truth" under the tent of religion. We need to defend the idea of religious truth or the truth of religion but, in the spirit of the old Enlightenment, without implicating ourselves in the mistaken idea of *the* true religion or undoing the separation of church and state, which protects us from that mistake. The concept of *the* true reli-gion is a fundamental conceptual mistake about both religion and truth.

So my idea is not simply to do again what the Enlightenment already has done effectively enough, which is to find a way to protect the rest of us from people who think that they are the privileged recipients of an Absolute Truth delivered from on high. The old Enlightenment can handle that. I want to argue against an underlying mistaken view of what true religion or religious truth is, which implies a fundamental mistake about both religion and truth embedded in the old Enlightenment. In other words we need to take up the question of religion and truth in radical and postmodern terms, where the powerful categorical walls erected in modernity are broken down, where "Reason" is taken down a peg or two and reinserted within a larger framework. In a general way, postmodernity must always find ways to "communicate" with premodernity, because they both elude the overgrowth of "categorial" thinking that marks modernity, but it must do so without becoming antimodern. Postmodernity must, on the one hand, pass through modernity but come out on the other end, while not, on the other hand, suffering a relapse into the premodern. It must be willing to learn something from premodernity without falling into nostalgia, and it must learn from modernity without embracing rationalism.

I hasten to add that the depiction I provide in terms of premodern, modern, and postmodern is a strictly heuristic device. It is a fiction that as a philosopher I reject but as an author I embrace, a ladder meant to be discarded later. If my critique of modernity lies in the critique of erecting strict and rigorous borders, then I certainly know better than to defend a rigid periodization such as this. That is why every significant "postmodern" philosopher refuses the term, and even Lyotard, who employed the term and provided the standard theory of it, tried to scramble the distinction and to say that the postmodern (as the production of the new) precedes the modern (the *modo*, the latest, the newest) and makes it possible. My use of it here is strictly for expository and economic purposes.

Hegel's Critique of the Enlightenment

In my view, modernity is marked by displacing truth as a focal concern and replacing it with Rationality. Truth is a substantive issue whereas rationality is a formal one. The truth of a work of art is not its formal perfection but the insight it gives us about our life. The truth of an ethical counsel is not its formal universalizability but its advice about living the good life. The truth of religious beliefs and practices is not reducible to ethics, much less to a formal right to practice religion; it is found in the insight it provides about the weal and woe of being human, about birth and death, joy and sorrow, faith and despair.

It is to Hegel's everlasting credit that he rejected the categorial thinking of modernity and made a profound critique of it from which modernity never recovered.[6] It was Hegel who saw that in modernity "truth" is
displaced by what the moderns were calling "reason" and who launched a
critique of Enlightenment Reason. That this would finally issue in postmodernity was hardly his intention! Hegel is the first great philosopher of
truth after premodernity, who returned truth to a place of honor. Hegel
criticized the Enlightenment for privileging a one-sided, lifeless, purely formal, ahistorical, and abstract *Verstand*, which he proposed needed to be
integrated into a full-bodied, concrete, historical, and substantial life of the
Spirit (*Geist*) and what he was calling reason (*Vernunft*). If in the view I
take we have a great deal more to learn about religion from Hegel than
from Kant, and from premodernity than from modernity, that is because
in both cases religion is treated as a substantive truth, not merely a formal
right or private choice. In short, premodernity and postmodernity communicate with each other on the question of religion because, for both,
religion is an event of truth, not merely a protected right or a mask worn
by ethics.

Hegel thought that the part of religion in which the rationalist philosophers were interested was its least interesting part, while they treated the
most interesting part of all as off limits, lying across the borders of pure
reason on the side of "revelation." The philosophers left out the substance
of Christianity, its *Sache*, its substantial truth. For it is precisely in the *content* of revelation, that the truth is revealed, where the truth means the life
of the Absolute, which is both substance and subject. In religion the Absolute bears the name of God, and in Christianity God is revealed in the
fullness of the divine life enunciated by the doctrine of the Trinity, in
the tripartite moments of God's life: God's life in itself (the religion of
the Father) and God's life as it abdicates its transcendence and enters into
space and time (the religion of the Son), in the Incarnation (the birth of
God), the Crucifixion (the death of God), the Resurrection (the rebirth of
God) and finally God's afterlife, the Ascension and sending of the Spirit
in and as the people of God (the religion of the Spirit). Hegel's metaphysical repetition of the Trinity shocked the theologians with what they mis-
took as his "pantheism"—what Mary-Jane Rubenstein calls their *pan*ic
at *pan*theism[7]—and he shocked the philosophers by openly defying the
categorial boundaries laid down by the Enlightenment between reason
and revelation.

Hegel's breakthrough cuts both ways. On the one hand, Hegel was saying that philosophy had everything to learn from religion, which has
something to tell us about the truth, because religion *embodies the truth*

and truth *assumes the form* of religion. Religion incarnates and substantial-izes the truth of the absolute Spirit for us in a concrete and imaginative mode. Religion is the way the truth achieves *Vorstellung*, the way the ab-solute sets itself forth (*vor-stellen*) in reality (which is its substance side) and also the way we image and imagine, visualize and envisage, narrate and tell ourselves stories about the absolute (which is its subjective side).[8] Reli-gion is the truth, the absolute truth, in the form of a *Vorstellung*. But of course, on the other hand, Hegel was also saying that religion does not quite understand itself, that religion requires philosophy to explain it to itself. Christianity has realized in a religious mode what philosophy alone can understand.

This was the Hegel who drove Kierkegaard to an outburst of irony and scorn, of parody and outrage, leading him to quip that it was as if God came into the world in order to arrange a consultation with German meta-physics. This was the Hegel who did not break with the Enlightenment in the sense that he agreed with the Enlightenment that Reason is a system and it encompasses everything, which is what Lyotard called "terror." Like Kierkegaard (and Schelling), I reject the notion that the *Vorstellung* can be monitored from above by absolute knowledge, that religion is a *Vorstellung* of something to which philosophy holds the key. But if the *Vorstellung* is not a presentation of the Absolute Spirit, then what is it? To simplify to an extreme I would say it is the presentation of an "event," which means the embodiment of a desire beyond desire, of a hope against hope, of a faith in the impossible. The event comes to pass in a multiplicity of ways in a mul-tiplicity of cultural forms of life—including but not confined to religion—which differ from each other rather as does one language or culture from another. That means it makes no more sense to ask which religion is the true religion than it does to ask which is the true language, the true form of art, or the one true culture. Consequently, the argument to be made against a modernist view of religion is not to defend its rationality against those who charge it with irrationality. We do not meet the charge of irra-tionality with the counterclaim that it is rational (a "warranted belief"). It is met by refusing to play by modernity's rules, refusing to be co-opted by modernity's misunderstanding. Religion is neither rational nor irrational in modernity's terms. There is a truth in religion—quite analogous to the truth in the work of art, which is its closest ally in this regard—which leaves the light of the Enlightenment completely in the dark.

We radical theologians reject the terms in which the Enlightenment has framed religion, the way innocent people object that they are being framed by the prosecution. Any religion that would emerge as rational in the terms set by Enlightenment reason would be a good deal less than religion. It might be ethics, but even then, it would be a lifeless ethics. It would be exactly what Hegel said it is, abstract, formal, and lifeless, because what the Enlightenment sees with the light of its Reason is blind to the substantive or substantial truth of religion (as well as of art and ethics), to what in German we call its *Sache*. Religious truth, as Latour says, is not a matter of information but a matter of transformation; it takes place in and as the truth of a form of life.[9] Flying beneath the radar of both the theism and the atheism of the Enlightenment, it has to do with a more elemental experience that precedes this distinction. Religious truth is not made accessible by a demonstration that proves it—no more than it is refuted by a critique that disproves it—but by a deeper "repetition" of what is going on there. But Hegel proposed a philosophical repetition of religion in terms of the Spirit, which claimed to be omniscient about what is going on in religion. What is needed is a repetition that confesses its unknowing, a deeply confessional repetition of religion.

Derrida's Repetition of Augustine

That is what we find in Jacques Derrida, a paradigmatic postmodern thinker (even though he would have properly rejected this description) in a text he called "Circumfession,"[10] dedicated to the *Confessions* of Saint Augustine, a paradigmatic premodern figure. Derrida neither submits Augustine to an Enlightenment inquisition, searching the saint's pockets for rationally warranted true beliefs, nor mocks Augustine for clinging to irrational superstitions. Instead, he stages a reenactment of the *Confessions*, a repeat performance of the text, in which he goes very far in reconstructing the scene of the *Confessions*, beginning with the crucial and elementary point that in this text Augustine is praying.[11] Readers of the *Confessions* feel they have come upon a man at prayer, whose back is turned to them, who addresses his words—*in litteris*, in writing—to "you" (*te*), "my God."[12]

But there is a problem. Augustine is praying to the God revealed in the Jewish and Christian Scriptures, and he can do so in community with his "brothers" in faith, in a book of common prayers handed down by the tradition, and he believes that God is there to hear his prayers and act upon them, albeit in ways too mysterious for him to comprehend. But to whom is Derrida praying, since, as he says, he "quite rightly passes for an atheist"?[13] Surely, then, what Augustine is doing makes sense, even if you do not share his faith, while what Derrida is doing is just a parody, an irreverent bit of impudence from an avant-garde writer who always has one trick or another up his sleeve and a devilish look in his eye. So the best his Enlightenment critics can do with Derrida is to solemnly conclude that his works are irrational, perhaps even "mad," certainly undeserving of an honorary degree at Cambridge. Augustine's religion is a true religion, even if you think religion itself is an illusion. Derrida's repetition is just a trick, a ruse, aimed at fooling us into thinking this is a real religion.

But Derrida says that his whole life long he has been asking himself Augustine's question, "What do I love when I love my God?" Notice the compound question, which assumes he loves God, that he loves something under the name of God, something he calls his God, the God of a certain faith and love. Only a fool would not love God. He confesses a faith and love in a certain God, albeit not the God of Augustine's faith—still a faith in something, but he knows not what, some *je ne sais quoi*. Notice, too, the name of the journal he is keeping is "Circumfession," which repeats both "confession" and "circumcision," the Christian Latin word for *bris*, used by the assimilated Algerian Jews. The word emphasizes the cut, including the literal cuts, the bedsores on his mother's body, but it also evokes an opening image of blood running like wine (*cru*), the blood of faith (*croire*), which is meant to signal a kind of ontological cut.[14] He is cut off, as he says at the end of the journal, from the truth in the sense of knowing the truth of his love and desire and his God, of what he loves and desires.

Truth for him takes place—it is an event—not in the domain of actuality, presence, essence, and identity, but in the open space between what is present and what is coming, a place where the present is exposed to what is to-come, to what he desires with a desire beyond desire, which is something unforeseeable. "Circumfession" is not *about* the event; it is itself a staging or performance (a per-ver-formance) of such an event. He is trying to take us by surprise by telling us about his religion, which we knew nothing about, that he is a man of prayers and tears and that he has been praying all his life. Who could have foreseen that? And to whom is he praying? (If I knew that, he responds, I would know everything.) For him to pray is to pry open the possible in search of the possibility of *the* impossible. Prayer takes place in the distance between the possible and the impossible. That unforeseeable in-coming (*invention*) of the unexpected (*tout autre*) is the event. This is what he calls, in another context and speaking of others than himself, a "religion without religion," a religion that *repeats* religion without sharing the dogmatic faith or rituals or communities of faith in the confessional religions.[15] It repeats the truth of religion, religious truth, but not in the sense of a true creedal assertion in a confessional religion; it is true religion, but not *the* true religion.

At a crucial point, Derrida cites an expression Augustine uses when Augustine speaks of his confessions in terms of "*facere veritatem*,"[16] doing or making (*poiesis*) the truth, as when he makes something by writing his confessions and does something by making a confession.[17] But the work done by the actual infinity of God in Augustine is done by the in-finitival *à venir* in Derrida. As such, its truth is steeped in un-truth, in not yet coming, in hovering before us as a risky chance, like a messiah who never shows up. Nothing is more demanding than the to-come, which presses with infinite urgency upon the present, making its transformation of the here and now imperative. Any such faith (*foi*) in the to-come cuts deeper than a particular belief in this or that, even as it cuts deeper than any reason we give for this or this. Such faith is the reason for the reasons we give, the deeper root both of giving reasons (*rationem reddere*) and of faith in the narrower sense of belief, the deeper root of the secular and the religious order, the deeper root of calculation, science and ethics, of art and politics. Such faith is the truth of a religion without religion, where religion is the stuff of what Augustine called the confessions of our restless heart (*cor inquietum*).[18]

The difference between Augustine and Derrida, then, is not that Augustine practices a true religion whereas Derrida is trying to pull off a ruse. The difference is that Augustine has a set of proper names to give to his desire, and Derrida's religion sustains a profound unnameability. Derrida's religion springs from an affirmative capacity to sustain uncertainty, which makes his prayer more truly wounded, his religion more truly prayerful and confessional, more truly religious, not less, more true to the restlessness of his own quasi-Augustinian somewhat atheistic ever restless heart.[19]

Conclusion

Rushing then to a conclusion, let me say this much.

1. Compared with the subtleties of Derrida's reenactment of Augustine's *Confessions*, the project of the Enlightenment, which is Inquisitorial, to put religion on trial by testing whether its faith is made up of warranted beliefs, failing which it is judged "irrational," is profoundly misguided and wrong-headed. It asks the wrong question, so that whatever answer it comes up with is irrelevant. It confuses faith with beliefs, having good reasons with pure Reason, and is blind to the deeper restlessness which precedes all reasons, and to the deeper experiential pre-propositional deposit of the event which precedes and follows every proposition.

2. The radical or "postmodern" religion of Derrida is a repetition of premodern wisdom, constituting an eccentric or decentered or chaosmic wisdom, which strangely is not immune to a certain moment of madness, to a certain foolishness of *the* impossible.[20] It was a source of some consternation to Augustine that, while everyone admits we desire happiness (*beata*

vita), we cannot all agree on what happiness is. For Derrida, such non-knowing and lack of consensus is not a lack but constitutive of happiness. For Derrida, wisdom begins and ends with a confession of our non-knowing, which does not debunk religion as irrational but repeats religion's truth. It does not repeat religion by reproducing the classical beliefs of confessional religion, but by repeating the events that take place *in* religion, which I am calling here the truth of religion or religious truth.[21]

8

Radical Theologians, Knights of Faith, and the Future of the Philosophy of Religion

My thesis is that the future of the philosophy of religion is rooted in what I call radical theology, which, I maintain, is the very thing that motivates our interest in the philosophy of religion and repays all our work. In what follows I treat radical theology as a form of what Johannes Climacus called "hidden inwardness," a religious passion that for the sake of propriety is kept discreetly out of public view, given that it is a mark of both bad taste and bad faith to wear one's religion on one's sleeve. On my hypothesis, were we ever to meet a radical theologian in the flesh, we would have the same reaction Johannes de Silentio describes on finally finding a knight of faith:

> The instant I lay eyes on him . . . I jump back, clap my hands, and say half aloud, "Good Lord, is this the man, is this really the one— he looks just like a tax collector." . . . [I] watch his slightest move- ment . . . a glance, a facial expression, a gesture, a sadness, a smile that would betray the infinite in its heterogeneity with the finite. No! I examine his figure from top to toe to see if there may not be a crack through which the infinite would peek. No! . . . He belongs entirely to the world; no bourgeois philistine could belong to it more. . . . No heavenly gaze or any sign of the incommensurable betrays him. . . . One would take him for a mercantile soul enjoying himself.[1]

As philosophy's hidden inwardness, radical theology is what is going on *in* the philosophy of religion while not being visible to the eye. It is "in" it not the way water is in a glass but the way an inner restlessness is disturbing something that gives the outward impression of stability. In radical theology we seek words for an infinite passion, for our deepest hopes and desires, for a faith that for all the world looks absurd. As such, radical theology is turned structurally toward the future, toward what is to come, for which we pray and weep. In radical theology the question is never what something is, but what it promises, what is promising, what is being promised *in* it, which requires a certain faith and hope in what seems absurd.

Infinite hopes and desires do not sit easily with the business as usual of the world, where we are taken up with finite projects and we try to avoid bad investments. Infinite hopes and desires are elusive, enigmatic, and resist objectification. That makes them suspect characters in the university, incommensurate with its methods and disciplines. But they are no less suspect to the "religion" of the confessional faiths, where a faith like this, a radical faith in the to-come, looks dark and dangerous, too unknowing and unorthodox. So the philosophy of religion—which harbors this infinite passion, this incommensurability—must for all the world appear to be a sober man, a mercantile soul, entirely commensurate with finitude and the world. It is asked to engage with infinite discretion in a covert operation, providing a cover of mundane respectability for radical theology, even at times offering it asylum from its persecutors. The philosophy of religion is asked to keep guard over a quasi-messianic secret, to keep it strictly to itself. Without the protection afforded by such a disguise radical theology would always be too mad for the academy and too heretical for the confessions. Radical theology occupies a place that is inside/outside philosophy and inside/outside religion, adopting their outward demeanor while being inwardly exposed to the abyss, taking care not to lace too tightly the garments of the "philosophy of religion" it dons in public. So just as Climacus said that humor is the incognito of the religious, the philosophy of religion (which could use a little humor) is asked to serve as the incognito of radical theology. Were we ever to meet a radical theologian, we would jump back and exclaim, "Good Lord, is this the man—he looks just like a philosopher of religion!"

Were it not for radical theology, the philosophy of religion would be a sober scholarly affair, at ease with itself and with the university, and even welcome in all the seminaries. Relieved of all suspicion, it would be left in peace, respected as a respectable discipline, a cool-headed inquiry into diverse bodies of beliefs and practices. As such it would be a perfectly proper chap in the faculty club, completely commensurate with the protocols and good manners of the university. All of which is perfectly true—up to a point, outwardly, on its face.[2] It is the destabilizing dislocating radical theology within that causes (I would say protects and preserves) the incommensurability—with itself, with the university, with confessional theology, with the world. The incommensurability lies in making a certain leap of faith, its faith in the to-come, which is analogous with the faith of the knight of faith in the absurd. Its faith is austere and groundless; its hope is quasi-messianic, the "quasi-" signifying both that this messiah does not actually show up and if *per impossibile* he did, we could not be sure that he will not be a monster. So the faith and hope to which radical theology gives form, a hope in a pure "to-come," is a faith in "*the* impossible," as Derrida likes to say. The to-come is not its "object" but what Heidegger calls its *Sache*, what Tillich calls its deepest matter of concern, or what the New Testament would call its treasure and its heart, and this because it is a matter not of knowledge but of faith and hope and love.

Striking the posture of an unorthodox Augustine who confesses before God, radical theology "circum-fesses" before God or death or the other, before I know not what,[3] the radical restlessness of its heart, praying and weeping for the coming of a completely unheard of and heretical messiah, calling for a new species of theologians, a new humanities, and a university to come. The figure of these coming theologians in this coming university is the secret hope of the philosophy of religion, the future it is calling for, the faith in the future that it "harbors," which means both to conceal and to keep safe, like a messianic secret, or like the hidden inwardness described by Johannes Climacus.

The Spectrality of Radical Theology

In radical theology, the open-ended force of desire and hope, uncontained by the disciplinary boundaries of religion, state, culture, or university, are given an unsteady, unstable, and spectral form. Beyond the "philosophy of" or the "theology of" this or that—religion or art or science—there lies the experience, the encounter, the engagement with the event that displaces and destabilizes any such stable formation. Radical theology is a theology of the event, its focus fixed on an obscure, restless, slightly spooky stirring going on *in* confessional theology, with matters from which confessional theology maintains a safe distance. The event can happen anywhere, *in* any inquiry or practice, *in* theology or philosophy, *in* the humanities or the sciences, *in* art or politics. Radical theology sets sail on the open seas of the to-come, the home shore out of sight, the other shore never reached, seeking to think the promise, which is structurally futural, always already what is coming, which is why this messiah never shows up.

The being of radical theology is always being-in. If we seek the "place" of radical theology we will find it *in* something else; its being is more *in*-sistent than *ex*istent or subsistent. It takes place *in* confessional theology, but it cannot be contained inside it, which is why it can also be found outside theology or religion—*in* literature, say, or politics, or science. We might say that its place is to be structurally displaced, never quite at home in any one place, and never safe or peacefully in place, exposing whatever it inhabits to the impact of the to-come, to the impingement of the future. Radical theology never quite gains its footing, since by dealing in events it is a matter of expecting the unexpected. Radical theology thus is futural through and through, as a structural matter and not merely as a matter of fact. Radical theology arises in response to the promise, and it calls for something new, for a new species of theologians, adapting a phrase from Nietzsche, in a "university to come," adopting a phrase from Derrida.[4]

Of course, radical theology does have a certain place, or enjoy a certain presence on the scene today—just where and how is one of my main concerns in these remarks.[5] But its place is always to be displaced, its home always provisional, always threatened by a certain homelessness, forced always to travel under an incognito. In Derrida's discourse, we would say its state is spectral, "*unheimlich*," meaning uncanny, a bit eerie, but literally "not-at-home," wandering like a ghost. In the discourse of the New Testament, it is like the son of man, having nowhere to lay its head. "Spectrality," says Derrida, is the subject matter not of ontology (what is) but of "hauntology" (the promise/threat).[6] As usual, when Derrida makes a quip, he is also being perfectly serious, because he is speaking of the event, humor being one of his favorite incognitos. The hidden inwardness of our knight of faith seems to be a matter of believing in ghosts. Look about and ask, Where is radical theology to be found, here and now? Where and how does it have a place—in the confessional religions or in the university? To what extent is it able to acquire what the Greeks called *ousia*, meaning both substance or essence and real estate! To what extent does radical theology acquire solid and substantial institutional body? The answer is, it does not quite exist, and yet it does not quite not exist; it is not quite living and not quite dead, like the "un-dead" of the horror movies.

But like any ghost worthy of the name, the specter has a reality or a force of a different sort. We ought not to say that radical theology exists, but it spooks. For it, to be is to spook. "*Es spukt*," Marx quipped, speaking of Max Stirner's critique of religion (as opposed, let's say, to Heidegger's *es gibt!*).[7] It spooks us, *in*sinuating a ghostly force into the life-world all around it—into the confessional religions and the university, into philosophy and religion, and especially into the sober and respectable figure of the "philosophy of religion," which is our concern here—and it gives none of them any peace. Ghosts see to it that neither the living nor the dead rest in peace.

Above all, as a discourse (*logos*) on God (*theos*), the spectral nature of radical "theology" causes a disturbance in the highest quarters, in God on high, in the name of God. For the name (of) "God" is also inhabited and disturbed by the event that transpires *in* the name of God. The event haunts and displaces the very being of God with the specter of what is going in and under that name, what is coming, what is calling, what calls, and what is called for in and under the name (of) "God." Radical theology raises the spectral prospect of a coming God, and its prayer is a call for a God to-come. At bottom, its subject matter, its *Sache*, its deepest concern, is not the future of religion, or of the philosophy of religion, but the future of God, whether, when all is said and done, there will have been God.

Radical theology enjoys—unless it suffers from—an ambiguous mode of existing without existence, a confounding mode of insistence without enjoying a robust and full-fledged existence. Radical theology is not a well-formed discipline that can be comfortably housed in the university, where it is not respectable to believe in ghosts. It cannot be condensed into a definitive creed or reassuring set of assertions that could be approved at a council or assembly of a confessional religion, which wants to be sure that the spirits with which it has commerce have not been dispatched by Beelzebub. So radical theology cuts a discomforting figure, and it makes a disconcerting call for a new species of theologians, for a university to come, for a religion to come, and even, God forbid, for a God to come. Nothing sacred, nothing present, nothing here and now, no essence, satisfies it, which is the essence of its restlessness with the present and the essence of its quasi-messianic future, of the to-come by which it is always and already inwardly disrupted. By a religion- or university-to-come I do not mean a coming institution belonging to the future-present but the force or call or solicitation of the to-come that provokes religion and the university today, in the present, that gives them something to think, to desire, to hope for. The to-come is *always* to come, as a structural matter. All we expect from religion and the universities of the present is for them to become more open to the to-come, to the unexpected, more hospitable to the in-coming of the unforeseeable, more welcoming of specters, more willing to be disturbed and ill at ease with their categories and concepts, their doctrines and definitions, their divisions and departments.

(Dis)placing Radical Theology

In order to address the question of the future of the philosophy of religion, I want first to distinguish radical theology from confessional theology. The task of confessional theology is to clarify the beliefs and practices of the confessional community, its self-understanding. Confessional theology therefore has a proper place—in the community, to be the place where the confessional community does its thinking. Radical theology does not report back to any confessional community, but rather to the human community at large. Radical theology touches on elemental issues of natality and mortality, of transcendence and finitude, of reverence, praise and gratitude,[8] purpose, hope and love, joy and sorrow—all issues that Tillich described as matters of ultimate concern, of common or universal interest, if not of common agreement. Radical theology belongs to what Derrida calls the "new humanities" found in the "unconditional university," the university to come, which reserves the right to ask any question, however dissident, however scandalous its questions may be to confessional authorities and traditions, to any authority, religious or secular.[9] Radical theology claims access to anything and everything that is going on in religion, even if the confessional authorities build walls around certain things and declare them "mysteries" unattainable by reason. Radical theology is, on its face at least, cosmopolitan and universal (its modern face), free and unfettered (its postmodern face), remembering we should not accept things at face value.

The "natural place" (as the ancients might have said) of confessional theology is the houses of worship and of learning conducted by the confessional community—its pastors at their preaching, its professors at their teaching in colleges and universities, seminaries, and divinity schools—all highly respectable places where the "radical" in radical theology renders it suspect or unwelcome. Radical theology does not conform to confessional authority, does not respect the distinction between orthodoxy and heresy. That suggests that the natural place of radical theology, by contrast, would be "secular" or nonconfessional institutions, like the "religion" or "religious studies" department of a secular university, where confessionalism is the cardinal sin.

But even here radical theology is a bit out of place, not quite welcome, a questionable figure, not because of the "radical" but because of the "theology." The ring of "theology" is spooky and unnerving in the ears of the secular university. Cool-headed secular academics say they are not afraid of ghosts, but they are afraid of people who believe in ghosts, the spirit-seers who worried Kant. That is why many secular institutions have no department of religion or religious studies at all, which they think would be out of place in a self-respecting enlightened university. Even the universities that do have such departments do so very cautiously, almost antiseptically, for fear of contamination. The theological and philosophical components of the department, which were dominant in the past, have been progressively displaced by anthropological, sociological, ethnological, and historical approaches to what is there called "religion." In these departments, "religion" is constituted as a perfectly proper "scholarly object" of study, not unlike the way one might have a scholarly interest in the study of Roman coins, meaning not as though your life depended on it. The difference between the confessional institutions and the secular ones is sharp; they adopt completely and symmetrically opposite positions in the matter of objectification. In a confessional institution, the working assumption is that it is necessary to believe in order to understand; if you are not "in" the confessional community, you will never quite "get it." The confessional faith is a lived or existential matter that cannot be completely theorized or objectified. In secular institutions, the opposite is the case: If you are "in" a confessional community, then your "objectivity" becomes an issue, and if you do believe, you must conduct yourself as if you do not, practicing a kind of methodological agnosticism, and check your beliefs at the door if you wish to maintain your respectability.

As a practical matter—a practice I am here trying to theorize—however, radical theology can and does gain entrance to these institutions, whether confessional or nonconfessional, by presenting its papers to the academic gatekeepers as "philosophy." To the members of the curriculum committee or the tenure committee or the acquisition editors of university presses, radical theology passes itself off as the "philosophy of religion." Like the knight of faith, the radical theologian gives every indication of being a sober fellow. This is a strategic solution (don't ask, don't tell) and the most common one, and it allows radical theology a respectable—if covert—place in the philosophy department of most institutions of higher education and even in the religion department of secular ones. The philosophy of religion provides a cover for radical theology, an incognito. But this arrangement is far from perfect and even, as I have been urging, a bit of a ruse, and this for two reasons.

First, there is the danger, which all too often is the reality, that in the confessional institutions, the "religion" in "philosophy of religion" will almost invariably mean the confessional one sponsored by the institution. That turns the whole thing into an exercise in apologetics, which is a compromised philosophy, and lends weight to Heidegger's well-known (if ironically very modernist!) complaint that a Christian philosophy is a square circle and a sham, so if philosophy wants to raise serious questions it needs to practice a methodological atheism.[10]

But there is a second and even more basic problem. The philosophy of religion concerns the beliefs and practices of the various "religions," which is a legitimate, respectable, and even urgent business for the university, especially today in a world turned upside down by religious extremists. But the subject matter of radical theology is not precisely "religion"—its structure, history, beliefs, and practices. It certainly involves offering a theory of religion, and, in my view, it finally isolates a certain religion that is nicely described as a "religion without religion."[11] But it is of some importance to see that its subject matter is not exactly religious beliefs and practices but, as I have been saying, what is going on *in* religion, which I contend is best theorized in terms of what Derrida calls the event. The subject of radical theology is what is going on *in* "religion, the religions, the religious,"[12] in what is called there God and the gods, gifts and grace, prayer and faith, hope and hospitality, love and compassion. The subject of radical theology is what Husserl called the things themselves, *die Sache selbst*, in other words, the things that religion is all *about*. Radical theology is not about religion, but about what religion is about. In Tillich's terms, its subject matter (*Sache*) is ultimately matters of "ultimate concern," matters that it theorizes and interrogates, questions and analyzes, just like confessional theology, but without regard to confessional authorities and without observing the limits imposed by the orthodoxies. Radical theology really is theology, but it is not confessional theology. Radical theology really is philosophical, but it is not precisely the philosophy of religion. Consequently it is a suspect character for both confessional theology and the university. It is brewing an ale calculated to please no one's taste.

That in turn suggests that radical theology is, most precisely of all, *philosophical theology* and that too is true enough and part of the working agreement that is struck with the institutional authorities. Radical theologians behave like philosophers, but ones who are literate in religious traditions and theological texts, the way philosophers of science need to be literate in physics or biology. They interrogate theological matters with a critical eye; they want to see for themselves; they cannot be put off by being told that it is all a mystery and a matter of supernatural revelation; they are not intimidated by bishops, archbishops, or the Bible. But this approach too has its limits. The very idea of what we call philosophical theology is constructed by distinguishing between "revealed" or "sacred" theology and "rational" or "philosophical" theology," where philosophy is restricted to the rational content of theology while leaving matters of faith and revelation to the doctors of sacred theology. The result is that the "radical" in radical theology is compromised by being inscribed within a "regional" distinction—natural reason up to here, supernatural revelation from there on in. In its most familiar form, philosophical theology takes up the question of the existence of God, the immortality of the soul, the freedom of the will, and the problem of evil. Enter the anthologies—Aquinas's "five ways," Anselm's "ontological argument," Hume's critique of miracles, and so on *ad infinitum*, maybe even *ad nauseam*. That will never do. Something has to change!

Radical Theology and Radical Hermeneutics

Hegel changed it. He showed that "philosophical theology" is a God-forsaken line of work, too thin, barren, and abstract an undertaking to serve as a fitting characterization of radical theology. Rational theology is just so much *Verstand* (rationalistic "understanding"), which is pretty much a term of abuse for Hegel, signifying an abstract, ahistorical, disembodied, one-sided rationalism, which allows itself to be distracted by the busy work of proofs, propositions, and entities. *Verstand* lacks the concrete robust life of the spirit that is accessible only to the full-bodied embrace of *Vernunft* (dialectical "reason"), which has its eye on what is going on *in* the proofs and propositions. *Verstand* results in pale and anemic creatures like Kant's reduction of religion to ethics or the modernist scholasticism of Christian Wolff, which Kant criticized under the name of cosmo-theology and onto-theology, the latter of which Heidegger set out to "overcome." Unlike philosophical theology, a radical theology is like *Vernunft*; it takes every interest in the "revealed" contents of theology, in its characteristic doctrines and concrete practices, in just the way that Hegel was above all interested in the Trinity and Incarnation and was, in that sense, a great Christian, even Trinitarian theologian—but in a radical mode.[13] So if radical theology is a kind of philosophical theology, which is true up to a point, it is a rogue, an outlaw, an illegal immigrant, or maybe even like one of those old Cynics who performed outrageous things in public. It refuses to observe the distinction between "revealed" and "rational," sacred or supernatural and natural theology, which defines philosophical theology.

What we learn from Hegel, who is the pivotal figure in the formation of radical theology, is that the "radical" in "radical theology" is not a *regional* marker but a *modal* one. Radical theology cannot be staked out as a regional subject matter whose borders are drawn by a critical distinction between rational and revealed, or the "natural light" and a supposedly "supernatural" light to which reason lacks access. In virtue of its very radicality, there is *nothing* in theology or religion—be it "faith," "mystery" or "revelation," "grace" or "prayer"—that is not accessible to radical theology, nothing in which it is not interested, no question it does not have the right to ask, no text or matter for which it does not seek an interpretation. The "radical" in radical theology does not mark a region but a point of view; it signifies the depth dimension in any and every region. The radical requires a different modality of thought, a way of understanding, an interpretative mode. Radical theology is a *hermeneutics* of what takes place in and under the name of God, of any name or belief or practice, be it a "revealed" truth or one born of "reason alone," be it an argument, an institution, a liturgy, or a politics. Radical theology is deeply interested in the founding "sacred scriptures" of the confessional traditions, in their parables and narratives and injunctions. These are all treated as so many serious meditations on the human condition, and even as "revelations," that is, as profoundly revelatory of our condition without the mystification of supernaturalism. Radical theology thus requires a taste for reading books of revelation, which requires a taste for literature, which in turn requires not only literary sensitivity to religious texts but also a historical-critical study of the origin and form of these texts. Radical theology is in no small part a meticulous history, genealogy, and phenomenology of what is happening in and under the name (of) "God," in everything that is written, made, and done under this name.

But if radical theology is deeply interested in revelation, it avoids the mystification of "Revelation," in caps, as it were a heavenly message delivered by angels to evangelists with their ears cocked heavenward, beyond human scope—whose proper interpretation is handed over to their institutional overseers. These religious authorities authorize themselves to say they are authorized by these texts. They are the very people who in fact have constituted these texts *as* revelation to begin with (canonization) and often redacted them to their own liking, burning what is not to their liking, not to mention the abyss of accidents to which they are vulnerable in being transmitted at first orally and then by copyists. Radical theology respects *every* revelation as "special," as idiosyncratic, wholly other (*tout autre*). It simply denies that any special revelation is definitive or exclusive—as if it comes at the cost of the "special" quality of other revelations, as if revelation were a zero-sum game, as if someone has won a game of guessing the secret name and the others have lost, as if the secret name was "revealed" to the former but not to the latter. One indication of how gratuitous a construction a "special revelation" is, is the regularity with which it turns out that the "special" revelation is inevitably made to "us," while the "others" were left in the dark by God. It is never the other way around.

In radical theology the "Sermon on the Mount" has a special revelatory force that consists in the shock it delivers to the sensibilities of a greedy and selfish world, in the topsy-turvy vision of the world it puts forth. It scandalizes the wisdom delivered by Greek philosophy or the so-called enlightened self-interest of common sense or the invisible hand of market forces, where greed is good. Such a special shock is the mark of any and every "revelation," which is therefore recast in radical theology as a "poetics"—an evocative discourse, calling on all the resources of syntax and semantics, to work up a unique sense of the human condition, of its magic, mystery, and misery. Revelations like this happen in *every* tradition; engendering a poetics of our condition, an imaginary, is pretty much what makes for a tradition in the first place. There are many such traditions, each of which is uniquely and idiomatically itself. If we speak of "special" revelation, that can only mean that every revelation is special, every other is wholly other (*tout autre est tout autre*), each one having a special character of its own. But if special revelation means enjoying a special privilege when it comes to having revelatory force, a privileged access to the truth, then no revelation is special, no more than there is one true culture, language, or work of art. But this does not mean that all such revelations are the same in the style of the old comparative religion, or to deny that they can be compared and contrasted and learn from one another.

We might say that as a mode of inquiry, radical theology follows the example of Jesus, who, to the great scandal of all, dined with sinners and associated with tax collectors. Radical theology, to the scandal of "philosophical theologians" or practitioners of "rational theology," does not fear to traffic in sacred scriptures, sacred doctrines, liturgical forms, and so on. That would be like a philosopher of science who feared trafficking in physics or biology. At the same time, radical theology, to the scandal of the confessional theologians, does not respect the suprahuman and exclusive authority the confession claims for its "revelation." As a result, again like Jesus, the foxes have their holes, the birds their nests, but radical theology has nowhere to lay down its head (Matt 8:20). If confessional theology has its place, radical theological is structurally out of place, displaced. For radical theology, these texts, traditions, and practices are not gifts delivered from on high. Instead, they make up a characteristic form of life (Wittgenstein), a distinct mode of being-in-the-world (Heidegger), or a particular historical experience of the world (hermeneutics). Such forms of life take place in multiple ways, constituting multiple forms of experience, a multiplicity that is quickly bruised and ultimately foreclosed by speaking too easily in Christian Latin of "religion." A revelation is a poetics, and radical theology is the *hermeneutics* of such poetics, a radical hermeneutic of its underlying experiences, whose predecessor is not Kant's abstract, rationalist, and reductionistic approach to religion, but Hegel's embrace of the concrete and historical.

Radical Theology as a Heretical Hegelianism

Radical theology belongs to the tradition launched by Hegel, not by Kant. Kant practiced a kind of philosophical regionalism, undertaking the "critical" task of marking off separate domains of inquiry and of enforcing a rigorous control of the borders he had drawn in the three *Critiques*. The touchstone of Kant's project is found in his guiding axiom that he has found it necessary to deny knowledge in order to make room for faith, the upshot of which is to reduce philosophical theology to apologetics.[14] Radical theologians, in contrast, are a hardier Hegelian lot who do not seek to sequester appearances from reality or to locate supernatural revelation safely beyond the reach of the missiles of natural reason. Far from keeping confessional theology safe, they seek to expose the danger, the groundlessness, the restlessness by which confessional theology is disturbed.

But that means that radical theologians differ from Hegel in a crucial and defining way. Hegel's hermeneutic has been well described by Catherine Malabou as a "speculative hermeneutic."[15] That is, Hegel held that everything in religion (not just its "rational" content) is of interest to philosophy and requires an interpretation—that is his breakthrough—an interpretation that can be supplied only by what he called "speculative thought"—that is the problem. Ultimate matters submit to an ultimate thinking that determines what they ultimately mean. So Hegel proposed to expose the speculative or metaphysical meaning of God and religion as a *Vorstellung* (representation), as the sensuous, pictorial, and narratival form taken by the absolute Spirit on its journey to absolute self-knowledge. We radical theologians, however, have no head for such heady Hegelian heights. We lack the *logos,* are bereft of the *Begriff* (concept), and fear flying too close to the sun of the absolute and final account with which Hegel purports to lay things out (*auslegen*) in his speculative hermeneutics. We agree with Hegel that religion is a *Vorstellung*, not of some metaphysical absolute, however, but of what unfolds in and under the name of God, of what we call the event, a word we have adopted here in order to do the least injury to our subject matter. Radical theology, then, is a theology of the event, a hermeneutics of the event, where hermeneutics is not "speculative" but "radical."

By the radicality of this hermeneutic I do not mean an interpretation that keeps things safe, that finds the ground on which we stand, or that attains the unshakable foundation of phenomena, which is the classical sense of "radical." I mean the opposite, one that expounds our radical exposure to groundlessness, our irreducible vulnerability to risk and uncertainty and to a certain unknowing, a certain uncertainty. Radical theology is not foundational theology; it does not propose the ground but exposes the groundlessness that goes all the way down. Radical hermeneutics means that interpretation goes all the way down and that there are neither rock-solid uninterpreted facts of the matter down below nor an overarching speculative penetration of phenomena that expounds their essential law up above. Radical hermeneutics means the willingness to put our own presuppositions at risk and that the exposure is without limit; the risk goes all the way down.

Classical Hegelianism, as Kierkegaard complained, is too knowing, too Gnostic, too much a know-it-all, and too much in league with the classical Christian theology of omnipotence, omnipresence, and omniscience. Classical theologians were so scandalized by Hegel that they failed to appreciate just how much he was on their side. So by radical, I mean a radical cut, a confession more circum-fessional than confessional where no one knows the "Secret." No one is somehow hardwired to the speculative essence of Being or God, of History or Spirit, all in the upper case. Radical hermeneutics is conducted exclusively in the lower case.

Such a hermeneutic can take the form only of a poetics. A "poetics" is a constellation of metaphors and metonyms, of parables and prose, of miraculous stories and historical memories, of myths and mysteries, of paradoxes and paradigms, in short, a discursive form that makes use of every resource possible in order to give words and deeds to an event, to give the insistence of this event existence in the world, allowing it to become a mundane word and deed. So by a "poetics" I do not mean the artistic adornment of a preconstituted idea, a literary illustration of a pregiven logos, a literary or artistic flourish added to an autonomous philosophical concept. I mean the very attempt to form, to forge, to constitute (*poiesis*) the event, to give it words and sensuous form, to constitute the mundane existence of the event. A poetics is always already a work in progress, a repetition forwards that is continually producing the actuality it tries to repeat, which is never fully constituted but is always in the making. A poetics gives the event a name, while the event, being essentially open-ended and to-come, graciously declines the nomination.

A poetics consequently cannot be kept confined in a disciplinary cell. It migrates across all the departments of the university, the "humanities," the "social sciences" and, today more than ever, the natural sciences, where the most wondrous and miraculous things of all seem to be taking place. It is not enough for theology simply to demythologize the old cosmology; it needs to engage the new and ever-changing cosmologies emerging almost daily. Its transdisciplinary character requires all the resources of the humanities—the literary capacity to interpret narratives, the historical resources required to understand the origin, genesis, and mutation of the founding stories and the institutions. It furthermore requires knowledge of contemporary particle physics and astrophysics, which have forever transformed the pre-Copernican imaginary in which traditional religious doctrines were born and nurtured, and of contemporary life sciences, evolutionary, genetic, which have utterly transformed the humanistic presuppositions of traditional theology. I think we are still absorbing the point made by Bultmann in the middle of the twentieth century.[16] The religious imagination of classical theology remains under the spell of a pre-Copernican imaginary, where the mythic split between heaven above, Hades below, and the earth in the middle merged with a Hellenistic metaphysics of the transcendent, unchanging, eternal, and supersensible being (above) and the immanent, changing, temporal world of becoming (below). That split was forever discredited by Hegel, which is Hegel's greatest achievement, and the beginning of radical theology, which means that the future of the philosophy of religion is tied up with the future of a philosophy of science. Finally, this poetics cannot be confined to academic quarters. It insinuates itself into pastors and their preaching,[17] and, beyond the religions and the groves of Arcadia, it wends its way into the interstices of the world, into the quotidian and micrological structures of everyday life and popular culture, which is another story and one I cannot take up here.

Deconstructing the Distinction between Radical and Confessional Theology

Before proceeding to a conclusion, I must concede what is by now obvious. I must make a confession, a circum-fession. The distinction on which everything thus far has depended—between confessional theology and radical theology—does not hold up. That does not grieve me; it is just as it should be. Just as I warned, the "radical" in radical thinking does not provide a ground but an exposure to groundlessness. Like any distinction worthy of the name, the ground gives out beneath this distinction. If a distinction is worth making at all, it is also worthy of being deconstructed. Otherwise it is a form of exclusionary terror. I have two things in mind in saying this.

First, the claim that radical theology is universal and cosmopolitan is a modernist fiction. Radical theology does not drop from the sky; it is not an exercise in the so-called absolute autonomy of thought, which is as much a myth as is pre-Copernican theological supernaturalism. To begin with, radical theology is a characteristically Western and philosophical undertaking, a work of Greco-European conceptualization, in the tradition of Western philosophy, from which it cannot be separated. Outside the Western philosophical tradition, such an undertaking might have little resonance. Furthermore, without ignoring or underestimating the presence of radical theology in preaching, it is too often the work of academics. When that happens, it submits (camouflages) itself to all the protocols of academe— the objectifying discourse, the rites of academic passage, the normalizing standards to be met for acquiring and maintaining an academic position, the disciplinary mechanisms of refereeing publications in the various academic journals and university presses. It is a creature of "Western philosophy" and a product of Western academic disciplinary protocols, which up to now have reflected a world of comfortable Euro-white males.

Second, we should take not entertain any illusions about the "purity" of radical theology; it is never pure of confessional theology of which it is the radicalization. It more often takes place *in* confessional theology, which also means that we must also be careful not to caricature confessional theology, not to reduce it to the reactionary religious right, or fail to realize that the most courageous and radical work is undertaken there. Radical theologians are by and large expatriates of the various confessional theologies, often even recovering fundamentalists, or ex-nuns or ex-seminarians. They are usually people trained in a confessional theology from which they later distanced themselves, with the result that everything they say about radical theology is the radicalization of the confessional theology that is always in the back of their heads, the way those who learn a foreign language retain their accent. Sometimes this confessional point of departure is first and foremost on their minds. In responding to my critics who take my version of radical theology to be a free-floating abstraction, I insist on its multiple debts to the Christian and larger biblical tradition, which is where I learned everything. My radical theology is a radical theology of the cross, of Paul, of Yeshua. I make no pretense to anything else. That is my life story.[18]

No one illustrates this better than Hegel himself, who went so far as to say that religion *is* Christianity, that Christianity is the absolute religion, and that every other religion is a predecessor that only imperfectly approaches or foreshadows absolute religion, a dialectical step along the way to the emergence of consummate and perfect revealed religion. Consequently, Hegel, the grandfather of the radical theologians, is also the greatest of the Christian philosophers, not because he was more pious than the philosophical-theological saints of the Middle Ages, who started each day with a prayer, but because his philosophy is an undisguised, unapologetic, and overt conceptualization of the Christian doctrines of the Trinity and Incarnation. Radical theology cannot pretend to some ahistorical transcendental status, even as it eschews the absolutization of any historical tradition, either of which would contradict the very meaning of "radical" as radically exposed to contingency, chance, and uncertainty. It says, like Augustine on the interpretation of the scriptures, let there be as many radical theologies as possible, so long as all of them are true.

Indeed, a fair amount, maybe *most* of what I am calling radical theology already takes place *in* the confessional theologies. When theologians working in confessional institutions exercise the freedom to think, the right to "ask any question" that I attribute to radical theology, they do so at great personal peril. In the past, if they incurred the wrath of the Inquisition, that could have cost them their lives. Today, it can cost them their livelihoods. Confessional theology is of an inherently unstable nature: The mission or commission to think through its confessional commitments requires that it be an exercise in *thinking*, and thinking cannot be what it is without reserving the right to ask any question, up to and including questioning its confessional presuppositions. Under the sheer force or pressure of thinking, confessional theologians frequently break through to radical theology. Once the work of thinking is launched, the underlying "events" that nourish radical theology will inevitably burn through and show up in the work of confessional theologians, exposing the contingent, constructed, and deconstructible makeup of the confessional community, which attracts the disapproving attention of the powers that be.

That this distinction breaks down, that there is all this mutual interaction and contamination, is not a rebuttal of radical theology; it is predicted by the radical in radical theology. After all, the confessional theologies are for the most part the only theologies that *exist*, upon which the *insistence* of radical theology is largely parasitical. They are the only theologies that have an institutional home (like the foxes and the birds of Matt 8:20), while radical theology is largely homeless, like the son of man. Except for occasional academic exercises, radical theology does not exist, not as such. Radical theology is not a competing religion, not a rival in a battle for confessional membership, does not engage in fund-raising. Still, it would be a sorry thing if the only place we find radical theology is in panels at the American Academy of Religion dedicated to the topic, where the participants read papers at one another written in a jargon that challenges the divine omniscience itself and keeps it safe from comprehension by other mortals down here on earth.

The Future of the Philosophy of Religion

But if radical theology does not *exist*, what then? All that remains to it is to *insist*—to persist as a hidden but insistent inwardness concealed by an outward existence whose demeanor betrays nothing of its incommensurability with the world. Radical theology insists both as a spectral disturbance hovering in the space between the mercantile business of the university and the madness of its concealed faith, and also as a not quite holy ghost in the space between the confessional theologies and a theological thinking to come. In radical theology, to be is to promise to be, to be as a maybe, to happen as a perhaps, to hover as an odd kind of quasi-messianic promise/threat. That brings us back to the future, to the to-come, which has been the guiding question all along. Radical theology is concealed from the world; it can never be robustly present and realized in existing institutional bodies; it smacks of spooks and dark spirits and mad poets. That is because it deals not with what is but with what is always coming, and it is constantly stealing away to its chambers where, with prayers and tears, it softly sighs come, *viens, oui, oui,* for something coming, which is the messianic secret it keeps to itself. It is not of this world because it is irreducibly futural, structurally turned to the world to-come, tuned and attuned to what is to-come. That does not refer to the difference between the temporal world and another eternal world behind the changing scenes of this one, as in the old Augustinian metaphysical dualism. It signifies another time, the hidden time, the hidden future of this world, a wholly other coming of the only world we know, a renewal of the world, a new worlding of the world, a hope in the promise of the world, the year of the Jubilee. It is concerned with events, with what is going on *in* what is present, with the promises that are being made by what is present.

The future of the philosophy of religion depends on offering an asylum for this madness, providing a safe place from its persecutors, hiding it in the attic. Radical theology whispers in the ear of the confessional theologies like the dwarf on Zarathustra's back whispering, "You know it, but you will not say it." It tempts confessional theologians to look down at the abyss over which they are suspended, reminds them of the contingency of their appearance in time, of the constructedness of their ancient narratives, of the violence of their origin. It haunts them with the spooky thought that had we been born in another time and place we would sing songs to other gods and in other languages, call for comings of an entirely different sort. It tempts them like Satan tempting Jesus, taunting them with the thought that what theology calls "grace" is, more austerely considered, the gratuitousness of an accident of birth. We are born without having been consulted, in a situation not of our own making, and the songs we sing salute our contingent circumstances, behind or beneath or within which lies something, we know not what, which we signify here as the event.

Just so, radical theology proves no less unnerving to the philosophers who faithfully believe that they do not depend on grace but credit themselves with an autonomy of thought that rises above contingency altogether, which is the future of an illusion if there ever was one. This lingering philosophical myth undergoes the most rigorous and unrelenting demythologization by being reminded of the historicality and constructedness of what it calls "philosophy" and "religion."

The future of the "philosophy of religion" depends on providing radical theology with a cover, offering it safe passage, serving as an incognito for what would look like messianic madness to the university and its protocols. In just the way that Johannes de Silentio said that humor must be the incognito of the religious—a joke about the inevitability of death and taxes, for example, is deadly serious—the philosophy of religion is asked to be the incognito of radical theology. It must give this mad quasi-messianic faith a professional demeanor, make it look respectable, even a little boring and humdrum, like a tax collector, like nothing more than a philosopher of religion.

Of itself, if it has a "self," radical theology has no place to lay down its head. No decisive "death of God" allows it to rest in peace, nor can it settle easily amid the comforts of the institutional life-world of the religions or the university. Its heterogeneity with the world consigns it forever to wander the world as a spirit. Its only refuge then is subterfuge. Underneath the propriety that the philosophy of religion maintains as a respectable player in the world, a scholarly chap of even temperament, there lies concealed something wild, lost, restless, erotic, uncertain, reeling under the blow of the to-come, trembling with the event of things unseen and unheard of, which sends it into the world as a sheep among the wolves of worldly institutions. The philosopher of religion is saying one thing, but something else is going on behind the scenes, a messianic secret that the philosopher keeps from the world. All the arguments about God and the soul, miracles and immortality, freedom and the problem of evil in the anthologies are allegories of something else, a cover for something quite other, *tout autre*, for what is going on *in* the philosophy of religion, which makes it interesting and a matter (*Sache*) of radical concern. Radical theology makes discreet, passing appearances in the philosophy of religion, like a strange fellow whom no one knows who keeps showing up in old photographs. The work that is done in the philosophy of religion looks for all the world like the business as usual of philosophy, but it is a secret agent, of another provenance, on a secret mission. It arises in response to a wild and strange call, which calls for what is to come, even as it itself arises as a call, calling come, *viens, oui, oui.* The philosophy of religion harbors, conceals, nurtures, and keeps safe the event of the call, a call that whispers a reminder of the may-being of being. This weak and uncertain voice of "maybe," ever soft and low, wends its winding way into everything that we describe in stable philosophical categories such as substance, essence, and presence, as matters of knowledge, science, and truth. The philosophy of religion contains the event of radical theology in the mode of being unable to contain it.

Seen from the point of view of the disciplinary structure of the university, radical theology is a hybrid and a misfit, an incommensurable. It defies the disciplinary boundaries that would separate it from literature, history, and the social sciences and, today more than ever, from the natural sciences. As a song to the poetry of the world, radical theology belongs everywhere and nowhere, lacking a proper home, even a proper name. It keeps several passports in its drawer depending on the country to which it seeks to gain illegal entry. It occupies the halls of philosophy and theology and secular religion and comparative literature departments, infiltrating them with an insistent, insidious unease about the constraints of their concepts, the insufficiency of their categories, and the limits of every project of objectification. It whispers in the ears of these disciplines that "religion" is a construction, as are "God" and "the gods," and that underlying these constructions lie the nonobjectifiable events that lay claim to us, that defy philosophical definition, scholarly objectification, and institutional codification, events that hold the promise of what is being promised in words of elemental evocativeness, which nothing guarantees will not be monsters. The "objects" of which we have undertaken a scholarly study, and such study is indispensable, are more deeply considered inescapable issues (*Sachen*) of life and death, of suffering and joy, of passion and compassion, which together make up the promise and the threat of the human condition, which cannot be more important and cannot be understood otherwise.

The university today is undergoing a massive reconfiguration under the combined impact of global capitalism, expanding bureaucratization and marketization, and revolutionary information technologies. Against this, radical theology holds out the hope that the present university can be deconstructed. Deconstructed does not mean destroyed but disseminated and disturbed in such a way as to allow the formation of new objects and modes of inquiry. Religion today is threatened by the ongoing polarization between fundamentalism and secularism. Against this, radical theology holds out the hope that religion can be deconstructed, that the practice of preaching and the constitution of doctrine and institution would allow the invention (in-coming) of the event. A religion to come and a university to come do not signify a future home—the to-come does not mean a future-present—but the very structure of the call and a structural openness to the event.

The philosophers of religion are asked to maintain the cool-headed calm of a stockbroker of the finite, negotiating deals within the institutions that house them. But inwardly they are as mad as the knight of faith who lives in virtue of the absurd; secretly they are tossed about by an infinite passion, ready for anxiety, exposed to the groundlessness that gives life its intensity and the future its promise. What they know but will not say is that it may very well be, perhaps, that their very subject matter is the "perhaps" itself, the promise/threat of the future, the "might be" that even works its way into God "al-mighty," the "maybe" in being, the force of the to-come that presses in upon everything that poses as present. Adopting the outward demeanor of the university, being inside/outside philosophy and religion, they think unthinkable thoughts, affirm the possibility of the impossible, dream of things completely unheard of, still to come. "Good Lord, is this the man, is this really the one—he looks just like a philosopher of religion."[19]

Theology in Trumptime
The Insistence of America

We have chosen the expression "Christian Nationalism" to get in the face of the Christian Nationalists—the phony nationalism of so-called Christians is what we mean. The expression is accusatory, a term of abuse for a corruption of both "Christian" and "nation." In theology, this is called blasphemy, idolatry, confusing a symbol with what it is a symbol *of*.

First as tragedy, November 8, 2016, then as farce, a sick joke—a narcissistic buffoon, a morally worthless con man, "Mr. President." In Trumptime, the stream of egregious offenses, normally unforgettable, career-ending, is so steady that examples become obsolete in a matter of hours. This is not deconstruction, as Steve Bannon thinks;[1] this is simple destruction. This is not a paradigm shift; this is the implosion or explosion of the prevailing paradigm, pure and simple, with nothing to replace it. If, as Heidegger says, the sense of Being goes back to the sense of time, this is the sense of time in Trumpworld, where nothing is and everything mutates, where even Heraclitus would complain about the fast pace of the flux. Parmenides would be horrified at the two-headedness, billowing clouds of confusion and contradiction, in tidal waves of deceit, denial, and dissemblance, of spurious, devious, misspelled duplicity, appeals to the basest instincts of the base, to the very worst instincts of the people. The corruption of the people, of "we the people" (woe to the people would be right), of the *nation*, as of the people of God. And this, God help us, in the name of Jesus, a name so badly abused, so defiled daily, that I prefer to say Yeshua, to decontaminate him from these so-called Christians.

185

In the blasphemous simulacrum that passes for *Christianity* on the Christian Right today, owning a gun is a right but having health care is a privilege; in the election of public officials, character matters, until does it not, until it serves the political interests of the Right to dismiss personal character, then it suffices to support a mendacious narcissist who brags about the obscene things he can do to women because he is rich and famous. In the blasphemous simulacrum which passes for "nationalism," these Christians rejoice in Christian militarism, just when Jesus said to put down their sword; when the Scriptures say to welcome the stranger, they dig in against the immigrants; they hold that bringing good news to the poor, feeding the hungry, and healing the lame is coddling people who are on the dole. Instead of the Good News, Fox News. Instead of the year of the Jubilee, when all debts would be forgiven, instead of the condemnation of the rich in the New Testament, they support a tax cut that represents a massive redistribution of wealth to those who are already obscenely wealthy. When Jesus said, suffer little children to come unto me, they approve of separating the children of refugees from their parents, of depriving women with unwanted pregnancies of medical insurance, proper prenatal medical care, and throwing those little children and their mothers on their own after they are born, like Hagar and Ishmael. It is surely such Christians as these that Jesus would have spit out of his mouth.

A nation is an event of natality. Nation means the natal place, the natal community, the place we are born and the people by whom and among whom we have been given birth. Our attachment to it is natal, natural. Such attachment is a fabric that is woven of all the lines of force of birth, all the corporeality and affectivity of familiar faces and places, of the childhood home, old friends, the old neighborhood, a gradually widening world that eventually embraces the national home and, increasingly, the global one, mother earth, which is the mother of us all. Birth is a matter of a gift we did not ask to receive, for which we are spontaneously grateful. The national is a primordial community, a primordial formation of the spirit; it is a natal language and literature, a spirit that inspires us with ideals and shape a form of life.

In this regard, the American nation has a marvelous novelty about it. It both is and is not a natal community; it is also and intrinsically an "intentional" community, whose very "idea" is to welcome the immigrant, those who have been displaced from their natal place and are welcomed here in order that they may make a new place for themselves and their children. In just the way that, as Derrida says, a "democracy" is an auto-deconstructive community, that is, one whose founding principle is to always expose those principles to public interrogation, to maintain their perpetually self-questioning reformability and deconstructibility,[2] so the American "nation" is an auto-deconstructive natality, one that maintains the instability of the very idea of natality, so that it can be the place of those who have lost their place, the place of the displaced. Such a nation of immigrants, wanderers, and pilgrims resonates with the biblical injunction to welcome the widow, the orphan, and the stranger and to provide a city of refuge.

So, these self-professed Christian nationalists subject us to two blasphemies, two obscenities, two sick jokes, two embarrassments—their so-called "Christianity" and their so-called "nation."

But make no mistake. We have also chosen our title in order to congratulate ourselves. *We* are not under accusation. So allow me to "flag" (if I may use this dangerous word here) the egregious mistake, both strategic and conceptual, that academic theorists and other learned despisers of religion on the Left have made in handing these two words over to the Right. This mistake was not made by Martin Luther King Jr. The civil rights movement was *driven* by the demands of *both* the Christian gospel *and* the very idea of America. This mistake was not made by Richard Rorty, whose *Achieving Our Country* went viral the day after the catastrophe. Eventually, he warned the Left—it was 1997—the abandoned trade unions and the blue-collar workers, the working white lower-middle class, would tire of having their manners corrected by postmodern professors and elect a "strong man" who would pretend to speak for them and proceed to undo forty years of progress on the left.[3] In *Achieving Our Country*—this title offends the ears of today's Left—Rorty urged loving the *nation*, "our country," the one that says, "Give me your tired, your poor, your huddled masses yearning to breathe free."

This America is, beyond a geopolitical entity, an idea, a prayer, a *dream*. The civil rights movement, King said, was "a dream deeply rooted in the American dream," in which all of God's people will be free, where freedom will ring from every mountainside.[4] Then, and only then, "will America be a great nation." Great, not with the hard power of an army but with the *soft power* of an idea that lifts up the powerless; first, not because of military and economic force, but because there the first are last and the last are first.[5]

Notice the temporal shift: King spoke of the day when America *will be* great, not "great *again*," which is the con job, the reactionary nostalgia, Trumptime, Fascist time.[6] King would not rebut this dog whistle to white supremacy, as do today's spineless, pandering politicians, by saying that America has *always* been great. That, too, is hypocrisy, a cruel joke. No nation founded upon European colonization, upon a near genocide of the indigenous population, and upon the backs of African bodies dragged here in chains, which, from Vietnam to Iraq, puts its poorest youth in harm's way for an unjust and spurious cause, where then as today poverty stretches from sea to polluted sea—no such nation can dare say that it has always been great. To all such nostalgia, to every such Fascist memory King would oppose a prophetic memory, what Johann Baptist Metz calls the *dangerous memory* of the dead, of what James Cone calls the lynching tree.[7]

To the Fascist dream of lost greatness, King opposed the prophetic dream of a greatness-to-come. King said that it *will be* truly great, for the *first time*, so the greatness is the greatness of the *dream*, like the dream of the DACA "Dreamers" today, the dream of the America *to-come*. The "great" belongs to *prophetic time*, to the adventive time of the event, of the to-come. My fellow democrats, there is no democracy, not yet, but it is coming.[8] My fellow Americans, there is no America, not yet, but it is coming, if only we can make it come. Not a phony America but the true one, where the truth makes us squirm, puts us on the spot, in the accusative, as Levinas says, which means that it is up to *us* to make it come true.

America insists; it does not exist. Its existence is up to us.

King's speech takes place in the time of the dream—of a *great nation*, one that would be, in the depths of its national heart, responsive to the call of the prophets and the gospel, to the imperative to bring good news to the poor, the hungry, the imprisoned. He dreams of the year of the Jubilee, which is a year not in calendar time but in theopoetic time, the time of the heart, the time of hope, the time of the impossible, the time of the to-come.

If the Christian Nationalism of the American Right is a *hypocrisy*, the message of the secular Left is *spirit*-less, devoid of both a *prophetic* vision and a *national* vision, the dream of a great nation. It lacks *Geist*, which I translate here as guts. In the face of the shameless charade of Christian Nationalism, the Left lacks the guts to cite the prophets and to dream of the year of the Jubilee when America *will* be great, when we will make it great, for the *first* time. The time of America is to-come.

Hoping against Hope
The Possibility of the Impossible

The Future Is Always Better

Voice of Skepticism: Let us be clear. Today, the situation is hopeless. There are no grounds for hope.

Voice of Hope: The future is always better.

Skepticism: How can you say anything so ridiculous? Look around you. Just look at the war being waged today by the children of Abraham, Jewish, Christian, and Muslim, a war over Jerusalem, both symbolically and substantively. The holy land is the land of holy wars. The future there is hopeless.

It is impossible today to have hope in the midst of a terrible intolerance to the immigrant, hostility to helpless families displaced by a war they did not start, in which they have no part. It is no longer possible to hope for hospitality to the widow, the orphan, and the stranger. How is possible to hope when children in flight from their war-torn homes wash up dead on the beaches?

It is impossible today to have hope in economic justice in a world of such incalculable greed that everything is calculated to further enrich the richest upper one percent and to further impoverish the poorest, to maximize inequality, to drive us further and further into the extremities of wealth and poverty.

It is impossible today to have hope in the midst of the harm we are doing to the environment, which the experts tell us is approaching the point of irreversibility. How are we supposed to reverse the irreversible?

It is impossible to hope in racial equality when African American and Hispanic men are incarcerated at a rate six times higher than white men. When it is almost impossible to convict a police officer who kills an African American.

It is impossible today to have hope in democracy, in the public institutions of democracy, when the democracy has been corrupted root and branch by money. It is impossible to believe in the impartiality of the judicial system when judges are nominated on the basis of political ideology. It is impossible to have hope in democratic elections when political campaigns turn on duplicity, not on truth, when everything is done to prevent the least powerful people from voting, when voting districts are manipulated. It is impossible to conduct a public discourse when it is corrupted by a media that has abandoned journalism in favor of the ratings and profits. Nothing is too malicious or misinformed or outright false to be "published" on the internet. Talk shows, radio and cable television networks fuel the fires of hatred, feeding the prejudices of entrenched believers, telling them only what they want to hear.

Hope: Has it not always been thus?

Skepticism: No, today the situation is much worse. Today, hope is impossible.

Hope: So what? Of course it is impossible. But that is why it is our hope. The future is always better, not because it is, but because that is our hope.

The Principle of Insufficient Reason

I have not come here to bring coals to Newcastle, to tell the Society of Pastoral Theology,[1] a group of people as diverse as this and as practiced in their various communities and ministries as you all are, about how to go about doing what you are already doing, and no doubt very well, without any help from me. What I have to offer is not a bit of strategic advice about how to be more effective in your work or how to deal with the daily obstacles you face. About that you all know more than I. It has been part of the prudence of the planners of this conference—unless it proves to have been their rashness—to provide for so wide a variety of perspectives as to be willing to indulge the musings of a philosopher.

I describe myself as a philosopher who tries to occupy the distance between philosophy and theology. My idea is not to synthesize the two, not to bring peace between them, but the sword. I want to let these ancient rivals disturb each other, to let each one give the other no peace, to let each keep the other off balance and unsure of itself. I am trying to breed a theological-philosophical hybrid, producing books that confound the categories of the shelving librarians. I have a special interest in hope. I put a lot of hope in hope, especially when we are pushed to the point of hoping against hope (Rom 4:18), which is when hope gets interesting. Surely that is what is called for when the topic is, as it is here, "suffering, extremism, violence and planetary crisis," whose barest outlines I have sketched above.

So I will treat this call to Pasadena as a call to follow my calling, which is to offer you a work of thought about hope, a bit of what in the academy is called "theory." Theory is not a word I like a lot, because it sounds indolent, idle, lazy, like it is the absence of practice, or opposed to practice. It inevitably provokes people to say, "That sounds good in theory but how does it work in practice?" But I am actually here under the opposite premise: What you are already doing is good in practice, and I am asking, how does it work in theory? Theory sounds a bit like the Enlightenment, whose motto was "dare to think," *sapere aude*. Like the Enlightenment, I am all for thinking, the more the better, and I am all for the trouble the Enlightenment made for the reign of religious violence and superstition and of authoritarian monarchies. But the down side of the Enlightenment was a tendency to confuse thinking with rationalistic calculation and the rule of method, which led to trouble.

Still, I like to think that the very fact that the Enlightenment *had* a motto, which took the form of an imperative, was a good sign, a sign that thinking was its passion, that it even admitted to having a passion. To dare to think is to dare to hope in thinking, to pledge one's troth to thinking, to love thinking. Were I ever pressed to come up with a motto for radical theology, I would say, "dare to hope," *sperare aude,* even if, especially if, it is not rational. The "principle of sufficient reason," according to Leibniz, one of the greatest Enlightenment philosophers, is that "every being has a sufficient reason for being." That is what led him to conclude that, since this world is, as he believed, the product of an omniscient, omnipotent, and omni-benevolent creator, it was the best of all possible worlds. That ontological optimism is where his idea of reason led him. As I think we would all agree today, it led him astray, as that proved to be too sanguine a view to take. Leibniz never lived to see the internet or a modern American political campaign. But it was just the sort of thing that one would be led to say by constricting thinking to reason and constricting reason to method instead of seeing in reason a capacity for the infinite, for the impossible.

Maybe there is hope for hope, after all. Hope against hope. Maybe the hopelessness with which I began is but the first word, not the last word on hope. Maybe the condition under which hope is possible is that it be impossible.

Were I ever invited by a Leibniz Society to give a talk—I have no hope that this will happen; I do not think it possible—my claim would be that faith, hope, and love, these three, all kick in directly in proportion to the *lack* of reason. The more rational, reasonable, probable, and likely a thing is, the more it is just a reasonable expectation and the less we require faith; we need faith just when things are beginning to look incredible. That is why faith is said to move mountains. The more likely it is that what we seek is about to happen, the better the bet, the less hope we need; that is the hope of a shrewd stockbroker. We need hope just when it is starting to look hopeless, like the body of a child washed up on the shore. That is why I am speaking of hoping against hope. Last, the more lovable are the people we love, and the more they love us back, the easier it is to love; even the tax collectors do that. We need love when the object of our love is unlovable and the ones we love do not love us back, or worse. That is why we are told to love our enemies. Faith, hope, and love, these three, seem to turn on a principle of unreason, of no-sufficient reason. Faith, hope, and love turn on a principle of insufficient reason.

The Folly of God

That insufficiency is formulated in a powerful way in Paul's notion of a *logos* of the cross, which he said, judged by the world's standard of wisdom, is foolishness, folly, nonsense (*folia*). So Paul is contrasting the wisdom of the world, of the Greek philosophers at Corinth, with the folly of God (1 Cor 1:18–25).[2] We are well advised not to transliterate *logos* as "logic," as it is anything but. Nor do we want to translate *logos* as *ratio*, reason, as was done in the Middle Ages. It is best to stick to something like "word" or "message" (NRSV). Paul is putting out the word about folly, about insufficient reason, when it comes to faith, hope, and love—and of a few other things, too, like forgiveness and hospitality, all of which follow the *logos* of the cross, the way of the cross. This is wisdom that is for all the world foolishness, and weakness as the world judges strength, even as for Leibniz it is simply irrational. Unhappily, we have a vivid example of this today, in the crudity and cruelty of Donald Trump, who regards nonviolent solutions precisely as "weakness," without realizing that, in what he would no doubt call "One Corinthians," this is precisely the weakness of God.

Viewed in the light of Leibniz's principle of reason, I would say that faith, hope, and love are "without reason" (*sine ratione*). They have no "grounds" (*logos* as *ratio* or *Grund*), or if they do, their grounds are groundless grounds. They belong to a schema that philosophers nowadays call "nonfoundationalist," which means not that they are simply mad but that they have a life of their own, that they run on their own, without anyone having to come up with a "foundation" for them. It was the point that Socrates was missing when he pressed for definitions, as if artists and people of practical wisdom could not do what they did in fact do if they could not define it to Socrates' satisfaction. In fact, requiring a foundation, a reason, for the virtues is a mark of degradation—like people who agree to be merciful or just only if there is something in it for them, a reward, preferably an eternal one. So they promise that for seventy years or so they will deal mercifully with the widow, the orphan, and the stranger just so long they are rewarded for their trouble! They demand an infinite return on a finite investment. Otherwise, they will tell these people to go bother someone else. This cynicism has sometimes been known to travel under the cover of leading a "Christian life"!

That is why faith, hope, and love not only can be but must be "without why," to invoke a saying that was prevalent in Rhineland mystics such as Meister Eckhart (*ohne warum*).[3] Eckhart seems to have picked up this expression from Marguerite Porete (*sans pourquoi*), which was one of the things that cost Marguerite her life at the hands of the Inquisition. The Inquisition was one of the reasons we needed an Enlightenment—to save us from the violence of people who confuse themselves with God Almighty, not to mention confusing the name of God with almighty power. Love is without why, the mystics said. That means, love is not in it for the payback, the return on its investment. Love is not part of an "economy"; it is not short-term pain for long-term gain. It is gratuitously, graciously, gracefully given. The kingdom of God is not a "reward" for love; it *is* love. Love is the way the world would look if God ruled, not the powers and principalities, and it is here and now, in the world. Love is the folly of God.

I own up to being a philosopher but of a highly hybrid sort, and hence I have had no compunction in dining with sinners, that is, with those whom the philosophers think sin against "reason." I have no compunction in making myself complicit with what are called the "theological" virtues, as the virtues itemized by Paul came to be known in classical theology. These virtues stand in contrast with what the philosophers call the four moral virtues, gleaned from Plato and Aristotle—prudence (practical wisdom), justice, fortitude (courage), and temperance (moderation). In the first century CE, a Roman scholar named Quintilian (Fabius Quintilianus), called these virtues the "four hinges of the world" (*quattuor cardines mundi*), the four hinges by which the legs of virtue sustain the table of life (from *cardo*, hinge). Together, they make for a well-hinged life in well-ordered world. So they came to be known as the four "cardinal" virtues. In the

Greco-Roman world, which thought of *deus* in terms of *natura*, and of *natura* in terms of necessity, the *rerum natura*, the order of the cosmos, wisdom lay in seeing the necessity in things, and virtue lay in accommodating our lives to this necessity. The wise man fits himself into this order, making himself commensurable with necessity. For individuals this means making themselves comfortable in their preassigned place and staying put, sheltering in place, we might say, against the winds of fate, a counsel that better served the interests of the men who proposed it than the women and the slaves, whom it left without hope.

But in the biblical view, wisdom was not foreign to folly, the folly of a God who is thought of not in terms of natural necessity but of making all things new, of the new being, of renewal. The name of God is the name of a promise, of a hope, of a "to-come," and the corresponding discourse is accordingly prophetic, messianic, eschatological, and the emphasis falls on the future. Accordingly, the characteristic virtues are future-oriented and transformative: faith in what does not seem possible, hoping against all the odds, loving the unlovable, saying yes to what is coming, yes to the future, to the coming year of the Jubilee. Justice is up ahead; it is coming. In sum, to call upon the name of God is to call for the coming of what we cannot see coming, which requires no little faith, hope, and love. If the Greco-Roman cardinal virtues provide the way to lead a well-hinged life, the theological virtues are for the unhinged, both according to Paul's *logos* of the foolishness of God, of God's folly, which in the French, *folie*, also means a little mad, and according to the un-Leibnizean principle of *in*sufficient reason. To the extent things make good sense, we don't need hope. To the extent things do not make sense, we do. When we say, "the future is always better," not because it is, but because that is our hope, we are prepared to make ourselves fools for faith, fools for love, fools for hope. Otherwise we are just cost accountants, stockbrokers of the infinite, hoping to get an eternal return on a temporal investment.

The Possibility of the Impossible

The logic, or alogic, or as I prefer to call it the "poetics" of hope, follows the dynamics of what Derrida calls "*the* impossible," by which he does not mean a simple logical impossibility, like "*p* & not-*p*."[4] The possible on Derrida's terms is what is foreseeable within the present or existing horizon of expectation. The possible is the expectable, the plannable, and it should not be taken lightly or dismissed, since without it out life would descend into chaos. This Derrida calls the "future present," the future we can see becoming-present. The foreseeable brings with it a host of obligations that concern what we should have been able to foresee—the future of our children, or of the planet, retirement, and so on. The possible is the sphere of things about which we cannot plead ignorance, and if we do, the ethicists will call it culpable ignorance. We should have known better.

By *the* impossible, Derrida means something that shatters the horizon of expectation, that breaks in upon us unexpectedly, that catches us unawares, by which the possible is inwardly disturbed. We are left scratching our heads. "That's impossible," we say. "How was that possible?" we ask ourselves. This Derrida calls the "absolute future," the one with teeth, the one we cannot see coming. So *the* impossible is not a logical but a phenomenological impossibility. It concerns what we cannot see coming, which Derrida calls the "event." For better or for worse—since sometimes the event means we are overtaken by an unforeseen disaster, which is what happens sometimes when you expose yourself to the coming of what you cannot see coming. Affirming the possibility of *the* impossible is risky business. It is to remain within the horizon of expectation, of the possible, of the tried and true.

But there is a drawback to living life entirely within the safe horizon of the possible, and it is considerable; if we pass our whole life thus, at the end of life we will discover that life has passed us by. Nothing happens, no events, nothing in-breaking, nothing transformative, no renewal, no new being. Nothing to make all things new. Playing it safe is also risky business. If life would descend into chaos without a relatively stable horizon of expectation, a life filled entirely with events, with uninterrupted in-breakings, with constantly shattered expectations, would descend into disabling trauma.[5] So the poetics of *the* impossible is very efficiently and felicitously condensed into a formula proposed by James Joyce, neither a classical cosmos nor pure chaos but a "chaosmos." As Derrida puts it, it is not a question of choosing between them; we live in the distance between the possible and the impossible. The relatively stable horizon of expectation is also relatively unstable, and it must be kept in a delicate off-balance, in a state of optimal disequilibrium, where we are ready for the coming of what we cannot see coming.

Of course, the unforeseeable future is going to come anyway, whether we like it or not. But Derrida, like the prophets—I think that with Derrida the Jewish prophets are never far away—is describing two different forms of life, two different modulations of living in the distance between the two. The one does everything it can to resist the coming of what it cannot see coming, takes every means to protect itself against it, and is only dragged kicking and screaming into the future. The other keeps the present off balance and tilts toward the future, just the way that walking is a controlled fall forward; it affirms the future, embraces it, is eager for what is coming. It says yes to the coming of what it cannot see coming and has a taste for risk. The first form of life is a kind of safety-first, risk-averse reactionary conservativism, which seeks to preserve the present. The second, which is riskier business and willing to take a leap, represents a progressive relationship with the world. In the second form of life, the only way to preserve or conserve a thing—be it a belief or a practice, a tradition or an institution—is to put it at risk. The first lives a life of little faith (*oligopistis*) and of such little hope (*oligo-elpis*) that its only hope is that nothing new is going to happen. The second lives a life of larger hope, of genuine hope, even if, especially if, the odds are against them, if it is foolish and without reason to hope.

That is why, in the face of this hopeless world we live in, the only possible response is hope in the impossible.

The Aporia of Hope

In biblical religion the impossible is associated with God, for with God, everything is possible, even the impossible (Matt 19:26). God makes all things new. That is our hope, and that I submit is what we centrally mean by God, namely, the possibility of the impossible. So, to put this Derridean point about the impossible in Tillichian terms, we might say the name of God is a symbolic way to affirm the possibility of *the* impossible. To put it that way implies this structure, hope in the impossible, is contained *in* the name of God but it is not contained *by* or confined *to* the name of God. It is uncontainable, and it might be found elsewhere, under other names, in other times and places, with or without the name of God or of what we call "religion" in a strict or narrow sense. It will be found anywhere in the culture, in art or science or politics, in the depths of culture, which Tillich calls the "ground of being," which is the seat and site of a religion in the deeper sense defended by Tillich. This ontological foundation does not remove the doubt from faith, or guarantee our hopes, of course, for guarantees do not give faith and hope but assurance, which removes the risk. But Tillich gives hope a groundless ground in being, in the ground of being. Hope calls for courage, not only the "moral" virtue of courage, one of the four hinges of the world, but a deeper *ontological* courage, a deeper affirmation of being, which Tillich calls the courage to be, a virtue of the unhinged.[6]

My views are close to Tillich but closer still to Derrida. Tillich's views are ontotheological, meaning that they tie God (*theos*) together with the ground of being (*to on*), and therefore with ground as a foundational *ratio*, whereas my pursuit is not precisely theo*logical* but theo*poetic*, meaning that I tie God together with a phenomenological form of life. Rather than a theological ground, a theopoetics turns on an abyss, or at least an *aporia*, like the possibility of the impossible. This means that I do not think that God is a supreme being or best thought of in the categories of being at all. I think that God, the name (of) "God," belongs to a poetics of the impossible.

Accordingly, I do not think that hope has a foundation in being but that it springs from the structure of time, and because time is tricky business, because the future is uncertain, its foundation is without foundation. That is the abyss or the aporia: The grounds of hope in time are groundless grounds, which, please note, is not the same as being utterly groundless or arbitrary. Hope is not utterly groundless but neither does it rest on solid grounds. Hope does not rest at all; it is restless with the future, which means it has an Augustinian restless heart (*cor inquietum*). Hope is not founded on a ground—being (*to on, ens*) or nature (*physis, natura*), essence (*essentia*), or substance (*ousia, substantia*)—for that would confine it to the possible, the reasonable, or even the necessary, making it almost an inevitable outcome, or at least a foreseeable outcome, the making explicit of what is already implicit, not the new being. A ground or essence provides being with a plan or a formula that time can follow and in which hope can be confident. But it is only when there is no plan, no foreseeable way forward, and hope still pushes forward, that we have to do with genuine hope. The motto for hope is dare to go where you cannot go; dare to affirm the possibility of what is impossible. The most economic formulation of the aporia is to say that the condition under which hope is genuinely possible is that it is impossible. Hope is, on this point, symmetric with the aporetic structure of loving the unlovable (the enemy), forgiving the unforgivable, and welcoming the unwelcome.

Still, we persist, we insist, we cannot resist asking, How is this—*the impossible*—possible? Why is it not utterly arbitrary? Why is this poetics not just a flight of pure fancy? Once again, the response to this question, which does not yield a ground or final answer, lies in time. We are turned to the future *by* time, *by* the temporality of our life. Time does not consult with us about this. We were not asked to sign on, to agree to the terms of temporality. It is not up to us. The future, the absolute future, is marked by a radical unforeseeability. The absolute future is not an invited guest but an unexpected visitation, which comes over us unawares. The unforeseeability of the future is imposed on us unconditionally; it is irreducible. Try though we might, we cannot stop it. In the very effort we make to turn away *from* it, we confirm how deeply we have been turned *toward* it, just the way a man running *from* his fears bears witness *to* his fears. For us, to live is to be turned toward the absolute future. There has never been a "theory" that can "see" (*theorein*) the future, the one we cannot see coming, and that fills us with fear and trembling. But, and everything depends on this, the absolute future is *no less* that by which we are lured, called, solicited. It is that for which we pray and weep, what we desire with a desire beyond desire, that of which we dream, that for which and in which we *hope*.

We hope without why, hoping against hope in the coming of what we cannot see coming. The impossibility of hope, on which the skeptic insists in the little dialogue with which I started, is the very staging of hope. The impossibility of hope is the condition of its possibility.

But *why?* That is the aporia, the no-way-out. If we have a good reason, it is not hope but a reasonable expectation. If it is utterly groundless, then it is not hope but an idle and arbitrary will-o'-the-wisp. Is there nothing between good reasons and arbitrary fancy? That is what I mean by a groundless ground. The groundless ground of hope means that it does not rest on a ground but that it is nonetheless *motivated*. Hope does not have a sufficient reason. Hope does not have a causal ground, but it does have a cause to fight for, a cause to hope in. Hope is not caused but motivated by a cause, by the absolute future, by its anything-is-possible open-endedness. The very openness of the future calls on us, solicits us, invites us to open ourselves to an unexpected visitation. Hope is not caused by a being or founded on a ground of being but motivated by an otherwise-than-being, a not-yet being. Hope is not caused by being, *être*, but elicited by a may-being, a *peut-être* (perhaps).[7] Hope is not caused, it is called up, called for, in the face of the cool course that being runs, affirmed in the face of the groundlessness of being. Hope is not the effect of a cause; it is a response to a call. Hope is not sustained by a cause; the cause is sustained by hope.

The Time of the Promise

I am describing the promise, the time of the promise, which elicits and solicits hope.

Surrounded on every side by being, essence, actuality, presence, by the powers that be (*ta onta*), the men (and it usually is men) of substance (*ousia*), the men who own all the real estate (*ousia* again!), the men who run the church or the state, who have the money or control the media, we hope and pray and weep for what has never been, not yet, but is promised. Whence this promise? Who is promising and what is being promised? The promise is what lies ahead of us in the future only because it has been handed down to us by the past. The promise is what is coming because it is what we have inherited; it is embedded in the world that was already running when we arrived on the scene, in a world that has filled our heads with words of elementary promise.

Like justice. Like the promise of justice, the time of justice, of prophetic justice, the inbreaking of justice, the dream, the desire, the prayer—to let justice flow like water over the land. Justice is always coming, never here, not entirely. Justice is found only here and there, making intermittent and transient appearances, not enough to quench our thirst but just enough to excite our desire, to inspire our hope. Justice is always a justice-to-come, always a messianic justice, where the messiah never shows up, is always promised—which is, I am saying, the very structure of our temporality. The "messiah" is an emblem of the to-come, an infinite emblem, not with the actual infinity of an omnipotent eternal being in the sky who will right every wrong and make straight the bent and crooked, but with the infinity of the infinitive, of the to-come, of temporality. Hope is *awakened* by the future, awakened by the promise inscribed in the future, by the future that is inscribed in the promise—like the biblical stories of God awakening the dead, those who sleep, to new life, stories that symbolize the new being. "Hope in resurrection" is a symbol of the promise, of awakening to the new being. Words that take the grammatical form of nouns, in the nominative, as if they were stable essences, that pass themselves off as essences, forms of being, are thoroughly penetrated by time. That is why Heidegger liked to turn nouns into verbs, and to say things like "the world worlds," or "language languages." Nouns are set into time like words set to music, temporalized through and through, so that they do not have an essence but a history, like the words of a story, or a song about a promise, about good news.

The biblical story is the story of the promise that Yahweh makes to the people of Israel to be their God, just so long as they promise to be his faithful people. He is the lord of history, of time, of the promise. In theopoetics, this does not make God the ground of the promise but an emblem of the promise, one of the symbolic names under which the promise is given, a way it is put into words, formed into images, cast into songs and stories, enacted in rituals, allowed to penetrate into the bones and bowels of the people of this story. In the time of the promise, time is there but there is no being there—no Supreme Being, no ground of Being, no hyperbeing (*hyperousios*). God calls, but when God calls, that is time's call, the call of the future in and under the name (of) "God." The call calls with or without the name (of) God. Time calls under this name or that, even and especially under the name of the nameless, where namelessness provides the best protection for the unconditionality of the call for hope and for the purity of the response. That is what I am arguing under the name of the "insistence" of God—that God does not exist; God insists. Hope is sustained by the insistence of God, not by God's existence. The name of God is not the name of a superbeing who makes good on his promises. God is not a superbeing who redeems our promissory notes, but the name of a promise. So even if God does not exist, do not give up hope in theology; that is not the end of theology, but the beginning.

We are told by the historians like Alan Segal that before the second century BCE there was no belief in the afterlife, and no thought of God as creating *ex nihilo*, among the ancient Israelites.[8] Indeed, an afterlife was considered polytheistic and as such strictly prohibited by their rigorous monotheism. Surviving death would produce deathless spirits who would rival the One God for attention and devotion. Those who return from the dead would pose a distraction to the single-mindedness of monotheism, a challenge to the power of God, and lead to soothsayers and diviners. The people might start praying to them, like the Canaanites or the Egyptians, not to the One God. That all changed when Antiochus IV (Epiphanes), sacked the city of Jerusalem in 167 BCE, defiled the temple, and issued an edict suppressing the Jewish religion, which led to the revolt of the Maccabees. Many faithful Jews, including women and children, were cruelly put to death, thus producing what the Christians would later on call the first "martyrs." The problem this defeat and persecution posed to the Israelites was significant: Were they to think that Yahweh is not faithful to his promise? That Yahweh cannot deliver the goods? The book of Daniel (12:1–4) proposes an innovative solution: God will awaken the dead from their sleep, vindicating those who lost their life for their faithfulness to him, and—this was a new twist on the idea—also raise up the those who shamed themselves by their complicity with the enemy in order to punish them.

That, I would say, is what the logicians call the fallacy of the *ignorantia elenchi*, drawing the wrong conclusion. Faced with defeat at the hands of the Hellenizers, the Israelites chose to hold on to the God of power at all costs; they upgraded his power to include the power to raise the dead from the dust and to create out of nothing. I propose they should instead have been led to rethink the name of God, not as the name of a superbeing with superpowers, but as the name of a promise, a promise that is sustained even in the face-to-face with death and defeat, even unto death and the cross. After all, as history shows, this sort of thing, death and persecution, will recur time and time again, and time and time again the Supreme Being fails to come to the rescue. At some point—perhaps when the environment can no longer sustain the libraries that must be built to hold the books of theodicy and martyrology aimed at coming up with a "sufficient reason" for all this—it should dawn on us that our hope in justice does not rest on the back of a Mighty Being who will come from on high to save us, no more than it is lodged deep below in the ground of being.

Hope in justice is sustained by the promise of justice that issues from the constellation of words and ideas, of narratives and parables, of beliefs and practices, of traditions and institutions, from the literature and the culture that "justice" engenders, that it throws off like sparks from a fire. Hope in justice is hope in the future that justice promises, hope in what is coming in and under that name, from the linguistic, prelinguistic and meta-linguistic forces that are unfolding in and under that name. That promise is the issue not of a being or ground of being but of being turned by time toward the future. The promise is the promise of a new being, of a coming being, of a renewal, of the being to come. The promise, the hope in the promise, is inscribed in our hearts by time, in virtue of which we are turned to the future, to what is to-come.

Conclusion

Skepticism: That all sounds lovely but it doesn't change anything. The cold truth is that justice is still impossible.

Other: So what? That is why it is our hope.

Skepticism: But when will all this happen?

Hope: In the year of the Jubilee

Skepticism: What year will that be?

Hope: The year of the Jubilee is not recorded in calendar time. It did not arrive when Jesus predicted it; it did not arrive when Paul predicted it. We have no record that it ever arrived.

Skepticism: Which amounts to admitting that it will never arrive.

Hope: From this we are not to conclude that it does not arrive, but only that its "arrival" does not take place in calendar time. It belongs to the temporality of the promise, of our hope in the promise, of our hope in the future. It is not a matter of days or weeks, months, or years, centuries or millennia.

Skepticism: That sounds like never, no time at all.

Hope: It belongs not to a chronology but to a kairology, happening here and there, whenever the shoots of justice manage to break through the crevices of cruelty. It belongs to an eschatology, not a violent apocalyptic one, when the Superbeing will make our enemies our footstool, but to a poetic eschatology, an eschato-poetics, a theopoetics of time.

Skepticism: I still don't get what you mean by hope.

Hope: Hope is what calls, what is called for, what is always calling. Hope in justice is hope in the call of justice, the promise of justice, the possibility of justice, even and especially if it is impossible. The impossible does not represent the destruction of hope; instead, the impossible takes the measure of its passion. The measure of the impossible is measureless, like the power of a picture flashed around the world of the dead body of a little boy washed up on a beach, far from his home, far from the arms of a woman weeping uncontrollably over her son, now lost forever. Hope is hope faced with that.

Like a Devilish Knight of Faith
A Concluding Quasi-Theological Postscript

He had the devil in his eye and he knew it. It was no small part of his enormous charm. If you are going to spend your whole life saying "come" to the coming of what you cannot see coming, it helps to have the devil in your eye. It also struck me as a rich theological trope—a theology with the devil in its eye, a bedeviling theology—and it gave me one of the best ideas I have ever had. A series of conferences in which we would bring him together with a group of distinguished theologians to discuss matters dear to his heart, the gift, forgiveness, hospitality, and the rest. This would be intimidating, he said. I smiled. I knew he would be the intimidator, not the intimidated. He had no academic preparation in theology, he said. I pleaded that the divinity schools and departments of religion were now beginning to realize that they had something to learn from deconstruction. Whatever his differences with Saint Paul might have been, there was always a pinch of Paul in Jacques Derrida, a will to travel the known world, to risk shipwreck and being bitten by serpents, in order to spread the good news. He agreed. I rejoiced.

The conferences were electrifying. He came to three of them and begged off the fourth because of what we were later grieved to learn would be a terminal illness. To this day people tell me how much these conferences touched their lives. When I escorted him into the auditorium at the opening session, the audience was instantly hushed. Elvis was in the building, we would joke. The first conference brought him together with Jean-Luc Marion, the leading Catholic philosopher of his generation who had worked under him at the École normale supérieure. Marion, eager to prove himself a pure philosopher, started out with a protest that he was not interested in "the religious meaning of the gift." Derrida, with a twinkle in his eye, could not resist; he rejoined that he was "interested in Christianity and in the gift in the Christian sense." This was going to be fun, and he was already having fun, enjoying the VIP treatment he received at Villanova, a Catholic university run by the Order of Saint Augustine, his memories of "*les Catholiques*" of his Algerian childhood in the back of his mind. At the customary grace before dinner that evening, I was struck by his demeanor—eyes closed, head bowed, the very soul of prayer. Impish, impious, and devilish, there was a piety about him that at bottom had to do with the solemnity of our mortality, with our trembling between life and death. I thought of Kierkegaard's line about the knight of faith: Good Lord, is this the man?

The third conference was my favorite, on Augustine and "Circumfession," the text in which he circumfessed himself a man of prayers and tears and exposed his circumcision, *in literis*, at least. Later on a lifelong philosopher of religion, clearly incensed and quite bedeviled by Derrida's late infiltration of the field (*sero te amavi!*), told me that he had nothing to learn from Derrida about religion and that he would thank him very much not to bare his circumcision! Held sixteen days after nine-eleven, we were worried that both the speakers—including Derrida, in China at the time—and most of the audience would be unable or reluctant to board a plane. But Derrida made it, as did nearly everyone else, and spoke movingly about those terrible days. Catherine Malabou was unable to attend because of the illness of her son, so Derrida volunteered to read her paper—on Heidegger and Derrida. The first time he came to the word "Derrida" in her manuscript he looked up and said (the devil in his eye), "that's me." There followed a memorable and extemporaneous commentary on his relationship with Heidegger.

"Deconstruction"—I am not convinced that this is the best word for his work—is not a position but a certain way of de-positioning, not a what but a how, a style of thinking otherwise, a devilish, impish, neo-Kierkegaardian, neo-Socratic mischievousness. Extending that style to theology, I sometimes quip, when I myself am feeling devilish, that Derrida is my favorite theologian. He himself was too rigorous, with too much respect for scholarly expertise, to tolerate any such claim. He was not a master of many fields but he had the unmistakable mark of genius, the ability to intervene creatively in a staggeringly wide range of fields, to inspire people who have spent their lives in those fields, to set them off in new and hitherto unsuspected directions. So instead of calling him a great theologian, which is not true, let us just say that his thought constitutes an enormous theological and religious provocation, which is quite true. He was an *agent provocateur* in theology as in many other matters.

He had an indelible memory of God, part of what he called his *nostalgeria*,[1] which went along with and disturbed his own deferred and deferential "atheism." Believers will find no better formula for their belief than what he believes of his own atheism, that he rightly passes for one: "*je passe à juste titre*"[2]—that is what others say about him, and they are probably right, but he himself does not know. His devilish intervention upon theology occurs at a strategic point, conjuring up the specter of God, the peculiar, spectral, and powerful way God lives on after the death of God. Nothing is ever simply dead. He feels about in the dark for the traces of an almost atheistic, almost Augustinian, almost Jewish covenant with the impossible, poking about like a blind man with a stick, or like a devilish knight of faith strolling the streets of Laguna Beach, the Left Bank, or Greenwich Village. Thank you, Jacques, for your prayers and tears and for having the devil in your eye. May God, or time, or memory, or life, or something, I know not what, be with you, wherever you are.

Acknowledgments

My thanks to the various publishers for permission to reprint the following essays.

"Tradition and Event: Radicalizing the Catholic Principle," in *The Challenge of God: Continental Philosophy and the Catholic Intellectual Tradition*, ed. Colby Dickinson, Hugh Miller, and Kathleen McNutt (London: Bloomsbury, 2019), 99–113.

"Proclaiming the Year of the Jubilee: Thoughts on a Spectral Life," in *It Spooks: Living in Response to an Unheard Call*, ed. Erin Schendzielos (Rapid City, S.D.: Shelter50 Publishing Collective, 2015), 10–47.

"Derrida and the Trace of Religion," in *A Companion to Derrida* (Blackwell Companions to Philosophy), ed. Zeynep Direk and Leonard Lawlor (Oxford: Wiley-Blackwell, 2014), 464–79.

"Augustine and Postmodernism," in *A Companion to Augustine* (Blackwell Companions to the Ancient World), ed. Mark Vessey (Oxford: Wiley-Blackwell, 2012), 492–504.

"On Not Settling for an Abridged Edition of Postmodernism: Radical Hermeneutics as Radical Theology," in *Reexamining Deconstruction and Determinate Religion: Toward a Religion with Religion*, ed. J. Aaron Simmons and Stephen Minister (Pittsburgh: Duquesne University Press, 2012), 271–91.

"Unprotected Religion: Radical Theology, Radical Atheism, and the Return of Anti-Religion," in *The Trace of God: Derrida and Religion*, ed.

Edward Baring and Peter E. Gordon (New York: Fordham University Press, 2015), 151–77.

"Forget Rationality—Is There Religious Truth?" in *Madness, Religion and the Limits of Reason*, ed. Jonna Bornemark and Sven-Olov Wallenstein, Södertörn Philosophical Studies 16 (Stockholm, Sweden: Elendars, 2015), 23–40.

"Radical Theologians, Knights of Faith, and the Future of the Philosophy of Religion," in *Reconfigurations of the Philosophy of Religion*, ed. Jim Kanaris (Albany: State University of New York Press, 2018), 211–36.

"Theology in Trumptime: The Insistence of America," in *Doing Theology in the Age of Trump: A Critical Report on Christian Nationalism*, ed. Jeffrey W. Robbins and Clayton Crockett, Westar Seminar on God and the Human Future (Eugene, Ore.: Cascade Books, 2018), 77–81.

"Hoping against Hope: The Possibility of the Impossible," *Journal of Pastoral Theology* 26.2 (2016): 91–101. http://www.tandfonline.com/doi/full/1.1080/10649867.2016.1244325.

"Like a Devilish Knight of Faith," *Oxford Literary Review* 36.2 (2014): 188–90.

Notes

Introduction: What Is Radical Theology?

1. See the results of the 2019 "Religious Landscape Study" by the Pew Research Center at https://www.pewforum.org/religious-landscape-study.

2. For an engaged and engaging presentation of this midcentury scene, John Robinson's classic *Honest to God* (Philadelphia: Westminster, 1963) has yet to be surpassed.

3. John D. Caputo, *The Mystical Element in Heidegger's Thought* (Athens: Ohio University Press, 1978; rev. ed.: New York: Fordham University Press, 1986); this was my first book.

4. Derrida uses this expression in *The Gift of Death*, trans. David Wills (Chicago: University of Chicago Press, 1995), 49.

5. For a valuable and comprehensive overview see *The Palgrave Handbook of Radical Theology*, ed. Christopher D. Rodkey and Jordan E. Miller (Cham, Switzerland: Palgrave Macmillan, 2018). The leading journal is *Journal of Cultural and Religious Theory* (www.jcrt.org). The *Journal for Continental Philosophy of Religion* (Brill) has also gotten off to a very good start.

6. It is perhaps this interweaving of radical and confessional theology in my work to which Joeri Schrijvers objects in his *Between Faith and Belief: Toward a Contemporary Phenomenology of Religious Life* (Albany: State University of New York Press, 2016), 133–292.

7. See Paul Tillich on "absolute faith" in *The Courage to Be* (New Haven, Conn.: Yale University Press, 1952), 171–76, and Arne Unheijm, *Dynamics of Doubt: A Preface to Tillich* (Philadelphia: Fortress Press, 1966), an inciting, insightful now forgotten introduction to Tillich.

8. See chapter 1.

9. In chapter 8, I suggest that radical theology, like the knight of faith, must look to all the world like a tax collector, that is, a philosopher of religion.

10. I say in principle because, in fact, as I point out in chapter 8 and in *The Insistence of God* (Bloomington: Indiana University Press, 2013), 70–72, this too is a fiction. Radical theologians for the most part report back to a largely western, mostly monotheistic academic audience and "submit to a vast and complex system of protocols and censorships, just like everybody else."

11. This is the fire I am trying to extinguish in chapter 5.

12. Jacques Derrida, "Circumfession: Fifty-Nine Periods and Periphrases," in *Jacques Derrida*, by Geoffrey Bennington and Jacques Derrida (Chicago: University of Chicago Press, 1993), 58, where Derrida says he speaks in "Christian Latin French." See also "Faith and Knowledge," in *Acts of Religion*, ed. Gil Anidjar (New York: Routledge, 2002), 40 where he problematizes *"la" religion*, in the singular.

13. See the elaboration of the concept of hermeneutics in John D. Caputo, *Hermeneutics: Facts and Interpretation in the Age of Information* (London: Pelican Books, 2018).

14. See Paul Tillich, "The Two Types of Philosophy of Religion," in Paul Tillich, *Theology of Culture*, ed. Robert C. Kimball (Oxford: Oxford University Press, 1959), 10–29, which is my candidate for the best essay ever written on the "philosophy of religion."

15. Gilles Deleuze, *The Logic of Sense,* trans. Mark Lester with Charles Stivale, ed. Constantin V. Boundas (New York: Columbia University Press, 1969), 149.

16. As I show in *The Insistence of God*, 147–48, mistaking the event as an essence or an ideality is exactly what throws Žižek off in reading my theology of the event.

17. Derrida would describe them as provisional effects of the play of *différance*, that is, as constructions and as such deconstructible. Tillich would say they are conditional forms of their unconditional content and as such subject to the Protestant Principle.

18. Martin Heidegger, *The Principle of Reason*, trans. Reginald Lilly (Bloomington: Indiana University Press, 1991), 16.

19. I orchestrate this motif in chapter 2, and then again in the final essay on hope (chapter 10).

20. Jacques Derrida, "Psyche: Invention of the Other," in *Psyche: Inventions of the Other*, vol. 1, trans. Peggy Kamuf and Elizabeth Rottenberg (Stanford, Calif.: Stanford University Press, 2007), 21–47.

21. In "Circumfession," 314, Derrida writes "You have spent your whole life inviting calling promising, hoping sighing dreaming, convoking invoking provoking, constituting engendering producing, naming assigning demanding, prescribing commanding sacrificing.".

22. I have developed this thematic in chapter 10.

23. See Jacques Derrida, *Margins of Philosophy*, trans. Alan Bass (Chicago: University of Chicago Press, 1982), 5–6; Jacques Derrida, "How to Avoid Speaking: Denials," in *Derrida and Negative Theology*, ed. Howard Coward and Toby Foshay (Albany: State University of New York Press, 1992), 73–74; and "Post-Scriptum," in *Derrida and Negative Theology*, 309–10. For a commentary, see John D. Caputo, *The Prayers and Tears of Jacques Derrida: Religion without Religion* (Bloomington: Indiana University Press, 1997), 1–19.

24. The atheists think the "radical" in this theology drives out the theology instead of constituting it (chap. 6); the Christian apologists think the theology drives out the radical instead of requiring it (chap. 5).

25. See Martin Heidegger's *What Is Called Thinking?* trans. Fred D. Wieck and J. Glenn Gray (New York: Harper and Row, 1968). Heidegger is exploiting the multivalence of the German "*Was Heisst Denken?*"

26. Tillich, *Theology of Culture*, 25.

27. Martin Heidegger, *Being and Time*, trans. John Macquarrie and Edward Robinson (New York: Harper & Row, 1962), §§56–57.

28. See Walter Benjamin's famous essay "The Concept of History," in *Walter Benjamin: Selected Writings*, vol. 4, *1938–40*, ed. Michael Jennings (Cambridge, Mass.: Belknap Press of Harvard University Press, 2003), 389–400. Derrida interprets this text in *Specters of Marx: The State of the Debt, the Work of Mourning, and the New International*, trans. Peggy Kamuf (New York: Routledge, 1994), 180–81n2. For a commentary see John D. Caputo and Jacques Derrida, *Deconstruction in a Nutshell* (New York: Fordham University Press, 1997), chap. 6.

29. Emmanuel Levinas, *Otherwise Than Being or Beyond Essence*, trans. Alphonso Lingis (The Hague: Nijhoff, 1981), 53–56.

30. Jacques Derrida, "The University without Condition," in *Without Alibi*, ed. and trans. Peggy Kamuf (Stanford, Calif.: Stanford University Press, 2002), 202–37.

31. Dietrich Bonhoeffer, *Dietrich Bonhoeffer Works*, vol. 8: *Letters and Papers from Prison*, ed. John W. de Gruchy, trans. Isabel Best, Lisa E. Dahill, Reinhard Krauss, and Nancy Lukens (Minneapolis: Fortress Press, 2010), 366.

32. Gilles Deleuze, *The Logic of Sense*, trans. Mark Lester with Charles Stivale, ed. Constantin V. Boundas (New York: Columbia University Press, 1969), 149; see also Ole Fogh Kirkeby, "*Eventum Tantum*: To Make the World Worthy of What Could Happen to It," *Ephemera* 4, no. 3 (2004): 290–308.

33. Martin Luther, *Heidelberg Disputation*, in *The Roots of Reform*, vol. 1 of The Annotated Luther, ed. Timothy J. Wingert (Minneapolis: Fortress, 2015), 98–99 (theses 19–21).

34. See Katharine Sarah Moody, *Will There Have Been God? An Introduction to the Radical Theology of John D. Caputo* (Lanham, Md.: Rowman and Littlefield, forthcoming).

35. See chapter 3, where I follow the history of Derrida's encounter with the name (of) "God."

36. Edmund Husserl, *Ideas Pertaining to a Pure Phenomenology and to a Phenomenological Philosophy*, vol. 1, trans. Fred Kersten (The Hague: Kluwer, 1998), §§47–55, §110.

37. Incredulity occurs midway between neutrality and denial. Incredulity disapproves but does not disprove; one can no more disprove the existence of a Supreme Being than of alien abductions. Incredulity just wrinkles its brow in disbelief.

38. Nor does it exclude; in fact, it includes the possibility of an "ecstatic naturalism" that gets past the idea of a dead inert matter being pushed around in empty space. We see this in Schelling and Tillich himself, and it is alive and well today in the work of Catherine Keller and Mary-Jane Rubenstein. I address the issues this raises, the way that theopoetics expands into cosmopoetics, in part 2 of *Cross and Cosmos: A Theology of Wounded Glory* (Bloomington: Indiana University Press, 2019).

39. That is an important part of the difference between Thomistic analogy and a Tillichian symbol.

40. See James S. Biello, *Ark Encounter: The Making of a Creationist Theme Park* (NewYork: New York University Press, 2018).

41. Tillich, *Theology of Culture*, 3–9, 40–51

42. See chapter 2 on the year of the Jubilee and chapter 9 on the critique of nostalgic time.

43. Rodkey and Miller, eds., *Palgrave Handbook of Radical Theology*, 8–13.

44. See James Cone, *A Black Theology of Liberation* (Maryknoll, N.Y.: Orbis Books, 2010). For Cone, if theology is not about liberation, it is not theology at all.

45. My preferred summary of these results is Geza Vermes, *Christian Beginnings: From Nazareth to Nicaea* (New Haven, Conn.: Yale University Press, 2013).

46. I have elaborated this theopoetics, what the God of Yeshua would look like, in *The Weakness of God: A Theology of the Event* (Bloomington: Indiana University Press, 2006) and in *Cross and Cosmos*.

47. See the discussion of Marx in chapter 2.

48. Derrida, "Circumfession," 58. See chapters 4 and 7. It is no mere coincidence that Augustine has been repeatedly taken up by postmodern thinkers who set out to repeat and reinvent his *Confessions*.

49. See the discussions of Hegel in chapters 5, 7, and 8.

50. See chapter 9.

51. See Jean Grondin, *Introduction to Philosophical Hermeneutics*, trans. Joel Weinsheimer (New Haven, Conn.: Yale University Press, 1994), 60–62. Grondin explains how this tripartite formulation of hermeneutics by J. J. Rambach (1737–1818), made famous by Gadamer, made its way into contemporary hermeneutics.

52. Derrida deploys this figure in Jacques Derrida, *Rogues: Two Essays on Reason*, trans. Pascale-Anne Brault and Michael Naas (Stanford, Calif.: Stanford University Press, 2005). This is the argument in chapter 8.

53. See chapter 1. For a comparable bit of resistance to authoritarianism from *within* the institution, see my account of Fr. John McNamee in *What Would Jesus Deconstruct? The Good News of Postmodernism for the Church* (Grand Rapids, Mich.: Baker, 2007), 118–34.

54. See chapter 10.

55. See Mary-Jane Rubenstein on "pan(icked) theology" in "The Matter with Pantheism," in *Entangled Worlds: Religion, Science and the New Materialism*, ed. Catherine Keller and Mary-Jane Rubenstein (New York: Fordham University Press, 2017), 159–66.

56. See Jason Horowitz, "Pope Says It's 'an Honor That the Americans Attack Me,'" *New York Times*, September 4, 2019. https://www.nytimes .com/2019/09/04/world/africa/pope-americans-attack.html?searchResult Position=6.

57. I elaborate what this displacement would look like in *On Religion*, 2nd ed. (London: Routledge, 2019); *Philosophy and Theology* (Nashville: Abingdon Press, 2006); and *What Would Jesus Deconstruct?*

58. Gianni Vattimo, *Belief*, trans. Luca D'Isanto and David Webb (New York: Columbia University Press, 1999), 1.

59. My interest in reconstruing the idea of reason in chapter 7 goes all the way back to *Radical Hermeneutics* (Bloomington: Indiana University Press, 1987), chap. 8.

60. In German *die Gift* means poison, an interlingual pun used by Derrida to signify the undecidability of gifts.

61. Paul Tillich, *The Socialist Decision*, trans. Franklin Sherman (New York: Harper & Row, 1977). I make use of this book in chapter 9.

62. See *Retrieving the Radical Tillich: His Legacy and Contemporary Importance*, ed. Russell Re Manning (Hampshire, UK: Palgrave Macmillan, 2015).

63. On the idea of ecstatic reason, see F. W. J. Schelling, *The Grounding of Positive Philosophy: The Berlin Lectures*, trans. Bruce Matthews (Albany: State University of New York Press, 2008), 202–3; and Paul Tillich, *Dynamics of Faith* (New York: Harper and Row, 1957), 87–88.

64. Derrida, "Circumfession," 291 (the French is *"sevrée de la verité"*).

1. Tradition and Event: Radicalizing the Catholic Principle

1. July 21, 2015, *Philadelphia Inquirer*. http://www.philly.com/philly/blogs /thinktank/On-gay-marriage-let-spirit-guide-the-church .html#puoCsq0wmIGYRQG8.99.

2. The work that David Tracy has done to think contemporary pluralism in terms of the hermeneutics of the tradition, drawing on Paul Ricoeur and Gadamer, is a case of taking the right approach, according to my point of view. See David Tracy, *The Analogical Imagination: Christian Theology and the Culture of Pluralism* (New York: Crossroad, 1981); *Plurality and Ambiguity: Hermeneutics, Religion, Hope* (San Francisco: Harper & Row, 1987).

3. Hans Küng, "Appeal to Rethink Infallibility," *National Catholic Reporter* 52:12 (March 25–April 7, 2016). See Hans Küng, *Infallible? An Unresolved Enquiry* (London: Continuum International, 1994).

4. Paul Tillich, *Dynamics of Faith* (New York: HarperCollins, 1957), 33, 112–13; *The Protestant Era*, trans. James Luther Adams (Chicago: University of Chicago Press, Phoenix Books, 1957).

5. See Mark Lewis Taylor, "Socialism's Multitude: Tillich's *The Socialist Decision* and Resisting the US Imperial," in *Retrieving the Radical Tillich*, ed. Russell Re Manning (New York: Palgrave Macmillan, 2015), 137–40.

6. The cross is a perfect symbol of the Protestant Principle: Anything, any book or ecclesiastical office that sets itself up as irreformable (unconditional) is to be crucified. See *The Courage to Be* (New Haven, Conn.: Yale University Press, 1952), 188. Whatever has been constructed is deconstructible.

7. John Dominic Crossan, "Our Own Faces in Deep Wells: The Future of Historical Jesus Research," in *God, the Gift and Postmodernism*, coedited by John D. Caputo and Michael J. Scanlon (Bloomington: Indiana University Press, 1999), 282–310.

8. Stanley Hauerwas (1940–) is a pacifist theologian and a critic of Reinhold Niebuhr's Christian realism. Hauerwas denies the notion of a "just war" and maintains that it is a creation of the post-Constantinian church. See his *The Peaceable Kingdom: A Primer in Christian Ethics* (Notre Dame, Ind.: University of Notre Dame Press, 1983)

9. Indeed, one of the oldest components of the Constantinian Church, the "just war" theory, was revisited in a conference held at the Vatican, April 11–13, 2016.

10. James L. Kugel, *The God of Old: Inside the Lost World of the Bible* (New York: Free Press, 2003), 125–36.

11. The grace of the Lord be on Brebeuf Preparatory School, a Jesuit institution in Indianapolis, for "respectfully declining" an archdiocesan directive to fire a teacher in a civil same-sex marriage. The archbishop said he would no longer recognize the school as Catholic, but I think the Spirit can no longer recognize itself in the archdiocese. See Derrick Bryson Taylor, "Jesuit School," *New York Times*, June 22, 2019.

12. I have defended this reading of the story in *The Weakness of God: A Theology of the Event* (Bloomington: Indiana University Press, 2006), 236–58. See also Ernst Käsemann, *The Testament of Jesus* (Philadelphia: Fortress Press, 1968), 9.

13. Richard Kearney, "Epiphanies of the Everyday: Toward a Micro-Eschatology," in *After God: Richard Kearney and the Religious Turn in Continental Philosophy*, ed. John Panteleimon Manoussakis (New York: Fordham University Press, 2011).

2. Proclaiming the Year of the Jubilee: Thoughts on a Spectral Life
    1. In its original publication—in *It Spooks: Living in Response to an Unheard Call*, ed. Erin Schendzielos (Rapid City, S.D.: Shelter50, 2015)—

this essay was accompanied by some two hundred pages of fascinating commentary by academics and non-academics, and by some quite wonderful and powerful graphics, which are not to be missed. This book is radical theology in action.

Jacques Derrida, *Specters of Marx: The State of the Debt, the Work of Mourning, and the New International*, trans. Peggy Kamuf (New York: Routledge, 1994), 166–77. See my commentary on this text in *The Prayers and Tears of Jacques Derrida: Religion without Religion* (Bloomington: Indiana University Press, 1997), 118–34.

2. Derrida, *Specters of Marx*, 65.

3. John D. Caputo, *Truth: Philosophy in Transit* (London: Penguin Books, 2013), chap. 5.

4. Derrida, *Specters of Marx*, 174.

5. Derrida, *Specters of Marx*, 41–44.

6. See Immanuel Kant, "What Is Enlightenment?" http://philosophy.eserver .org/kant/what-is-enlightenment.txt (accessed June 2014).

7. Derrida, *Specters of Marx*, 75.

8. Slavoj Žižek and John Milbank, *The Monstrosity of Christ: Paradox or Dialectic*, ed. Creston Davis (Cambridge, Mass.: MIT Press, 2009). This debate revolves entirely around which of these positions is the true materialism. I have tried to settle the hash of both positions in *The Insistence of God: A Theology of Perhaps* (Bloomington: Indiana University Press, 2013), chap. 7.

9. Caputo, *Insistence of God*, 97–103. I spell out my case in detail in chapter 5 in the current volume.

10. See John D. Caputo, "The Weakness of the Flesh: Overcoming the Soft Gnosticism of Incarnational Christianity," in *Intensities: Philosophy, Religion and the Affirmation of Life*, ed. Steven Shakespeare and Katharine Sarah Moody (Surrey, Eng.: Ashgate, 2012), 79–94.

11. Jean-François Lyotard, *The Postmodern Condition: A Report on Knowledge*, trans. Geoff Bennington and Brian Massumi (Minneapolis: University of Minnesota Press, 1984), xxiv.

12. Jacques Lacan, *The Triumph of Religion, preceded by Discourse to Catholics*, trans. Bruce Fink (Cambridge: Polity Press, 2013), 64.

13. Gianni Vattimo, *Belief*, trans. Luca D'Isanto and David Webb (New York: Columbia University Press, 1999). I give a more nuanced account of the intertwining of confessional and radical theology in the Introduction, and in Caputo, *Insistence of God*, chapter 4.

14. Jacques Derrida, "Circumfession: Fifty-Nine Periods and Periphrases," in *Jacques Derrida*, by Geoffrey Bennington and Jacques Derrida (Chicago: University of Chicago Press, 1993), 155.

15. Jacques Derrida, *Rogues: Two Essays on Reason*, trans. Pascale-Anne Brault and Michael Naas (Stanford, Calif.: Stanford University Press, 2005), 110.

16. Johann Baptist Metz, *Faith in History and Society*, trans. D. Smith (New York: Crossroads, 1980), 109–15.

17. http://poetry.rapgenius.com/Robert-frost-the-span-of-life-annotated#note -2172683 (accessed June 2014).

18. Derrida, *Specters of Marx*, 174.

19. For Levinas, the ethico-religious subject is not the agent subject of the "I am capable of" but the responsible subject, the "me," *me voici*, put in the accusative by the coming of the other. Emmanuel Levinas, *Otherwise Than Being, or Beyond Essence*, trans. Alphonso Lingis (The Hague: Nijhoff, 1981), 53–56.

20. Jean-Luc Marion, *Being Given*, trans. Jeffrey Kosky (Stanford, Calif.: Stanford University Press, 2002), 199–247.

21. I work out this dream in *Insistence*, chapter 2.

22. *Hegel's Lectures on the Philosophy of Religion*, one-volume edition: *The Lectures of 1827*, ed. Peter Hodgson (Berkeley: University of California Press, 1988), 75–77.

23. Catherine Keller, *The Face of the Deep: A Theology of Becoming* (London: Routledge, 2003).

24. Martin Heidegger, "A Letter on Humanism," in *Heidegger: Basic Writings*, ed. by D. F. Krell, 2nd ed. (New York: Harper & Row, 1993).

25. In John D. Caputo, *Cross and Cosmos: A Theology of Wounded Glory* (Bloomington: Indiana University Press, 2019), Interlude 1, 167–80, I meditate on the various locutionary powers of the "it."

26. Derrida, *Specters of Marx*, 136.

27. Paul Tillich, *Theology of Culture*, ed. Robert Kimball (Oxford: Oxford University Press, 1959), 25.

28. I elaborate this in *Prayers and Tears*, 26–41.

29. Derrida, *Rogues*, xiv. In Derrida, the "unconditionals," such as justice, are always a weak force, without the "force of law."

30. *The Complete Mystical Works of Meister Eckhart*, trans. and ed. Maurice O'C Walshe (New York: Crossroad, 2009), 83–90 ("Intravit Jesus in quoddam castellum").

31. For an insightful study of preaching and postmodernism, see Phil Snider, *Preaching After God: Derrida, Caputo, and the Language of Postmodern Homiletics* (Eugene, Ore.: Cascade Books, Wipf and Stock, 2012). See also Robert M. Price, *Preaching Deconstruction*, with a foreword by Thomas J. J. Altizer (Mindvendor, 2014); Christopher D. Rodkey, *Too Good to Be True: Radical Christian Preaching, Year A*, with foreword by Peter Rollins and an afterword by Thomas J. J. Altizer (Alresford, Hants, UK: John Hunt Publishing, Christian Alternative, 2014).

32. Even someone as selfless as Louis Massignon (1883–1962), founder of Badaliya ("substitution"), a community of Christians in Egypt who were to be witness to Christ in the Islamic world, admitted that conversion to Catholicism may indeed be the object, or at least the result, of his work, but if it is to happen, it is to happen freely, without any pressure being applied on the part of the Christians. Cited by Derrida in *Acts of Religion*, ed. Gil Anidjar (New York: Routledge, 2002), 376n36.

33. Marguerite Porete, *The Mirror of Simple Souls*, trans. Ellen L. Babinsky (New York: Paulist Press, 1993), 19 (101). See also 43 (122–23), 49–51 (127–29), 66 (142). I cite by chapter with the pagination in parentheses.

3. Derrida and the Trace of Religion

1. Jacques Derrida, "Circumfession: Fifty-Nine Periods and Periphrases," in *Jacques Derrida*, by Geoffrey Bennington and Jacques Derrida (Chicago: University of Chicago Press, 1993), 154–55.

2. Jacques Derrida, *Margins of Philosophy*, trans. Alan Bass (Chicago: University of Chicago Press, 1982), 5–6.

3. Jacques Derrida, "How to Avoid Speaking: Denials," in *Derrida and Negative Theology*, ed. Howard Coward and Toby Foshay (Albany: State University of New York Press, 1992), 309–10.

4. Hélène Cixous, "Promised Belief," in *Feminism, Sexuality and Religion*, ed. Linda Martín Alcoff and John D. Caputo (Bloomington: Indiana University Press, 2011), 130–60.

5. Jacques Derrida, *Speech and Phenomena and Other Essays on Husserl's Theory of Signs*, trans. David Allison (Evanston, Ill.: Northwestern University Press, 1973), 98–99 (although notice the mistranslation of *ou* as "where" instead of "or").

6. Jacques Derrida, *Writing and Difference*, trans. Alan Bass (Chicago: University of Chicago Press, 1978), 182,

7. Jacques Derrida, *Of Grammatology*, corrected edition, trans. Gayatri Chakravorty Spivak (Baltimore: Johns Hopkins University Press, 1997), 71.

8. Derrida, *Of Grammatology*, 323n3.

9. Derrida, "Circumfession," 155.

10. Jacques Derrida, *The Animal That Therefore I Am*, ed. Marie-Louise Mallet, trans. David Wills (New York: Fordham University Press, 2008).

11. Jacques Derrida, *Acts of Religion*, ed. Gil Anidjar (New York: Routledge 2002), 47.

12. Robert Detweiler, ed., "Derrida and Biblical Studies," *Semeia: An Experimental Journal for Biblical Criticism* 23 (1982); Louis Mackey, "Slouching towards Bethlehem: Deconstructive Strategies in Theology," *Anglican Theological Review* 65, no. 3 (1983): 255–72. Carl A. Raschke, *Alchemy of the Word* (Missoula, Mont.: Scholars Press, 1979).

13. Jacques Derrida and John D. Caputo, *Deconstruction in a Nutshell: A Conversation with Jacques Derrida* (New York: Fordham University Press, 1997), 8.

14. Derrida, *Acts of Religion*, 242–43.

15. Derrida, *Acts of Religion*, 251–58.

16. Søren Kierkegaard, *Fear and Trembling*, in *Kierkegaard's Writings*, VI, *Fear and Trembling* and *Repetition*, trans. and ed. Howard Hong and Edna Hong (Princeton, N.J.: Princeton University Press, 1983), 54–121.

17. Jacques Derrida, *The Gift of Death*, trans. David Wills (Chicago: University of Chicago Press, 1995), 58–73.

18. Jacques Derrida, *Given Time, I: Counterfeit Money*, trans. Peggy Kamuf (Chicago: University of Chicago Press, 1991), 30.

19. Derrida, "Circumfession," 3.

20. Derrida, *Given Time*, 6.

21. Derrida, "Circumfession," 40, 183.

22. Derrida, *Acts of Religion*, 326–28.

23. Derrida, "Circumfession," is the case in point. On the "perverformative"—every new performance of *x* will pervert *x*, for better or worse—see Jacques Derrida, *The Post Card: From Socrates to Freud and Beyond*, trans. Alan Bass (Chicago: University of Chicago Press, 1987), 136.

24. Jean-Louis Chrétien, "The Wounded Word: Phenomenology of Prayer," in *Phenomenology and the Theological Turn: The French Debate*, ed. Dominique Janicaud et al. (New York: Fordham University Press, 2000), 147–75.

25. Derrida, *Gift of Death*, 49.

26. Jacques Derrida, *Politics of Friendship*, trans. George Collins (London: Verso 1997), 29–30.

27. Jacques Derrida, "Psyche: Inventions of the Other," in *Psyche: Inventions of the Other*, trans. Peggy Kamuf and Elizabeth Rottenberg (Stanford, Calif.: Stanford University Press 2007), 1–47.

28. Michael Naas, *Derrida From Now On* (New York: Fordham University Press, 2008), 62–80.

29. Jacques Derrida, *Rogues: Two Essays on Reason*, trans. Pascale-Anne Brault and Michael Naas (Stanford, Calif.: Stanford University Press, 2005), xiv–xv.

30. Jacques Derrida, *Negotiations: Interventions and Interviews: 1971–2001*, trans. Elizabeth Rottenberg (Stanford, Calif.: Stanford University Press 2002), 362.

31. Jacques Derrida, "An Apocalyptic Tone That Has Recently Been Adopted in Philosophy," in *Raising the Tone of Philosophy*, ed. Peter Fenves (Baltimore: Johns Hopkins Press, 1993), 164.

32. Derrida, *Politics of Friendship*, 35, 42.

33. Slavoj Žižek and John Milbank, *The Monstrosity of Christ: Paradox or Dialectic*, ed. Creston Davis (Cambridge, Mass.: MIT Press, 2009).

34. T. J. J. Altizer et al., eds., *Deconstruction and Theology* (New York: Crossroad, 1982); Mark C. Taylor, *Erring: An A/theology* (Chicago: University of Chicago Press, 1984).

35. Quentin Meillassoux, *After Finitude: An Essay on the Necessity of Contingency*, trans. Ray Brassier (London: Continuum, 2008).

36. Dan Zahavi, *Husserl's Phenomenology* (Stanford, Calif.: Stanford University Press, 2003).

37. Derrida, *Negotiations*, 367.

38. See chapter 5.

39. Martin Hägglund, *Radical Atheism: Derrida and the Time of Life* (Stanford, Calif.: Stanford University Press, 2008). I give a fuller refutation of this book in chapter 6.

40. Hägglund, *Radical Atheism*, 31.

41. Derrida, *Negotiations*, 105, 94.

42. John D. Caputo, *Against Ethics: Contributions to a Poetics of Obligation with Constant Reference to Deconstruction* (Bloomington: Indiana University Press, 1993); this book is written in the spirit of Derrida and Lyotard.

43. Derrida, *Acts of Religion*, 248; Derrida, *Gift of Death*, 71.

44. Jacques Derrida, "Epoché and Faith: An Interview with Jacques Derrida," in *Derrida and Religion: Other Testaments*, ed. Yvonne Sherwood and Kevin Hart (London: Routledge, 2005), 39.

4. Augustine and Postmodernism

1. See *Polygraph: An International Journal of Culture and Politics*, 2008 (19/20), Special Issue, "Cities of Men, Cities of God: Augustine and Late Secularism," ed. R. Leo.

2. Mark C. Taylor, *After God* (Chicago: University of Chicago Press, 2007), 1–42.

3. John D. Caputo, *Philosophy and Theology* (Nashville, Tenn.: Abingdon Press, 2006), 44–50.

4. Giorgio Agamben, *The Time That Remains*, trans. Patricia Dailey (Stanford, Calif.: Stanford University Press, 2005); Alain Badiou, *Saint Paul: The Foundation of Universalism*, trans. Ray Brassier (Stanford, Calif.: Stanford University Press, 2003); Slavoj Žižek, *The Puppet and the Dwarf: The Perverse Core of Christianity* (Cambridge, Mass.: MIT Press, 2003).

5. Jean-Luc Marion, *God without Being*, trans. Thomas Carlson (Chicago: University of Chicago Press, 1991), 83.

6. Jean-Luc Marion, *In the Self's Place: The Approach of St. Augustine*, trans. Jeffrey L. Kosky (Chicago: University of Chicago Press, 2008), 9–10.

7. Marion, *In the Self's Place*, §§1–2; *God without Being*, 25–52; Jean-Luc Marion, *Being Given*, trans. Jeffrey Kosky (Stanford, Calif.: Stanford University Press, 2002), 27–39.

8. Marion, *God without Being*, 36.

9. Marion, *Being Given*, 199–247.

10. Marion, *In the Self's Place*, 100.

11. Marion, *In the Self's Place*, 40–50.

12. References to the *Confessions* are to book, chapter, and line (for those who want to consult the Latin).

13. Jacques Derrida, "How to Avoid Speaking: Denials," in *Derrida and Negative Theology*, ed. Howard Coward and Toby Foshay (Albany: State University of New York Press, 1992), 133n3.

14. Marion, *In the Self's Place*, 85–86; Jean-Luc Marion, *The Erotic Phenomenon*, trans. Stephen E. Lewis (Chicago: University of Chicago Press, 2007), 16–22.

15. Marion, *In the Self's Place*, 54–55.

16. Marion, *God without Being*, 105.

17. Dominique Janicaud, "The Theological Turn in French Phenomenology," in *Phenomenology and the "Theological Turn,"* ed. Dominique Janicaud et al., trans. Bernard G. Prusak (New York: Fordham University Press, 2000).

18. Marion, *In the Self's Place*, 74–80.

19. Marion, *In the Self's Place*, 80–87.

20. Marion, *In the Self's Place*, 108.

21. Marion, *In the Self's Place*, 118–19.

22. Marion, *In the Self's Place*, 131–32.

23. Marion, *In the Self's Place*, 101; Martin Heidegger, *Phenomenology of Religious Life*, trans. Jennifer Anna Gosetti and Matthias Fritsch (Bloomington: Indiana University Press, 2004), 142, 148.

24. *dissilui, Conf.* 11.29.39.

25. Marion, *In the Self's Place*, 223.

26. Marion, *In the Self's Place*, 225–27.

27. Marion, *In the Self's Place*, 233–34.

28. Marion, *In the Self's Place*, 326–27.

29. Marion *In the Self's Place*, 328.

30. Marion, *God without Being,*103.

31. *Conf.* 10.6.9.

32. Marion, *In the Self's Place*, 243–47.

33. Martin Heidegger, *Being and Time*, trans. John Macquarrie and Edward Robinson (New York: Harper & Row, 1962), 43–44.

34. Heidegger, *Being and Time*, 492n7.

35. Heidegger, *Phenomenology of Religious Life*, 151–55.

36. *Conf.* 10.30.41; Heidegger, *Phenomenology of Religious Life*, 155–78.

37. Heidegger, *Being and Time*, 215–16.

38. Heidegger, *Phenomenology of Religious Life*, 153.

39. Heidegger, *Being and Time*, 492n.vii.

40. Heidegger, *Phenomenology of Religious Life*, 185.

41. Heidegger, *Phenomenology of Religious Life*, 221.

42. On "use" and "enjoyment," see *On Christian Doctrine*, trans. D. W. Robertson Jr. (Indianapolis: Library of Liberal Arts, 1958), 9–10 (book 1, chaps. 3–5).

43. Heidegger, *Phenomenology of Religious Life*, 212–13.

44. In John D. Caputo, *Cross and Cosmos: A Theology of Wounded Glory* (Bloomington: Indiana University Press, 2019) I have elaborated a radical theology of the cross that takes it point of departure from this distinction in the *Heidelberg Disputation*.

45. John E. van Buren, *The Young Heidegger: Rumors of a Hidden King* (Bloomington: Indiana University Press, 1994) 162–67.

46. Marion, *Being Given*, 259–62.

47. Jacques Derrida, "Circumfession: Fifty-Nine Periods and Periphrases," in *Jacques Derrida*, by Geoffrey Bennington and Jacques Derrida (Chicago: University of Chicago Press, 1993), 211.

48. Jacques Derrida, *Monolingualism of the Other; or, The Prosthesis of Origin*, trans. Patrick Mensah (Stanford, Calif.: Stanford University Press, 1998), 1–5.

49. Derrida, "Circumfession," 177. On the metropole, see *Monolingualism of the Other; or, The Prosthesis of Origin*, trans. Patrick Mensah (Stanford, Calif.: Stanford University Press, 1998), 41–43.

50. Derrida, "Circumfession," 38–39.

51. Derrida, "Circumfession," 155; Jacques Derrida, "Epoché and Faith: An Interview with Jacques Derrida," in *Derrida and Religion: Other Testaments*, ed. Yvonne Sherwood and Kevin Hart (New York: Routledge, 2005), 28–31, 46–47; Derrida, "Roundtable," in *Augustine and Postmodernism: Confessions and Circumfession,* ed. John D. Caputo and Michael J. Scanlon (Bloomington: Indiana University Press, 2005), 38–39.

52. Jacques Derrida, "Faith and Knowledge," in *Religion*, ed. Gianni Vattimo, trans. Samuel Weber (Stanford, Calif.: Stanford University Press, 1998), 9–10.

53. Robert Dodaro, "Loose Canons: Augustine and Derrida on Their Selves," in *God, the Gift and Postmodernism*, ed. John D. Caputo and Michael Scanlon (Bloomington: Indiana University Press, 1999), 79–111.

54. Derrida, "Epoché and Faith," 39, 45; Derrida, "Faith and Knowledge," 8, 40, 51.

55. Mark C. Taylor, *Erring: An A/theology* (Chicago: University of Chicago Press, 1984), 6.

56. Derrida, "Circumfession," 154–55.

57. Richard Kearney, *Debates in Continental Philosophy* (New York: Fordham University Press, 2004), 140.

58. Derrida, "Circumfession," 122. SA means variously Saint Augustine, *savoir absolu* (Hegel), and "signifier" (*signifians*) (de Saussure, Lacan).

59. Derrida, "Circumfession," 115; cf. Aug., *Conf.* 10.12.33.

60. Jacques Derrida, "Response to Malabou," in Caputo and Scanlon, *Augustine and Postmodernism*), 139.

61. Derrida, "Response to Malabou," 138.

62. Derrida, "Circumfession," 48–49; cf. Aug., *Conf.* 10.1.1, echoing John 3:21).

63. Caputo and Scanlon, Introduction to *Augustine and Postmodernism,* 4.

64. Kearney, *Debates in Continental Philosophy*, 150.

65. Derrida, "Faith and Knowledge," 17–18.

66. Derrida, "Circumfession," 26–31.

67. Derrida, "Circumfession," 80.

68. Derrida, "Circumfession," 172, 213, 217.

69. Derrida, "Circumfession," 117–19.

70. Derrida, "Circumfession," 314–15.

71. Derrida, "Circumfession," 28.

72. See chapter 7, for a complementary presentation of "Circumfession."

73. Jean-François Lyotard, *The Postmodern Condition: A Report on Knowledge*, trans. Geoff Bennington and Brian Massumi (Minneapolis: University of Minnesota Press, 1984), xiv.

74. "Late have I loved you"; *Conf.* 10.27.38. Jean-François Lyotard, *The Confession of Augustine*, trans. Richard Beardsworth (Stanford: Stanford University Press, 2000), 2, 55–56.

75. Lyotard, *Confession of Augustine*, 17–18, 74–75.

76. Lyotard, *Confession of Augustine*, 56.

77. James J. O'Donnell, "Augustine's Unconfessions," in Caputo and Scanlon, *Augustine and Postmodernism*, 212–21; Elizabeth A. Clark, "On Not Retracting the Unconfessed," in Caputo and Scanlon, *Augustine and Postmodernism*, 222–43.

78. Lyotard, *Confession of Augustine*, 27–28.

79. Lyotard, *Confession of Augustine*, 36.

80. Lyotard, *Confession of Augustine*, 18–20.

81. Lyotard, *Confession of Augustine*, 36.

82. Lyotard, *Confession of Augustine*, 56–57.

83. Lyotard, *Confession of Augustine*, 35–36,

84. For further reading, see *Augustine and Postmodern Thought: A New Alliance against Modernity*, ed. L. Boeve, M. Lamberigts, and M. Wisse (Leuven: Peeters, 2009), which is a splendid collection of studies by close readers of Augustine who bring Augustine into dialogue with postmodern theory, including "Radical Orthodoxy," a neo-Augustinian theological movement that makes a selective use of postmodern theory; the rich notes in this volume contain many helpful bibliographical references. I strongly recommend the essays on Derrida by Dodaro (note 53, above) and all the essays in Caputo and Scanlon, eds. *Augustine and Postmodernism*, which contains helpful studies of the deployment of Augustine by Heidegger, Lyotard, and Ricoeur. John D. Caputo, *The Prayers and Tears of Jacques Derrida: Religion without Religion* (Bloomington: Indiana University Press, 1997) is a comprehensive presentation of Derrida where the Augustinian analogy is uppermost in mind. Van Buren (note 45) and Benjamin Crowe, *Heidegger's Philosophy of Religion* (Bloomington: Indiana University Press, 2007) demonstrate how Heidegger emerged from his early study of Kierkegaard, Luther, and Augustine. W. J. Hankey, "Re-Christianizing Augustine Postmodern Style," *Animus* 2 (1997) is a lively and lucid intervention on several issues of interest to this topic. See also the *Revue de Métaphysique et de Morale* (July 2009), a special issue titled "St. Augustin, penseur de soi: Discussions de l'interprétation de Jean-Luc Marion." See also Johanna Schumm, *Confessio, Confessiones, Circonfession: Zum literarischen Bekenntnis bei Augustinus und Derrida* (Munich: Wilhelm Fink Verlag, 2013).

5. On Not Settling for an Abridged Edition of Postmodernism: Radical Hermeneutics as Radical Theology

1. *Reexamining Deconstruction and Determinate Religion: Toward a Religion with Religion*, ed. J. Aaron Simmons and Stephen Minister (Pittsburgh: Duquesne University Press, 2012).

2. By "exclusive" I mean privileged access, that something has been revealed to a certain number of people but not to everybody and that if you don't believe it you are at worst wrong or at best merely in the dark. A statement like "Jesus is uniquely God Incarnate" is treated as representationally true or false, representing a supernatural state of affairs unknowable unless it is revealed, something that has been revealed to Christians, who are defined by this privilege. Christians accept its truth, and anyone who denies it is wrong; anyone who has never heard of it is at a disadvantage; and those who have heard it and ignore or reject it put themselves at a disadvantage. The latter problem beset St. Paul, who was worried about his own people, the Jews, who rejected Christ. Paul claims the advantage of privileged access, that he was given the special privilege of being visited by the risen Christ, which authorized him to assure those whom he managed to reach that he was right about this proposition. It is really not much consolation to other traditions, which know or care little or nothing about Christianity, to learn that in this charitable exclusivism they are not regarded as "entirely incorrect." From such "charity" may the Lord protect us. Why not a theory that the *others* are the ones who got privileged access and *we were left out*? Wouldn't that be even more charitable? We don't need charity here; we need justice, doing justice to others, a judicious analysis of religious truth that justly recognizes that nobody has any privileged access in matters like this, which is the advantage of seeing that we have to do here with symbols and *Vorstellungen*, with theopoetic differences, not competing representational assertions and special privileges.

3. See J. Aaron Simmons, "Apologetics after Objectivity," in *Reexamining Deconstruction*, 35.

4. See John D. Caputo, *Truth: The Postmodern Search for Wisdom* (London: Penguin Books, 2015).

5. Stephen Minster, "Faith Seeking Understanding," in *Reexamining Deconstruction*, 83.

6. Mark Twain was good at exploring these accidents of birth. His memorable *The Tragedy of Pudd'inhead Wilson* explores the fate of two babies switched in the cradle, one the son of a slave who was quite white, the other the son of a wealthy man, and the utterly different people they became as a result. Imagine the same switch of infants between Christian and Islamic families or lands.

7. *Kierkegaard's Writings*, 12.1, *Concluding Unscientific Postscript to "Philosophical Fragments,"* trans. and ed. Howard Hong and Edna Hong (Princeton, N.J.: Princeton University Press, 1992), 118.

8. Quentin Meillasssoux, *After Finitude,* trans. Ray Brassier (London: Continuum, 2008), 28–49. For a further reflection on Meillassoux, see chapter 3.

9. Minister, 82–83.

10. I elaborate exactly what ontological weight is carried by phenomenological statements in John D. Caputo, *Cross and Cosmos: A Theology of Wounded Glory* (Bloomington: Indiana University Press, 2019), 227–40.

11. Simmons, 25–30.

12. Simmons, 26.

13. Simmons, 33.

14. Simmons, 43–44. Stephen Minister makes the same mistake by saying that Derrida holds no positions, a statement he makes in almost perfect innocence of Derrida's distinction between positions and affirmations; Minister, 76.

15. Jacques Derrida, *Monolingualism of the Other; or, The Prosthesis of Origin*, trans. Patrick Mensah (Stanford, Calif.: Stanford University Press, 1998), 4.

16. Although I delimit formal logic, I want no part in dismissing it. Having attended graduate school in the days before there were many "continental" programs to speak of, I had a completely traditional philosophical education. I was prepared in mathematical logic under Hugues Leblanc, who was a student of Quine at Harvard, who had a special interest in the method of "natural deduction" developed by Gerhard Gentzen (1909–45), which I had begun to use in an early publication on Kant's critique of the ontological argument. The work I did on axiomatization and formal systems helped me later on understand Husserl, structuralism, and the analogous use of the notion of formal undecidability in Gödel and Derrida.

17. Martin Heidegger, *Of Time and Being*, trans. Joan Stambaugh (New York: Harper & Row, 1969), 2, 25.

18. John D. Caputo, *The Weakness of God: A Theology of the Event* (Bloomington: Indiana University Press, 2006), chap. 11.

19. John Milbank makes a "complete *concession*" to the idea that Christian theology is a "contingent historical construct"; see *Theology and Social Theory* (Oxford: Blackwell, 1993), 2. For a lively criticism of this movement, see *Deconstructing Radical Orthodoxy: Postmodern Theology, Rhetoric and Truth*, ed. Wayne J. Hankey and Douglas Hedley (Aldershot, Eng.: Ashgate, 2005).

20. In the Introduction to this volume, I identify this as the process of entering Yeshua into theopoetic space. In my opinion, the most sensible *historical* account is found in Geza Vermes, *Christian Beginnings: From Nazareth to Nicaea* (New Haven, Conn.: Yale University Press, 2013).

21. See Bruce Benson's response to Simmons in *Reexamining Deconstruction*, 61–68.

22. I continued this project in *Cross and Cosmos*, where I propose a radical or postmodern rendering of Luther's *Heidelberg Disputation*.

23. Minister, 77–85.

24. Minister, *Reexamining Deconstruction*, 340–42.

25. For a constructive account of the relationship between continental and analytic philosophy of religion, see Nick Trakakis, *The End of Philosophy of Religion* (London: Continuum: 2009).

26. Jacques Derrida, *Rogues: Two Essays on Reason*, trans. Pascale-Anne Brault and Michael Naas (Stanford, Calif.: Stanford University Press, 2005), 110.

27. See John D. Caputo, *On Religion*, 2nd ed. (London: Routledge, 2019); *What Would Jesus Deconstruct? The Good News of Postmodernity for the Church* (Grand Rapids, Mich.: Baker, 2007); *Philosophy and Theology* (Nashville, Tenn.: Abingdon, 2006). I should point out that some of the contributors to *Reexamining Deconstruction* lack tenured positions and to their credit are testing other borders—between continental and analytic philosophy, even as their interest in religion could make secular philosophers (and hiring committees) uncomfortable.

28. John D. Caputo and Jacques Derrida, *Deconstruction in a Nutshell: A Conversation with Jacques Derrida*, edited with a commentary (New York: Fordham University Press, 1997), 168–78.

29. See the exchange between Jeffery Robbins, Clayton Crockett, Victor Taylor, and me, on the one hand, and Donald Wiebe, on the other hand, in *The Council of Societies for the Study of Religion Bulletin* 37, no. 2 (2008): 31–48 and *The Council of Societies for the Study of Religion Bulletin* 37, no. 3 (2008): 77–86.

30. John D. Caputo, *The Insistence of God* (Bloomington: Indiana University Press, 2013), 87–116; and "The Perversity of the Absolute, the Perverse Core of Hegel, and the Possibility of Radical Theology," in *Hegel and the Infinite: Religion, Politics, and Dialectic*, ed. Clayton Crockett, Creston Davis, and Slavoj Žižek (New York: Columbia University Press, 2011), 47–66.

31. *Hegel's Lectures on the Philosophy of Religion: One Volume Edition: The Lectures of 1827*, ed. and trans. Peter C. Hodgson (Berkeley: University of California Press, 1988), 80–85.

32. Catherine Keller, *The Face of the Deep* (London: Routledge, 2003).

33. Of course, as Hegel himself points out, there are concepts *in* theology—the conceptual apparatus of dogmatic theology—but they are constructions that remain within the imaginative framework of the *Vorstellung*. One might distinguish concepts *in* theology from concepts *of* theology.

34. This point, that my "without" implies a certain phenomenological reduction, or as I would say radicalization, one that is profoundly different from Marion's neo-phenomenology, was singled out by Kevin Hart, in an essay titled "Without," to which I have responded. Jean-Luc Marion and I (following Derrida) have very different, even opposite ideas of "without." Hart was the first one to make an argument against me on behalf of the "with," but with considerably more sensitivity to how the "without" works in the work of Jacques Derrida than the arguments made in *Reexamining Deconstruction*. Kevin Hart, "Without," in *Cross and Khora: Deconstruction and Christianity in the Work of John D. Caputo*, ed. Neal Deroo and Marko Zlomsic (Eugene, Ore.: Pickwick Publications, Wipf and Stock, 2010), 80–108, and my response, "Only as Hauntology Is Religion without Religion Possible: A Response to Hart," 109–17.

35. Minister, "A Response to J. Aaron Simmons," in *Reexamining Deconstruction,* 71. That the concrete traditions are and should feel "haunted" goes to the heart of what I am arguing.

36. Slavoj Žižek and John Milbank, *The Monstrosity of Christ: Paradox or Dialectic,* ed. Creston Davis (Cambridge, Mass.: MIT Press, 2009), 254.

6. Unprotected Religion: Radical Theology, Radical Atheism, and the Return of Anti-Religion

1. The present chapter appeared in a longer and more fully elaborated form in "The Return of Anti-Religion: From Radical Atheism to Radical Theology," *Journal of Cultural and Religious Theory* 11, no. 2 (2011): 32–125. http://www .jcrt.org/archives/11.2/caputo.pdf.

2. Martin Hägglund, *Radical Atheism: Derrida and the Time of Life* (Stanford, Calif.: Stanford University Press, 2008). Hereafter referred to as *RA.*

3. Quentin Meillassoux, *After Finitude: An Essay on the Necessity of Contingency,* trans. Ray Brassier (London: Continuum, 2008), 18. For robust rebuttals of Meillassoux, see Adrian Johnston, "Hume's Revenge: À Dieu, Meillassoux," and Martin Hägglund, "Radical Atheist Materialism: A Critique of Meillassoux," in *The Speculative Turn: Continental Materialism and Realism,* ed. Levi Bryant, Nick Srnicek, and Graham Harman (Melbourne: re.press, 2011), 92–113 and 114–29, respectively.

4. Michael Naas, *Derrida From Now On* (New York: Fordham University Press, 2008), 62–80; see especially 239n5, in which Naas succinctly states my views on Derrida and religion with a judiciousness absent from *RA.*

5. Christopher Watkin, *Difficult Atheism: Post-Theological Thinking in Alain Badiou, Jean-Luc Nancy, and Quentin Meillassoux* (Edinburgh: Edinburgh University Press, 2011), 3–11.

6. Jacques Derrida, "Circumfession: Fifty-Nine Periods and Periphrases," in *Jacques Derrida,* by Geoffrey Bennington and Jacques Derrida (Chicago: University of Chicago Press, 1993), 58.

7. Clayton Crockett, "Surviving Christianity," *Derrida Today* 6, no.1 (2013): 29–33. Crockett has since published a superb book on Derrida which continues this rebuttal of Hägglund: Clayton Crockett, *Derrida after the End of Writing: Political Theology and the New Materialism* (New York: Fordham University Press, 2018). See also Neal DeRoo, "The Dangers of Dealing with Derrida—Revisiting the Caputo-Hägglund Debate on the 'Religious' Reading of Deconstruction," *Religious Theory: E-Supplement to Journal of Culture and Religious Theory* (http://jcrt.org/religioustheory), Part 1, June 26, 2018; Part 2, July 3, 2018; Part 3, July 11, 2018.

8. "STD," I cannot resist adding, is not far from "S.T.D.," the abbreviation for *sacrae theologiae doctor.*

9. As Derrida once pointed out, he first found the paradigm of phenomena constituted by their impossibility in Husserl's fifth *Cartesian Meditation,* where the alter ego is internally constituted by the impossibility of experiencing the

experiences of the other person. Were that impossibility not possible, the phenomenon would be ruined. Jacques Derrida, "Hospitality, Justice, and Responsibility," in *Questioning Ethics: Contemporary Debates in Philosophy*, ed. Mark Dooley and Richard Kearney (London: Routledge, 1999), 71.

10. John D. Caputo, *Radical Hermeneutics: Repetition, Deconstruction, and the Hermeneutic Project* (Bloomington: Indiana University Press, 1987), 1–7.

11. In making Derrida's atheism into a "position," a "thesis," Hägglund undoes everything that is interesting about Derrida's atheism, all the undecidability and the faith embedded in it. Derrida says that while he "rightly passes" as an atheist, he cannot say he *is* an atheist. "I can't say, myself, 'I am an atheist.' It's not a *position*. I wouldn't say, 'I am an atheist' and I wouldn't say, 'I am a believer' either. I find the statement absolutely ridiculous. . . . Who *knows* that? . . . And who can say, 'I am an atheist?'" Jacques Derrida, "Epoché and Faith: An Interview with Jacques Derrida," in *Derrida and Religion: Other Testaments*, ed. Yvonne Sherwood and Kevin Hart (New York: Routledge, 2005), 47.

12. Jacques Derrida, *On the Name*, ed. Thomas Dutoit (Stanford, Calif.: Stanford University Press, 1995), 64.

13. Jacques Derrida, *Paper Machine*, trans. Rachel Bowlby (Stanford, Calif.: Stanford University Press, 2005), 96.

14. John D. Caputo, *The Weakness of God: A Theology of the Event* (Bloomington: Indiana University Press, 2004), 113. Hereafter referred to as *WG*.

15. Catherine Malabou, *What Should We Do with Our Brain?* trans. Sebastian Rand (New York: Fordham University Press, 2008), 69.

16. Derrida, *Paper Machine*, 79.

17. Jacques Derrida, *Rogues: Two Essays on Reason*, trans. Pascale-Anne Brault and Michael Naas (Stanford, Calif.: Stanford University Press, 2005), 90.

18. Derrida, *Rogues*, 135, 142, 151, respectively.

19. Jacques Derrida, *The Beast and the Sovereign*, vol. 1, trans. Geoffrey Bennington (Chicago: University of Chicago Press, 2009), 110.

20. Jacques Derrida, *Without Alibi*, ed. and trans. Peggy Kamuf (Stanford, Calif.: Stanford University Press, 2002), 202.

21. Derrida, *Without Alibi*, 204–5.

22. Derrida, *Without Alibi*, 206.

23. Jacques Derrida, "The Force of Law," in *Acts of Religion*, ed. Gil Anidjar (New York: Routledge, 2002), 243.

24. Nor is the undeconstructible an "essential meaning" clothed in the materiality of a word, which is Žižek's misunderstanding of my view of the event. Slavoj Žižek and John Milbank, *The Monstrosity of Christ: Paradox or Dialectic*, ed. Creston Davis (Cambridge, Mass.: MIT Press, 2009), 256–60. This is a debate about whether Christianity or atheism is the true materialism!

25. Jacques Derrida, *Given Time: I. Counterfeit Money*, trans. Peggy Kamuf (Chicago: University of Chicago Press, 1991), 30.

26. The "desire" of Madame de Maintenon would be to "give what she cannot give"; "that is the whole of her desire. Desire and the desire to give

would be the same thing, a sort of tautology. But maybe as well the tautological designation of the impossible" (Derrida, *Given Time*, 4–5).

> For finally, if the gift is another name of the impossible, we still think it, we name it, we desire it. . . . In this sense one can think, desire, and say only the impossible, according to the measureless measure of the impossible. . . . If one wants to recapture the proper element of thinking, naming, desiring, it is perhaps according to the measureless measure of this limit that it is possible, possible as relation *without* relation to the impossible. (29)

27. Derrida, *Acts of Religion*, 254.
28. Derrida, *Rogues*, 74.
29. Derrida, *Given Time*, 29. Emphasis added.
30. Derrida, *Given Time*, 6.
31. Derrida, *Given Time*, 29.
32. Derrida, *Given Time*, 29. Emphasis added.
33. Derrida, *Given Time*, 30.
34. Allow me to note in passing the evolution of Derrida's use of "experience." In *Given Time* he consigns "experience" to the order of presence in order to affirm the impossible beyond presence and experience. In *Psyche* he defines deconstruction as the "experience of the impossible" beyond presence. From the impossibility of experience to the experience of the impossible. See Derrida, *Acts of Religion*, 244, and *Psyche: Inventions of the Other*, vol. 1, trans. Peggy Kamuf and Elizabeth Rottenberg (Stanford, Calif.: Stanford University Press, 2007), 15.
35. Derrida, *Given Time*, 30.
36. Jacques Derrida, *Of Grammatology*, corrected edition, trans. Gayatri Chakravorty Spivak (Baltimore: Johns Hopkins University Press, 1997), 60.
37. Derrida, *Of Grammatology*, 60–62.
38. Jacques Derrida, *Glas*, trans. Richard Rand and John Leavey (Lincoln: University of Nebraska Press, 1986), 151–62a, where the word "quasi-transcendental," which largely replaces "ultra-transcendental," is introduced at the end of a sentence split by an eleven-page break. See my *More Radical Hermeneutics* (Bloomington: Indiana University Press, 2000), 95–101.
39. The merit of Hägglund's book is to show that *différance* is not an immaterial being or a transcendental form. It can "take place" only in a material substance, only by spatially inscribing time and temporally inscribing space (*RA*, 27), taking off from Derrida's reference to a new transcendental aesthetics, beyond Kant's and Husserl's (Derrida, *Of Grammatology*, 290). We see such an "aesthetics" already when Derrida argued that by calling upon the "danger" of "writing" to explain the "origin of geometry" Husserl implied that the constitution of "ideal" objects requires a material-technological substance; this does not undermine ideal objects but explains how they are constituted. *Différance* is formally indifferent to the distinction between phonic and graphic

or any other material substance, but it is not indifferent to the material substance in general. Its (quasi-)formality is "found," as it were, only in the "materiality" of space-time, of "spacing-timing," which is what *différance* "is," if it is. But of itself, *différance* neither is nor is not, is neither ideal nor real, is neither a form nor a material substance, is "not more sensible than intelligible," is no more a matter of materialism than of formalism or idealism, just because it supplies the quasi-condition, "before all determination of the content," under which all such differences are constituted. The constitutive force of *différance* lies in the invisible (or inaudible) play of differences between visible (or audible) things, the "pure movement which produces difference," like the spacing between "ring, king, sing," the interval, the space, the imaginary slash between them (Derrida, *Of Grammatology*, 62). It "is" the between "itself," *s'il y en a*. It is, as such, the difference as such, which as such does not exist. So it is as inadequate to say Derrida is a materialist or a realist as to say he is an idealist; the less confusing thing to say is that he is not an anti-materialist, an anti-realist, or an anti-idealist.

40. Derrida, *Of Grammatology*, 61.

41. See "The Becoming Possible of the Impossible: An Interview with Jacques Derrida," in *A Passion for the Impossible: John D. Caputo in Focus*, ed. Mark Dooley (Albany: State University of New York Press, 2003), 26–27. This is an interview of Derrida by Mark Dooley about *The Prayers and Tears of Jacques Derrida*, followed by my reply to Derrida, "A Game of Jacks," 34–49. On the question of the religious turn, see Edward Baring, "Theism and Atheism at Play: Jacques Derrida and Christian Heideggerianism," in *The Trace of God: Derrida and Religion*, ed. Edward Baring and Peter E. Gordon (New York: Fordham University Press, 2015), 72–87.

42. Hägglund thinks that Levinas, who spent a good deal of World War 2 in a Nazi work camp, is defeated by this question (*RA*, 89)—without ever discussing Levinas's own reply. Hägglund does his best to distance Derrida from Levinas (*RA*, 94–100), even on this point, their common notion that our obligation to the singular other is always divided by the other others (the "third"). Hägglund labors under the misunderstanding that Levinas is some kind of Neoplatonist who thinks that when you die you enjoy eternal happiness outside of time, whereas that was Levinas's critique of Kierkegaard's Christian eudaemonism. Quoting Levinas saying that the dream of "happy eternity," meaning eternal happiness in Kierkegaard's Christianity, needs to be demythologized into fecundity (children) and the endless time it takes to do good (more time, either a new idea of time or a time of messianic vigilance), Hägglund mistakes Levinas's reference to "the eternal" as a Neoplatonic absolute *outside* time (*RA*, 133), also missing Levinas's opening for a distinctively Jewish "death of God" theology. Interestingly, both François Laruelle and Ray Brassier single out Levinas for having identified the very *structure* of the "real," even if it is restricted to the reality of the other person. Levinas reduces "religion" (other-worldly) to ethics (time) more radically than does Kant's *Religionbuch*, with

assumptions as merciless as Nietzsche's about the myth of the *Hinterwelt*. Levinas thinks that when you die, you rot, that you sur-vive only by living-on in more time (he is one of Derrida's sources on this point!), or in your children, and that life is postponing death. Hägglund notes this last point, but simply laments that Levinas should have been more consistent about it! (*RA*, 91).

43. In *RA*, 85, Hägglund conflates this point with the "non-ethical opening of ethics." But these are two different matters. The nonethical opening of ethics is archi-writing, *différance*, opening the space in which one can constitute ethical and legal categories, like good and bad, legal and illegal; that pre-ethical "violence" or archi-writing is what Lévi-Strauss missed in his Rousseauizing of the Nambikwara (Derrida, *Of Grammatology*, 139–40). Archi-violence (= archi-writing) is to be distinguished from "the common concept of violence" (112). From this Hägglund concludes that the relation to the other cannot be "ethical" as such, which does not follow.

44. Derrida, *Of Grammatology*, 61–62.

45. Jacques Derrida, *The Gift of Death*, trans. David Wills (Chicago: University of Chicago Press, 1995)71; Derrida, *Acts of Religion*, 248.

46. Derrida, *The Beast and the Sovereign*, 108.

47. Jacques Derrida, *Negotiations: Interventions and Interviews: 1971–2001*, trans. Elizabeth Rottenberg (Stanford, Calif.: Stanford University Press, 2002), 105; cf. 182.

48. Derrida, *Negotiations*, 94.

49. Jacques Derrida, "An Apocalyptic Tone That Has Recently Been Adopted in Philosophy," in *Raising the Tone of Philosophy*, ed. Peter Fenves (Baltimore: Johns Hopkins University Press, 1993), 164. Cf. Derrida, *Psyche*, 45.

50. Derrida, *Negotiations*, 94, adding: "One must think the event from the 'Come [*viens*]' and not the reverse."

51. John D. Caputo, *The Prayers and Tears of Jacques Derrida: Religion without Religion* (Bloomington: Indiana University Press, 1997).

52. Derrida, "Apocalyptic Tone," 162. In the middle of the account of citationality, Derrida says the *singularity* of the "come" is "absolute," that is, each usage (John of Patmos's, his, etc.) is unique, and "divisible," that is, repeatable (not absolutely singular) (165). Hägglund cites this text and effec-tively undermines it with his gloss. Omitting the reference to "singularity," he says the "come" is "absolute because it is the condition of everything," but that is reduced to meaning that events can only be events by succeeding one another (*RA*, 46). So for Hägglund the text announces (quite *un*apocalyptically!) the absolute being of space and time. Never a word about the prayer, the injunction, the call, the appeal, which is "beyond being" (Derrida, "An Apocalyptic Tone," 166). The text is simply deposited in the bank accounts of radical atheism, despite the fact that it undermines the central premise of *Radical Atheism*, the mistaken idea that events have a purely descriptive status in deconstruction.

53. Derrida, "Apocalyptic Tone," 165.

54. Derrida, "Apocalyptic Tone," 166.

55. Derrida, "Apocalyptic Tone," 166.

56. Derrida, "Apocalyptic Tone," 167.

57. Jacques Derrida, *Margins of Philosophy*, trans. Alan Bass (Chicago: University of Chicago Press, 1982), 12.

58. Derrida, *Of Grammatology*, 323n3.

59. As Jacques Derrida said to Kevin Hart when asked about "supernatural" grace (as opposed to the grace of the event), "deconstruction, as such, has nothing to say or to do. . . . Deconstruction has no lever on this. And it should not have any lever." "Epoché and Faith: An Interview with Jacques Derrida," in *Derrida and Religion: Other Testaments*, ed. Yvonne Sherwood and Kevin Hart (New York: Routledge, 2005), 39.

60. Jacques Derrida, "Roundtable," in *Augustine and Postmodernism*, ed. John D. Caputo and Michael Scanlon (Bloomington: Indiana University Press, 2005), 38–39. See above, n. 11.

61. Mark C. Taylor, *Erring: A Postmodern A/Theology* (Chicago: University of Chicago Press, 1985).

62. Caputo, *Prayers and Tears of Jacques Derrida*, 14.

63. Derrida, *Margins of Philosophy*, 6.

64. Caputo, *Prayers and Tears of Jacques Derrida*, §1.

65. John D. Caputo, *The Mystical Element in Heidegger's Thought* (New York: Fordham University Press, 1982), 222–40.

66. Jacques Derrida, "Afterw.rds: or, at least, less than a letter about a letter less," trans. Geoffrey Bennington, in *Afterwords*, ed. Nicholas Royle (Tampere, Finland: Outside Books, 1992), 200.

67. "The Becoming Possible of the Impossible: An Interview with Jacques Derrida," in *Passion for the Impossible*, ed. Dooley, 28.

68. Derrida, *On the Name*, 76.

69. I am chided for misunderstanding Derrida on this point (*RA*, 116), but when the "correct" understanding is set forth, it simply repeats what I have said for thirty years and is the basis of my disagreement with Jean-Luc Marion. See Caputo, *The Prayers and Tears of Jacques Derrida*, §§3–4, especially pages 45–48; and Caputo, *More Radical Hermeneutics*, chap. 10.

70. Before I published *The Prayers and Tears of Jacques Derrida* I sent the typescript to Derrida, who responded by saying, "You read me the way I love to be read, just where things remain the most risky, the most obscure, the most unstable, the most hyperbolic" ("vous me lisez comme j'aime être lu, là où les choses restent le plus risquées, le plus obscures, le plus instables, le plus hyperboliques"), and he added, "Thank you from the bottom of my heart, and I know, from reading you, that you understand what I mean by this better than anyone" ("Je vous en remercie du fond du coeur, et je sais, à vous lire, que vous comprenez mieux que quiconque ce que je veux dire par là . . ."). Personal correspondence, Feb. 24, 1996. In his interview with Mark Dooley, Derrida expresses his interest in seeing theology opened up in a deconstructive mode ("The Becoming

Possible of the Impossible," 23–24), as he does also in "The Force of Law," in Jacques Derrida, *Acts of Religion*, 236; "Epoché and Faith: An Interview with Jacques Derrida," 27–50. The latter was an interview that Sherwood, Hart, and I conducted with Derrida at a memorable plenary session of the American Academy of Religion in 2002. I introduce all this not as an *auctoritas*, which would only return the gift to the donor. Indeed, in both the "Edifying Divertissements" of *The Prayers and Tears of Jacques Derrida* and in *Weakness of God* I take deconstruction where Jackie, "a little black and Arab Jew," cannot go— into a deconstruction of Christian theology, which gives "God" and theology some time (remembering that *donner* also includes *donner un coup*). My point is to show that Derrida and I share a common interest in letting deconstruction reopen and reinvent theology, a project close to the heart of deconstruction, not least because deconstruction has a heart, but quite foreign to *Radical Atheism*.

71. Jacques Derrida, *Learning to Live Finally: The Last Interview*, trans. Pascale-Anne Brault and Michael Naas (Hoboken, N.J.: Melville House, 2007), 31; Derrida, *Rogues*, 158.

72. John D. Caputo, *Against Ethics* (Bloomington: Indiana University Press, 1993), 15–19.

73. Derrida, "Circumfession," 154.

74. Hägglund is mistaken to say that I gloss the "rightly pass for an atheist" passage (Derrida, "Circumfession," 155) by claiming that for me Derrida is merely an atheist about a Hellenistic God, which is a "finite creature," but not about the biblical God, which is not a finite creature (*RA*, 227n61). I have consistently maintained that the name of God is an effect of the play of traces, that every "God" is a finite creature. What interests me in this passage is the *play* in the name to which Derrida confesses when he says "rightly pass." That is what they say about me and they are right, but there are so many other voices in me that cannot be arrested by this intimidating word, which is what Hägglund undertakes to do by trying to freeze-dry the a/theological effect of deconstruction as "radical atheism." In the passage Hägglund cites (Caputo, *The Prayers and Tears of Jacques Derrida*, 334–36), and in *The Prayers and Tears of Jacques Derrida* generally, I am arguing that to approach Derrida by way of "negative theology" is to overemphasize Christianity and Neoplatonism and to have no ear for Derrida's Jewish side, which is tuned to the sensuous and strange images of God in the Tanakh. Derrida is not an orthodox Jew, still less a Christian. He is even a bit of an Arab. When Hägglund goes on to sketch the mortal God in the rest of that note, he joins me in the project of constructing a weak theology.

75. "For there are those who say that what I am doing is really a hidden or cryptic religious faith, or that it is just skepticism, nihilism or atheism. He [Caputo] has never shared these prejudices" ("The Becoming Possible of the Impossible: An Interview with Jacques Derrida," in *Passion for the Impossible*, ed. Dooley, 23).

76. Caputo, "Game of Jacks," 36.

77. Derrida's work both shocks and emancipates confessional believers by showing that their faith is co-constituted by a non-faith, that they can only "rightly pass" for Christians (or anything else), an exquisite formula paralleling Johannes Climacus's refusal of the compliment of "Christian" as he is only trying to become one. On Augustine's use of *facere veritatem,* see Confessions, 10.1; cf. Derrida, "Circumfession," 47–48.

78. François Laruelle, in *Future Christ: A Lesson in Heresy* (trans. Anthony Paul Smith [London: Continuum, 2011]), uses the "future Christ" as a figure of immanence rather than of a transcendent being come down to earth to authorize the Inquisition and burn heretics.

79. Derrida, "Circumfession," 3.

80. And in several books consequent upon this work: *The Insistence of God: A Theology of Perhaps* (Bloomington: Indiana University Press, 2013); *The Folly of God: A Theology of the Unconditional* (Salem, Ore.: Polebridge Press, 2016); *Cross and Cosmos: A Theology of Wounded Glory* (Bloomington: Indiana University Press, 2019).

81. Derrida, *Rogues,* 157; cf. xiv–xv, 114; "Epoché and Faith," 42: "If it is as weak and vulnerable that Jesus Christ represents or incarnates God, then the consequence would be that God is not absolutely powerful."

82. Martin Hägglund, "The Autoimmunity of Religion," in *The Trace of God,* 178–98.

83. When Schelling says that God is not a being but a life, and hence subject to suffering and death (see Slavoj Žižek, *The Parallax View* [Cambridge, Mass.: MIT Press, 2006], 184–85), the radical atheism of *Radical Atheism* becomes a prolegomenon to radical theology. When invited once to replace *khora* with the God of love, I declined because that would load the dice and remove the risk. See James H. Olthuis, "Testing the Heart of Khora: Anonymous or Amorous," and my response, "The Chance of Love," in *Cross and Khora: Deconstruction and Christianity in the Work of John D. Caputo,* ed. Neal Deroo and Marko Zlomsic (Eugene, Ore.: Pickwick, 2010), 174–96.

84. It is this "dangerous memory" of suffering and of the dead that I see inscribed in Derrida's gloss on Luke 9:60 about letting the dead bury the dead (Caputo, *The Prayers and Tears of Jacques Derrida,* 147). Glossing this text, I do not side with Jesus, who is saying something very sassy, especially to Jews (it meant: seek the Kingdom of God first and put everything else second), but with Derrida, that this would be injustice. Absolute life, I say, "constitutes, for Derrida, the very definition of 'absolute evil,'" which is, alas, always possible. When I mark the difference between the impossible that we love and the impossible we may end up with, like the difference between the democracy to come and the National Socialism to come, Hägglund complains (*RA,* 141–42) that I am denying that the promise of justice is haunted by the threat of injustice, denying that as a structural matter laws that do justice to some sell others short, or the memory of some is the forgetting of others. Those are things I point out clearly in other contexts, and the

complaint is simply groundless. Caputo, *The Prayers and Tears of Jacques Derrida*, 202–5.

85. Derrida says that he writes with a mixture of tragedy and laughter and that "Jack [Caputo] understood that he had to do the same with me. He understood that he had to make serious jokes" ("The Becoming Possible of the Impossible: An Interview with Jacques Derrida," in *Passion for the Impossible*, ed. Dooley, 25–26).

86. Hägglund, "Autoimmunity of Religion," 178–98.

87. "For me, God is precisely the one who would share my desire for the impossible, even if he doesn't respond to, or satisfy that desire. This is a dream" ("The Becoming Possible of the Impossible: An Interview with Jacques Derrida," in *Passion for the Impossible*, ed. Dooley, 29). See Derrida's remarks on the endless fluctuation between God and the impossible (ibid., 28) and my commentary on this passage in Caputo, "Game of Jacks," 38–39. One of the many things sold short in *Radical Atheism*, chapter 4, is Hent de Vries's important argument that for Derrida the name of God is paradigmatic of every name, of the name itself, as that which is always already written under erasure, under the logic of the *sans*.

88. Caputo, *The Insistence of God*, 24–38.

89. When my gloss on the New Testament sayings on the "Kingdom of God" is cited (*RA*, 121), the text I am glossing is confused with my point.

90. "Creation is quite an 'event,' which means it opens up a long chain of subsequent and unforeseeable events, both destructive and re-creative ones, and the creator is just going to have to live with that undecidability that is inscribed in things" (*WG*, 72).

91. "The whole drama of creation follows a simple but bracing law: without the elements, there is no chance in creation, and without chance, there is no risk, and without risk and uncertainty, our conception of existence is an illusion or fantasy" (*WG*, 74). "The two narratives have a kind of good news/bad news structure: 'Good, yes, yes, but.'" (*WG*, 75). This position is explicit in Derrida, but it is various ways prefigured in Jacob Boehme, Schelling, and Tillich.

92. As Derrida said to Dooley, "Don't forget that Jack Caputo speaks of religion *without* religion" ("The Becoming Possible of the Impossible: An Interview with Jacques Derrida," in *Passion for the Impossible*, ed. Dooley, 22).

93. Derrida, *Gift of Death*, 49.

94. Jacques Derrida, *On the Name*, ed. Thomas Dutoit (Stanford, Calif.: Stanford University Press, 1995), 69.

95. Caputo, *Prayers and Tears of Jacques Derrida*, 6–12, and Caputo, *More Radical Hermeneutics*, chap. 10.

96. Derrida, *Learning to Live Finally*, 24.

97. Jean-Louis Chrétien, "The Wounded Word: The Phenomenology of Prayer," trans. Jeff Kosky, in *Phenomenology and the "Theological Turn": The French Debate* (New York: Fordham University Press, 2001).

98. Jacques Derrida, *H.C. for Life, That Is to Say . . .* , trans. Laurent Melesi and Stefan Herbrechter (Stanford, Calif.: Stanford University Press, 2006), 2; cf. 36. See Hélène Cixous, *Insister of Jacques Derrida*, trans. Peggy Kamuf (Stanford, Calif.: Stanford University Press, 2007), 179; "Promised Belief," in *Feminism, Sexuality and Religion*, ed. Linda Alcoff and John D. Caputo (Bloomington: Indiana University Press, 2011), 146.

7. Forget Rationality—Is There Religious Truth?

1. See the classic study of *intellectus*—a simple intuitive insight—by Pierre Rousselot, *L'intellectualisme de Saint Thomas* (Paris: Alcan, 1908). Eng. trans.: *Intelligence: Sense of Being, Faculty of God*, trans. Andrew Tallon (Milwaukee: Marquette University Press, 1999).

2. Jean-François Lyotard, "What Is Postmodernism?" in *The Postmodern Condition*, trans. Geoff Bennington and Brian Massumi (Minneapolis: University of Minnesota Press, 1984), 77–81. For a felicitous postmodern deployment of the sublime in religion which moves in a psychoanalytic direction, see Clayton Crockett, *Interstices of the Sublime: Theology and Psychoanalytic Theory* (New York: Fordham University Press, 2007).

3. Martin Heidegger, *What Is a Thing?* trans. Vera Deutsch and W. B. Barton (Chicago: Gateway Editions, 1968).

4. The sympathetic antipathy of the sublime also anticipates the *mysterium tremens et fascinans* of the holy in Rudolf Otto, *The Idea of the Holy: An Inquiry Into the Non-rational Factor in the Idea of the Divine and Its Relation to the Rational*, trans. John W. Harvey (Oxford: Oxford University Press, 1958). Otto offers a richer approach to religion that is opened up by Kant but never explored by Kant, who was content to reduce religion to ethics.

5. Jacques Derrida, *Rogues: Two Essays on Reason*, trans. Pascale-Anne Brault and Michael Naas (Stanford, Calif.: Stanford University Press, 2005), 118–59.

6. For a further discussion of Hegel and radical theology, see chapters 5 and 8.

7. Mary-Jane Rubenstein speaks of "pan(icked) theology" in "The Matter with Pantheism," in *Entangled Worlds: Religion, Science and the New Materialism*, ed. Catherine Keller and Mary-Jane Rubenstein (New York: Fordham University Press, 2017), 159–66.

8. For an outstanding account of *Vorstellung* in Hegel, see Catherine Malabou, *The Future of Hegel: Plasticity, Temporality, and Dialectic*, trans. Lisabeth During (New York: Routledge, 2005).

9. Bruno Latour has been saying a number of very sensible things about the distortion of religion by Enlightenment Rationality in "'Thou Shalt Not Take the Lord's Name in Vain'—Being a Sort of Sermon on the Hesitations of Religious Speech," *RES: Anthropology and Aesthetics*, no. 39 (2001): 215–34; *On the Modern Cult of Factish Gods*, trans. Catherine Porter and Heather MacLean (Durham: Duke University Press, 2010).

10. See chapter 4 for a fuller discussion of "Circumfession."

11. Jacques Derrida, "Circumfession: Fifty-Nine Periods and Periphrases," in *Jacques Derrida*, by Geoffrey Bennington and Jacques Derrida, trans. Geoffrey Bennington (Chicago: University of Chicago Press, 1993). See also chapter 4, for another presentation of this text. For commentary and discussion of this text, including a round-table discussion with Derrida, see *Augustine and Postmodernism: Confessions and Circumfession*, ed. John D. Caputo and Michael Scanlon (Bloomington: Indiana University Press, 2005).

12. For a close analysis of confessing in writing, see Johanna Schumm, *Confessio, Confessiones, Circonfession: Zum literarischen Bekenntnis bei Augustinus und Derrida* (Munich: Wilhelm Fink Verlag, 2013).

13. Derrida, "Circumfession," 155.

14. Derrida, "Circumfession," 3–6.

15. Jacques Derrida, *The Gift of Death*, trans. David Wills (Chicago: University of Chicago Press, 1995), 49.

16. *The Confessions of St. Augustine*, trans. Rex Warner (New York: Penguin Books, 1963), bk. 10, c. 1, p. 210. Augustine is glossing John 3:23: "*poion ten aletheian.*"

17. Derrida, "Circumfession," 48.

18. *Confessions of St. Augustine*, 1.1.17. This is also the point of Martin Heidegger, *The Principle of Reason*, trans. Reginald Lilly (Bloomington: Indiana University Press, 1991). I am influenced here—and in my *Truth: The Search for Wisdom in the Postmodern Age* (London: Penguin Books, 2013)—by the history of truth and the critique of the "principle of reason" in modernity in Heidegger's book, but my emphasis is on Derrida's messianic version of this history, not a blinding manifestation of being at the beginning but the hope of the coming of something unforeseeable.

19. See chapter 4 for a complementary presentation of "Circumfession."

20. I refer to the foolishness of the logos of the cross in 1 Corinthians 1, which has been suggestively analyzed by Stanislas Breton, *A Radical Philosophy of Saint Paul*, trans. Joseph N. Ballan (New York: Columbia University Press, 2011), where the wisdom of the world, the pride of being, is displaced by the foolishness of *ta me onta*, those whom Derrida calls "rogues," the outsiders. I am linking the logic of the cut in Derrida's "Circumfession" with the logic of the cross in Paul.

21. My thanks to Marcia Sá Cavalcante Schuback for her insightful comments on the first version of this essay from which I have greatly benefited.

8. Radical Theologians, Knights of Faith, and the Future of the Philosophy of Religion

1. *Kierkegaard's Writings*, vol. 6, *Fear and Trembling* and *Repetition,* trans. and ed. Howard Hong and Edna Hong (Princeton, N.J.: Princeton University Press, 1983), 38–39. For "hidden inwardness" and humor as the incognito of the religious, see *Kierkegaard's Writings*, 12.1, *Concluding Unscientific Postscript to "Philosophical Fragments,"* trans. and ed. Howard Hong and Edna Hong (Princeton, N.J.: Princeton University Press, 1992), 499–501.

2. See Wesley J. Wildman, "Reforming Philosophy of Religion for the Modern Academy," in *Reconfigurations of the Philosophy of Religion*, ed. Jim Kanaris (Albany: State University of New York Press, 2018), 253–69, which makes a splendid case that there is a perfectly proper role for the philosophy of religion that the university should respect and the college curriculum committee should welcome.

3. Jacques Derrida, "Circumfession: Fifty-Nine Periods and Periphrases," in *Jacques Derrida*, by Geoffrey Bennington and Jacques Derrida (Chicago: University of Chicago Press, 1993), 58.

4. Jacques Derrida, *Without Alibi*, ed. and trans. Peggy Kamuf (Stanford, Calif.: Stanford University Press, 2002), 202; Jacques Derrida, *Politics of Friendship*, trans. George Collins (London: Verso, 1997), 34, 41, 43.

5. See *The Palgrave Handbook of Radical Theology*, ed. Christopher D. Rodkey and Jordan E. Miller (Cham, Switzerland: Palgrave Macmillan, 2018). See also the *Journal of Cultural and Religious Theory* (www.jcrt.org) and the *Journal of Continental Philosophy of Religion*, where a great deal of this kind of work is published.

6. The motif of "specter" and "hauntology" is found in Jacques Derrida, *Specters of Marx: The State of the Debt, the Work of Mourning, and the New International*, trans. Peggy Kamuf (New York: Routledge, 1994), 10 (and throughout).

7. Derrida, *Specters of Marx*, 136.

8. See Tyler Roberts, "Reverence as Critical Responsiveness: Between Philosophy and Religion," in *Reconfigurations of the Philosophy of Religion*, 189–210.

9. Derrida, *Without Alibi*, 202–3.

10. Martin Heidegger, *An Introduction to Metaphysics*, trans. Ralph Manheim (New Haven, Conn.: Yale University Press, 1959), 7; *History of the Concept of Time: Prolegomena*, trans. Theodore Kisiel (Bloomington: Indiana University Press, 1985), 80. See chapter 5, where radical thinking is shrunk down to an instrument of apologetics.

11. Jacques Derrida, *The Gift of Death*, trans. David Wills (Chicago: University of Chicago Press, 1995), 49.

12. Jonathan Smith, "Religion, Religions, the Religious," in *Critical Terms for Religious Studies*, ed. Mark C. Taylor (Chicago: University of Chicago Press, 1998), 269–84.

13. *Hegel's Lectures on the Philosophy of Religion*, one-volume edition: *The Lectures of 1827*, ed. Peter Hodgson (Berkeley: University of California Press, 1988), 84–85, 92, 402–4.

14. See chapter 5 for more on my case against the Kantians.

15. Catherine Malabou, *The Future of Hegel: Plasticity, Temporality, and Dialectic*, trans. Lisabeth During (New York: Routledge, 2005), 167.

16. Rudolf Bultmann, *New Testament and Mythology and Other Basic Writings*, ed. Schubert Ogden (Philadelphia: Augsburg Fortress Press, 1984).

17. See Phil Snider, *Preaching after God: Derrida, Caputo, and the Language of Postmodern Homiletics* (Eugene, Ore.: Cascade Books, Wipf and Stock, 2012).

18. I tell this story, beginning with my life in a Catholic religious order, in *Hoping against Hope: Confessions of a Postmodern Pilgrim* (Minneapolis: Fortress Press, 2015).

19. Kierkegaard, *Fear and Trembling*, 38–39. For further development of this divine madness, see John D. Caputo, *The Folly of God: A Theology of the Unconditional* (Salem, Ore.: Polebridge Press, 2016).

9. Theology in Trumptime: The Insistence of America

1. Stephen Bannon speaks of the "deconstruction of the administrative state." See https://www.realclearpolitics.com/video/2017/02/23/stephen _bannon_pillar_of_trumps_platform_is_deconstruction_of_the _administrative_state.html.

2. Jacques Derrida, *Politics of Friendship*, trans. George Collins (London: Verso, 1997), 101–6, a book from which Steve Bannon could learn a thing or two about the deconstruction of democracy. See also the approach to democracy developed in Jacques Derrida, *Rogues: Two Essays on Reason*, trans. Pascale-Anne Brault and Michael Naas (Stanford, Calif.: Stanford University Press, 2005).

3. Richard Rorty, *Achieving Our Country: Leftist Thought in Twentieth-Century America* (Cambridge, Mass.: Harvard University Press, 1998), 89–90.

4. Delivered on the occasion of the March on Washington, August 28, 1963, the "I Have a Dream . . ." speech by Martin Luther King Jr. can be found at https://www.archives.gov/files/press/exhibits/dream-speech.pdf.

5. Joseph Nye Jr., *Soft Power* (New York: Perseus Books, Public Affairs, 2004).

6. In *The Socialist Decision*, trans. Franklin Sherman (New York: Harper & Row, 1977), Paul Tillich, defending Christian socialism, opposes prophetic time to reactionary Fascist time and criticizes the soullessness of secular Marxist socialism. As a result of this book, originally published in Germany in 1933 and directed against the Nazis, Tillich was dismissed from his professorship at the University of Frankfurt and emigrated to the United States.

7. Johann Baptist Metz, *Faith in History and Society*, trans. David Smith (New York: Crossroads, 1980), 109–15; James H. Cone, *The Cross and the Lynching Tree* (Maryknoll, N.Y.: Orbis Books, 2011). See my account of Cone in *Cross and Cosmos: A Theology of Difficult Glory* (Bloomington: Indiana University Press, 2019), 86–105.

8. This is the leitmotif running throughout Derrida's *Politics of Friendship*.

10. Hoping against Hope: The Possibility of the Impossible

1. This essay was delivered at the annual meeting of the Society of Pastoral Theology, on the topic of "suffering, extremism, violence and planetary crisis," which met in Pasadena, California, in June 2016, a few months before the

fateful presidential election which would pose an even greater challenge to hope. The position staked out in this paper is developed at greater length in John D. Caputo, *Hoping against Hope: Confessions of a Postmodern Pilgrim* (Minneapolis: Fortress Press, 2015).

2. I follow the logic of this folly in John D. Caputo, *The Folly of God: A Theology of the Unconditional* (Salem, Ore.: Polebridge Press, 2016).

3. See *The Complete Mystical Works of Meister Eckhart*, trans. and ed. Maurice O'C Walshe (New York: Crossroad, 2009), 129 ("Ego Eligi Vos de Mundo"). The "without why" motif is brilliantly played off Leibniz's principle that "nothing is without reason" in Martin Heidegger, *The Principle of Reason*, trans. Reginald Lilly (Bloomington: Indiana University Press, 1991). See also *Hoping against Hope*, 24–30.

4. See Jacques Derrida, *Psyche: Inventions of the Other*, vol. 1, trans. Peggy Kamuf and Elizabeth Rottenberg (Stanford, Calif.: Stanford University Press, 2007), 23–47.

5. Derrida was interested in events that break up the sedimented horizon of everydayness, but in *Hermeneutics: Facts and Interpretation in the Age of Information* (London: Penguin/Pelican, 2018), 219–43, I discuss the opposite phenomenon: nurses who work in pediatric oncology whose working day is made up of the daily trauma of events of the most terrible kind, of the uninterrupted disruption of everydayness,.

6. This is, in a nutshell, the argument sustained throughout the classic work of Paul Tillich, *The Courage to Be* (New Haven, Conn.: Yale University Press, 1952).

7. I have explored this suggestion in greater detail in *The Insistence of God: A Theology of Perhaps* (Bloomington: Indiana University Press, 2013).

8. Alan F. Segal, *Life after Death: A History of the Afterlife in Western Religion* (New York: Doubleday, 1989), 248–81.

Like a Devilish Knight of Faith:
A Concluding Quasi-Theological Postscript

1. Jacques Derrida, *Monolingualism of the Other; or, The Prosthesis of Origin*, trans. Patrick Mensah (Stanford, Calif.: Stanford University Press, 1998), 52. This book contains a moving autobiographical account of growing up a *pied noir* in Algeria

2. Jacques Derrida, "Circumfession: Fifty-Nine Periods and Periphrases," in *Jacques Derrida*, by Geoffrey Bennington and Jacques Derrida (Chicago: University of Chicago Press, 1993), 155.

Index

John D. Caputo is the Thomas J. Watson Professor Emeritus of Religion at Syracuse University and the David R. Cook Professor Emeritus of Philosophy at Villanova University who writes and lectures on religion in the postmodern condition. His most recent books are *Cross and Cosmos: A Theology of Difficult Glory* (Indiana University Press, 2019); *On Religion*, 2nd ed. (Routledge, 2019); *Hermeneutics: Facts and Interpretation in the Age of Information* (Penguin/Pelican, 2018). He is best known for *Radical Hermeneutics* (Indiana University Press, 1986), *The Prayers and Tears of Jacques Derrida* (Indiana University Press, 1997), and *The Weakness of God: A Theology of the Event* (Indiana University Press, 2004), which received the American Academy of Religion Award for work in constructive theology. He has addressed wider- than-academic audiences in *What Would Jesus Deconstruct?* (Baker Academic, 2007) and *Hoping against Hope* (Fortress, 2015). There are several studies of his work, including Štefan Štofanik, *The Adventure of Weak Theology: Reading the Work of John D. Caputo through Biographies and Events* (SUNY Press, 2018); "John Caputo: Faiblesse de Dieu et déconstruction de la théologie," *Études Théologiques et Religieuses* 90, no. 3 (2015): 313–16; Phil Snider, *Preaching after God: Derrida, Caputo, and the Language of Postmodern Homiletics* (Wipf and Stock, 2012); and Zohar Mihaely, *Holy Anarchy: John Caputo and the Challenge of Religions Today* (Tel Aviv: Resling Publishing, 2020).

Perspectives in Continental Philosophy
John D. Caputo, series editor

Emmanuel Falque, *The Wedding Feast of the Lamb: Eros, the Body, and the Eucharist*. Translated by George Hughes.

Emmanuel Falque, *Crossing the Rubicon: The Borderlands of Philosophy and Theology*. Translated by Reuben Shank. Introduction by Matthew Farley.

Colby Dickinson and Stéphane Symons (eds.), *Walter Benjamin and Theology*.

Don Ihde, *Husserl's Missing Technologies*.

William S. Allen, *Aesthetics of Negativity: Blanchot, Adorno, and Autonomy*.

Jeremy Biles and Kent L. Brintnall, eds., *Georges Bataille and the Study of Religion*.

Tarek R. Dika and W. Chris Hackett, *Quiet Powers of the Possible: Interviews in Contemporary French Phenomenology*. Foreword by Richard Kearney.

Richard Kearney and Brian Treanor, eds., *Carnal Hermeneutics*.

A complete list of titles is available at http://fordhampress.com.